Girl Unbroken

Girl Unbroken

A Sister's Harrowing Story of Survival from the Streets of Long Island to the Farms of Idaho

Regina Calcaterra and Rosie Maloney
with Jessica Anya Blau

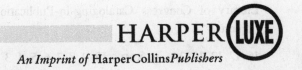

HARPER **LUXE**

An Imprint of HarperCollinsPublishers

HarperCollins books may be purchased for educational, business, or sales promotional use. For information please e-mail the Special Markets Department at SPsales@harpercollins.com.

FIRST HARPERLUXE EDITION

ISBN: 978-0-06-249706-2

HarperLuxe™ is a trademark of HarperCollins Publishers.

Library of Congress Cataloging-in-Publication Data is available upon request.

16 17 18 19 20 ID/RRD 10 9 8 7 6 5 4 3 2 1

To Rosie:
Mia bambina, je t'aime.
—Gi

To Daniel, Alexis, and Brody:
I am reminded daily that you are the
reasons why I persevered.
You have blessed me with boundless happiness and I am
honored that I get to be the one that you call Mom.
—with unconditional love, Mom (Rosie)

You have to walk that lonesome Road
You have to walk it by
Yourself
And there's nobody whose going to
Walk it for
You.
—R. CALCATERRA (AGE 9)

Contents

Author's Note

When I wrote *Etched in Sand,* I revisited the harrowing details of my own journey while deliberately remaining conservative with how much I shared of my siblings' own stories. In fact, it was Rosie, my youngest sister, who I was the most protective of, a heightened instinct that to this day I have yet to shed. Although I was steadfast about not disclosing her experiences, I also knew that her story would inspire those caped in darkness to push through toward the light.

At the urging of *Etched in Sand*'s readers, who for the past three years kept inquiring about Rosie's welfare, Rosie was inspired to tell her story. Rosie and I embarked on the journey of writing *Girl Unbroken* together. For her it was tremendously empowering; for me it was a heartfelt labor of love—an everlasting gift that will constantly remind her how resilient she truly is. In order to tell it well, we felt it necessary to write it in Rosie's voice, in the first person narrative, so readers can share her journey alongside her just as they did alongside me in *Etched in Sand*.

Girl Unbroken is the true story of Rosie's experiences shortly before she was removed from the care of her older sisters and the atrocities she endured after our mother dragged Norman and her across the country and far away from those who loved them the most. All of our siblings consented to the publication of *Girl Unbroken* and the use of our actual names in the following pages. However, some people's names have been changed in order to protect their anonymity, including but not limited to Rosie's and Norman's foster parents, relatives both living and deceased, and those our mother associated with. Specifically worth noting is Rosie's stepfather, whom we refer to with the pseudonym of Clyde Hapner. Also referred to with pseudonyms are some of the towns where Rosie and Norman predominantly resided when in Idaho, along with their landmarks and occupants. For ease of description, Rosie's high school boyfriends were consolidated into one character as were her caseworkers and they each are represented by pseudonyms.

In the acknowledgments of *Etched in Sand,* I thanked Rosie: *Boundless love and adoration to Rosie, who has her own story to tell, which I'll encourage her to do . . . only when she is ready.* And now she is ready . . .

—Regina Calcaterra

Introduction

We were five kids with five different fathers— one jailed and then dead, two missing, and two unknown. Our mother, Cookie, was more gone than there, more drunk than sober, more mentally ill than mentally well. Cookie blew in and out of our lives like a hurricane, blind and uncaring to everything in her path. Once she arrived, she dispensed beatings, or tied my sister Gi naked to the radiator, or called all my sisters sluts and whores simply because in spite of the fact that they were starving, exhausted, and without heat in many New York winters, they remained beautiful, strong-willed, self-reliant, and loving. Cookie just couldn't rip all that good out of them, but they hid it from her the best they could, storing all their sweetness and good will in me and our brother, Norm. Norm and

I were the babies, the little ones, the ones they wanted to save.

My sister Gi looked at me as her do-over. Everything that had been missing from her childhood, she brought to mine. Gi read to me, she piled clothes on top of me to keep me warm. She bathed me, brushed my light brown hair, and taught me how to count to ten in English, Spanish, and French.

During the storms of my mother being home and in the calm of her absence, the only thing I knew for sure was that Gi would make everything okay. In this way, I was always safe, loved, and cared for. I was her Rosie, her sweetie, her *bambina*.

When she was nine years old, Gi wrote a poem that her teacher saved and gave back to her years later.

You have to walk that lonesome Road
You have to walk it by
Yourself,
And there's nobody whose going to
walk it For
You.

R. Calcaterra

We didn't know it then, but that poem and those words were words I would have to live by before I turned nine. Gi walked with me as far as she could. But in the end, there was nothing she could do to hang on to me when our mother and the county social workers decided I'd be better off without my siblings.

This story is about the missing years when my sisters weren't there to save me. These were the years I had to walk the lonesome road. And you can bet that as soon as I was upright and strong enough, I walked that road straight back to the people who loved me.

Girl Unbroken

1
Foster Things

Gi told me we were moving again. If you count foster homes and living in cars, where I, as the youngest, slept in the footwell, we'd moved at least fifteen times already. And I was only eight years old. This move was worse, though. In this move, I was losing my sisters.

The oldest of us, Cherie, had already left to live with her husband and new baby. The rest of us had found ourselves, once again, to be wards of the state: Camille at seventeen, Gi, almost fourteen, Norm, twelve, and me.

We were in an upstairs bedroom of a house we called the Toad House, because it was drab gray with big front windows that looked like hooded eyes. My clothes were in this room but I'd never slept here. Gi, Norm, and I were like a litter of pups, curling up every night in the living room together where we felt safe.

Months ago, our mother, Cookie, had abandoned the four of us in the Toad House. Later that same day, Camille moved into her best friend's house. She didn't want to leave us behind, but she thought maybe if she had a real home and didn't have to worry about food, she could get a few odd jobs and make enough money to buy food for us. When Cookie finally returned two nights ago, she beat Gi so violently that there were raised bruises like purple walnuts running from her brow to her cheek. Around Gi's swollen and now-lopsided lips were craggy lines of scabs. Gi thought it was probably her social studies teacher, Mr. Brown, who called Social Services the next day. Gi told me she hadn't realized how bad she looked until she saw Mr. Brown's face turn white at the sight of her. It's always harder to ignore the truth when you see that truth in someone else's eyes.

Now Cookie was in the kitchen with a silver-haired social worker, and another social worker sat in the living room. She was a pretty blonde-haired lady who looked just like Mrs. Brady from *The Brady Bunch*.

"Why can't I go with you?" I asked Gi. We were looking out the window at the two gray cars parked on the gravel driveway. One was waiting to take Norm and me away; the other was for Gi and Camille. After Gi learned that Social Services was snooping around, she called Camille at her friend's house. Camille rushed home to take care of us.

"There are too many of us to fit in the same car, love bug." Gi was as skinny as a piece of licorice, losing her hair from malnutrition and the stress of having to steal food just to make sure Norm and I would keep growing.

"But we always fit in one car!"

"Not this time," Gi said. Tears streaked down her face.

I grabbed Gi's licorice leg and said, "But you always said that we are so skinny we can all be folded up to fit anywhere. And we are *really* skinny now. We can fit in the same car!"

"Well, maybe we can, but the home that you're going to prefers little kids like you and Norm because you're cuter, sweeter, and easier to hug." Gi picked me up and squished me in her arms. I could feel her bones and muscles and all her love coming out at me. Cookie, our mother, had arms as big as my belly. All that bubbling flesh, and she never used any of it to love us. There were boyfriends, however, men who got a charming, purring version of Cookie reserved just for them. Sometimes Cookie paid the rent with her flesh. Watching Cookie, I absorbed a quick lesson, barely understood at the time but later fully digested, of just how much utility the female form can hold.

"I'm not a baby," I told Gi.

She brushed my hair with her darting fingers and said, "You will always be my baby, *mia bambina*." Gi stopped talking for a minute, as if something were stuck in her throat. Her lumpy face was wet with tears. And then finally she said, "I'm so sorry, *mia bambina*. I'm so, so sorry."

"But you didn't do anything wrong! You were protecting me!" I started to touch my sister's face but pulled my hand away when I remembered how much those walnut bruises had hurt when I'd touched them last.

"I was supposed to take care of you forever," Gi said, and she began crying again.

With everything we'd endured, and everything we'd seen, you'd think we'd also seen a lot of crying. But we were scrappy, willful, and driven. We knew how to get a loaf of bread out of a grocery store with no cash in less than sixty seconds. We knew how to manage landlords, bill collectors, our mother's old boyfriends, enraged wives (whose husbands had slept with Cookie), and nosy neighbors as they hunted down Cookie. We could convince an entire school system that we had a mother and a house—the only two things that could prevent us from getting split up and placed in separate foster homes. And we knew how to run from our mother when she was drunk as a rabid raccoon and ready to focus her heft and her misery on any one of us who got in her way. Especially Gi. Gi was the one with the father who had broken Cookie's heart. In this way, I might have been luckiest. My father didn't break Cookie's heart—he just went to prison. And when he got out of there, he was murdered before he could break her heart.

In all of that, through all of that, no, we rarely cried. Until this day, when Gi just couldn't stop.

My sister put me down and busied herself by sorting through my scavenged clothes, which she'd previously arranged on the floor by color.

"This will be the perfect outfit for when you meet your foster parents." Gi sniffed back her tears as she lifted a pair of purple velour pants with a matching top that had lilies embroidered around the neckline. The outfit was spotless and shiny clean.

In spite of the chaos in our lives, in spite of the fact that our mother wouldn't buy tampons for herself and instead used dirty washcloths that she left around the house, in spite of the uncountable rodents and their droppings that filled every crack in every house we lived in (like a grubby brown confetti thrown as a *hurrah* each time we moved in), my sisters kept things clean. They scrubbed, they organized, they folded . . . and they picked. The year we had lice, Gi, Camille, and Cherie tore through our scalps until we bled red polka dots. Like most of our homes, there was no hot water, and so no way to wash away the lice. We threw out our clothing, and at night we went to the Salvation Army, where we rummaged through the Dumpster until we'd found enough to replace what had been tossed away. This was how we got our clothes every season, every year. This is how I got my pretty velour outfit. "Here we go." Gi pulled the top over my head and then stood there, her chest chugging up and down as she cried some more. It never occurred to me then that this had likely been some girl's outgrown Easter outfit, worn on a day when a bunny delivered baskets of candy and there was a ham for dinner—two things I'd never yet had.

"My arms." I wagged my hands inside as if I were trapped. Gi laughed, still crying, and helped thread my limbs into the sleeves.

"You're going to look perfect for your new family." Gi tucked my hair behind each ear and then held the elastic-waist pants open so I could step into them.

"I don't need a new family." My family was the only one I wanted. There was no difference between the heart that beat inside me and the hearts of my sisters and brother, beating outside of me. We were a single entity.

Gi cried harder now. She kissed me on my forehead and cheeks and then loaded my folded clothes into the Hefty bag. On top of the clothes she placed my favorite games: Candy Land, Parcheesi, and Operation. If we were missing parts to the games, Gi, Cherie, and Camille would always compromise by using random chess and checker pieces or pebbles so that all three games were complete. In a fractured life, my sisters were always trying to make things whole again.

We came downstairs. Norm sat silently on the couch in the living room, waiting to be told what the next move was. Cookie was still in the kitchen; she could hear us, but she couldn't see us. There was an awkward bashfulness around Cookie after she'd let loose with one of her barbaric beatings. It was as if Cookie's violence were a vicious animal caged inside her flesh and she had to be real still to keep it from busting out again. Of course, she'd never let that animal out in front of a social worker.

Gi dropped the Hefty bag on the living room floor. I wrapped my arms around her leg again and turned away from Mrs. Brady. Camille came downstairs carrying Norm's bag of clothes. She set his bag beside mine.

"What's in there?" Mrs. Brady asked. Her voice wasn't like the mother's on the TV show. This woman sounded hard, official, as if her throat was made of steel.

"Their clothes," Camille said. You could tell Camille and Gi were sisters—she was a lighter, more round-eyed version of Gi.

"And some games," Gi said.

"Take the games out." Mrs. Brady stood and smoothed out her beige skirt.

"But these are their games that they love to play," Gi said.

"Take them out. There will be games there." She looked toward the door. It was time to go.

"But they have all the pieces," Camille said. "They're whole games."

"TAKE THE DAMN GAMES OUT!" Cookie shouted from the kitchen. We were all startled at the sound of her voice.

Two days earlier, on Tuesday, our mother had come home with a carton of milk and a box of macaroni and cheese. She was drunk and angry because she had just fought with her latest boyfriend. There were no hellos or kisses. Cookie dropped the bag of groceries on the kitchen table, then dropped herself onto the couch and immediately fell asleep on her stomach. Her face was turned to one side, smashed up as if there were no bones. She snored so loudly and deeply that Norm and I laughed. "It sounds like a big old man," I said, and we laughed even harder.

Gi made the macaroni and cheese, and the three of us sat on the living room floor eating the macaroni and cheese and drinking glass after glass of milk until the entire carton was gone. Gi and Norm finished their meals first and were relaxing with full bellies while I still ate. When I was done, I placed my glass on my plate and stood to clear my dishes. With my first step, my glass fell and broke on the wood floor next to Cookie's boneless face. My mother instantly jumped up and lunged toward me. She grabbed my hair and shouted, "You stupid little twat!" When she jerked my head back, I dropped my plate and that broke too. Gi and Norm jumped up, and Gi pushed Cookie away from me. The fight that followed was so terrifying I could only see it as a series of frozen snapshots. There was broken glass; there was Cookie with her wooden-heeled shoe thrust into my sister's back, and her face, and her arms, and her legs; there was blood covering Gi's face; there was Cookie's enormous body on top of Gi's stringy one; there were words—Gi screaming and Cookie saying over and over again that she wished Gi had never been born; and there was Norm and me, both of us hollering, begging for Gi to stop fighting back so maybe our mother would finally stop beating her.

"Please, can we have the games?" I whispered to my sisters, ignoring the social worker.

"There are a lot of kids where they're going, and there is no extra room for games," Mrs. Brady said. My sisters gave each other a look—their expressions were so similar it was like watching only one of them in a mirror. Gi opened my bag and removed the games.

Camille held Norm's hand and Gi carried me to the car. She sobbed in my neck as her footsteps crunched across the gravel. There was a pudgy man with hair all over his face waiting at one car. At the other car, where Mrs. Brady put my and Norm's Hefty bags, was a big pink-faced man. He opened the back door and let my sisters crawl all over Norm and me as they hugged and kissed us good-bye. Mrs. Brady got in the front seat and immediately put on her seatbelt. Her back was stiff as she stared out the front windshield.

"*Je t'aime,*" Gi whispered in my ear, then she and Camille got out of the car. I reached up and felt my face, wet and slippery from my sisters' tears.

Just as the man was closing my door, Cookie trampled out of the house like a drunken elephant.

"MY BABIES," she wailed.

The man hurriedly got into the front seat and slammed his door. A sturdy click sounded before Cookie was at the window, her fists thudding against the glass.

"Don't open the windows," Mrs. Brady said without turning to look at us.

"My babies!" Cookie cried. "Don't worry, my babies! I'll get you back!" I watched my mother in her spandex jumpsuit bounce around outside my window. Her insincere pleading didn't feel real—it was like watching a play at school. Norm was as impassive as I. What struck me at that moment was not Cookie's emotions, rather it was how tight her clothing was and how much her body jiggled in spite of being bound in fabric.

I scooted up and looked out the front window as Camille and Gi got into the car parked in front of ours. Cookie didn't put on a show for them. They knew things at the time that I sensed but couldn't articulate until later: Cookie only wanted us for the welfare checks. It was money that benefited Cookie alone. Between mental illness and a fierce alcohol addiction, Cookie was walled into a windowless tunnel of her own desires. There wasn't room in there for another being, even ones as pipe-cleaner scrawny as me, my sisters, and Norm.

Cookie ran alongside the car, screaming as we

backed out of the driveway. Her giant breasts heaved up and down, almost in slow motion as she tried to keep up. We were only one house away when she stopped running, pulled a cigarette from her jumpsuit pocket, and lit up. Norm and I looked out the back window and watched the car Gi and Camille were in. We couldn't see them, but we could see their silhouettes in the backseat. A bone-thin arm was waving at us—it was Gi's arm, I knew. That arm, not Cookie's hysterics, got me crying. And once I was crying, Norm cried too. We tried to keep it down, sniffling, our heads rocking as we sobbed. Mrs. Brady talked to us from the front seat. She wanted us to know that no one had room enough for four kids. And even if they did, the people who would take little kids didn't want big kids. And the people who would take big kids didn't want little ones.

When we pulled up to a stoplight, Gi and Camille's car pulled right up beside us. Gi had her face against the window and was mouthing words to me: *Je t'aime, mia bambina, je t'aime.* Camille lunged forward so she was beside Gi and for a moment I thought they'd jump out and get in our car. But then their car turned right and ours turned left. A sound came out of me. Not a scream, more of a gasp. It was as if something had been pulled straight from my gut. I was crying harder than ever.

"It's okay," Norm said. He swallowed away his tears and put his arm around me. "Now it's my turn to take care of you."

Minutes later, we stopped in front of a sad-looking Victorian house. In the front yard were three cars, one of which was up on blocks and had no trunk or hood cover. Between the cars on the weedy dirt were bikes, skateboards, and wagons. Each one had something missing: a wheel, a seat, handlebars.

"Time to go, kiddos," Mrs. Brady said, and she stood at the open back door.

"I want my sisters!" I cried and wedged myself against the backseat, refusing to leave.

"Norman, help your sister out of the car. Now." Mrs. Brady said. The real Mrs. Brady would have used humor, or maybe she'd bring brownies or cookies out to the car. This Mrs. Brady was all business.

Norm, who was always pragmatic, said, "Ma'am, this looks like a bad place. And if Rosie doesn't want to go, I think we better not go."

Mrs. Brady lifted her shoulders and huffed. The pink-faced driver got out of his seat, opened the other back door and lunged across the seat. He grabbed my legs and pulled while I kicked and screamed. Norm held on to me, a determined gritty look on his face.

Once I'd slipped free of Norm and was left trembling on the ground, my brother scrambled out and picked me up. "We don't have a choice," he said. "But don't worry, we won't be here too long anyway."

At the front door, on the cement stoop, was a thin woman with stringy brown and gray hair. She wore black leggings and an oversized Popeye sweatshirt. In the same hand in which Popeye held his pipe, she held her cigarette. She looked us up and down, her nose and lips contracted as if we smelled, and then she dropped her cigarette on the stoop and stomped on it with her white canvas sneaker. This was something I'd seen Cookie do many times, although Cookie was fond of high-heeled shoes that made a horse's clop-clop when she walked.

"Thought you got lost," she said. Her voice was like crushed ice.

"This one took a little longer than usual," Mrs. Brady said.

"So these are the two, huh?" Her eyes were tiny blue pinpoints that she drilled into me for a second before drilling them into Norm.

"This is Norman and Rosanne," Mrs. Brady said. "Kids, meet Mrs. Callahan, your new foster mother."

"I want Gi," I whispered.

"I got you," Norm whispered back.

"They look too skinny to me," Mrs. Callahan said.

"I don't want no finicky eaters, you hear? What I serve, they eat. This ain't no diner and I ain't no short-order cook."

"I'm sure they'll appreciate anything you put in front of them. They haven't had a real meal in weeks." Mrs. Brady gave a forced smile, and I wondered if she didn't like Mrs. Callahan.

"And the stipend sure don't give me enough money to buy them separate meals! It barely covers the cost of keeping them here. I do this outta generosity, you hear? You gotta be a giving and generous soul to spend your own money on people like this." Mrs. Callahan's nose lifted again. I wondered if she was part dog and that's why she kept sniffing at us.

"I'm sure they'll appreciate all your good will and all your good meals," Mrs. Brady said. "Won't you, kids?"

"Yes, ma'am," Norm said, and he put his hands on my ears to stop me from shaking my head *no*.

"Becky will show them around," Mrs. Callahan said and then she shouted into the house, "Becky! Now!"

A second later, a freckle-faced, open-mouth-breathing girl a little taller than Norm appeared. She wore small wire-rim glasses and had brown hair cut in the shape of an upside-down salad bowl on her head. When she stood still, her body made the letter S: shoulders slumped forward, back rounded at the top, stomach bulging, butt out. Below all that her legs splayed out wide, feet pointing into a V.

"Show 'em around the house," Mrs. Callahan said, and she walked the social worker to the car, leaving Norm and me with splatter-footed Becky.

"C'mon," Becky said and waddled away with Norm and me following, "Mom said we weren't getting no more grimy rent-a-kids, but lookee lookee—" Becky looked back at us, as if to make sure we knew that we were the rent-a-kids to which she was referring.

We entered the kitchen. Becky said, "This is the kitchen. Obviously." Norm and I looked at each other, trying not to smirk.

"You're not allowed to touch anything in here. Ever. Unless you get permission from my mom, but she'll never give you permission so don't even ask." Becky picked up a wrapped Twinkie off the counter, opened it, and ate it in three giant bites while Norm and I watched.

Becky was still chewing the Twinkie when we followed her into the living room. "Living room," she said. "Obviously."

Norm squeezed my hand, and I bit my lip so I wouldn't laugh.

"You're not allowed to go in this room. Ever."

"Obviously," Norm whispered. Becky didn't seem to hear and galumphed away and then up the stairs, her feet slapping each step heavily. Norm and I followed quietly.

We stopped outside a bathroom with brown and yellow tiles, a sliding shower door, and a toilet that was missing the lid. Norm and I looked at each other, holding back our smiles. We'd had far worse. In fact, as far as bathrooms went, this was one of the better ones.

"Bathroom. Obviously." This time Becky dragged out the word. As if the bathroom were even more obvious than the other rooms. "You and the other rent-a-kids have to keep it clean and you're only allowed to use it in the day."

"What if we have to go at night?" Norm asked.

"Hold it in," Becky said.

"Obviously," Norm said.

"Or use the bucket." A jagged little smile slipped across Becky's mouth.

"Bucket?" Norm laughed, and I giggled.

"You're not gonna laugh when the door is locked and you hafta smell that bucket," Becky said.

We followed Becky down the hall to a wood-paneled room with four sets of bunk beds and a single bulb hanging from the ceiling. The switch for the light was in the hallway, outside the room. Becky turned it on.

"Bunkroom. Obviously." Becky pointed to the small stretch of wall where there was no bed. "Sit there an' wait for my mom."

Norman and I did as we were told. We both kept our eyes on Becky, all curved and splatty in the doorway. After a couple of seconds she turned her head and shouted into the hallway, "MA! I'M DONE WITH THE TOUR!"

Mrs. Callahan showed up, and Becky stepped further into the room.

"I don't want no trouble outta you two, you hear?" Mrs. Callahan said.

Norm and I both nodded.

"You do everything we say, and we'll all get along fine. And don't think you can be sneakin' around behind my back 'cause I got eyes and ears all over this house."

I thought of floating eyes and detached ears bobbing against the ceiling like forgotten party balloons.

"And Becky here"—Mrs. Callahan pointed at Becky, who stared at her mother with open-mouthed wonder—"sees everything. There ain't nothin' that gets by her. You got it?"

"Yes," Norm said, and he nudged me until I said yes too.

"You wanna tell the rules or me?" Mrs. Callahan said to her daughter, who had yet to close her gaping mouth.

"You," Becky said.

"Fine. Rule One: all foster things in the bunkroom at eight p.m. with lights out."

Becky smiled at the words *foster things,* and I wondered if she'd replace *rent-a-kid* with that.

"Rule Two," Mrs. Callahan continued. "The bunkroom door stays locked from eight until six the next morning. Rule Three: if you have to go to the bathroom after eight, you use the bucket." Mrs. Callahan nodded at Becky, who smiled and rushed to the closet. She slid open the door and pointed up and down with her thick arm at the blue plastic bucket.

"Can I tell 'em about bucket duty?" Becky grinned.

"Yup. Make it quick," Mrs. Callahan said.

"You gotta carry the bucket downstairs," Becky's voice swung up as if this were a question, "and you can't spill it or you'll get in trouble. And then you take it in the backyard and you dump it into the poop hole." Now she was really smiling. As if the word *poop* brought her particular pleasure.

"Rule Four," Mrs. Callahan continued. "You can't use the bathroom more than three times a day. This ain't no toilet paper factory. And when you use toilet paper, don't use more than three squares for number one and six squares for number two."

I was wondering how she would know how many squares anyone used when Mrs. Callahan said, "Becky will know if you use too much and she'll tell me."

"Obviously," Norm whispered, so quietly that I felt the words more than I heard them.

Norm and I spent the remainder of the afternoon on our bunk bed: Norm on top, me on the bottom. We were told the other kids had after-school activities and wouldn't be home until late. Staying away from Becky and Mrs. Callahan seemed like a wise idea, so Norm and I planned to sign up for as many after-school activities as we could the following day.

Around five, Mrs. Callahan showed up in the doorway. Becky, her slumpy, open-mouthed shadow, hovered nearby. Behind them was a row of four kids varying in height from bigger than Camille and Gi to smaller than me. I quickly did the math: eight beds, six kids big and small. There was room for Gi and Camille after all. My eyes burned with tears of frustration.

"Here are two more trouble makers for ya." Mrs. Callahan pointed at Norm and me. "These things seem a little dense to me, so you better tell them the rules again." She turned and went down the stairs with Becky following. Our bunkmates filed in, each of them watching us as if we were cats about to claw them.

Black-haired Brian was the first to speak. He was creaky and stiff with legs that moved like they were made of aluminum pipes and arms that he spastically bent and straightened like folding yardsticks. Brian stuttered when he spoke, and his eyelids fluttered like nervous butterflies.

"I'm th-th-thirteen," he said, after telling us his name. "Hopefully I'll s-s-s-stop twitching when I'm f-f-f-fourteen, 'cause no one likes t-t-t-t-to hang out with a twitcher."

I thought I would hang out with a twitcher, but I was too shy to say so and, also, I figured a thirteen-year-old boy wouldn't want anything to do with an eight-year-old girl.

A little blond boy hung over the edge of the bunk bed, his hands dangling like he was about to jump into a handstand. "I'm Charlie," he said. "I'm nine and my parents are in jail but I've got grandparents who like to see me when they have time. Are your parents in jail?"

Norm shook his head no and I shook my head yes—though I knew my previously jailed father was dead. Charlie didn't notice. He just kept talking.

"That's Hannah." Charlie pointed to the girl in the

bunk below him. Then he pointed to the boy in the bunk across from him. "And that's Jason. They're brother and sister, just like you. Hannah is ten and Jason is—"

"I'm eleven," Jason said.

"Hannah doesn't speak," Charlie said. Hannah didn't look up. With her head dropped like that I could see how knotted her wavy hair was. I felt bad for her that she didn't have a sister like Gi to comb out her hair every night and every morning. And then I felt bad for myself because who was going to comb my hair now?

"Hannah hasn't talked in a year," Jason said. "But I like talking, so I do it all the time." Hannah continued to look at her knees, Brian jerked and spasmed, and Charlie hung like a little white-haired chimp while Jason monologued about how his dad lost his job and started getting drunk every day. His dad didn't mean to hurt anyone, Jason claimed, but he couldn't help himself when he was drunk and so the social worker thought Jason and Hannah were better off here while their parents worked things out.

And then Jason asked, "So why are you here?"

I looked at Norm so that he would answer. I didn't want to say what was in my head: *We're here because two nights ago, my mother beat my sister so badly her entire body looked like a swollen, purple piece of meat; we're here because we were so hungry, we stole butter from the grocery store and ate it raw; we're here because we had no hot water and no heat all through last winter; we're here because our mother takes off for months at a time, and when she returns she drinks and curses and smokes and brings strange men into the house.*

Norm said, "We're here because our mom is too busy to take care of us."

"What about your dad?" Jason asked.

I looked at Norm again. He and I had the same last name, Brooks, though we had different fathers. Norm was a real Brooks and he was the only one of the five of us who was born while Cookie was married to his father. Gi and my oldest sister, Cherie, had Cookie's maiden name, Calcaterra. Camille's last name was completely different. No one, including Camille, knew where the name came from. When we asked her about Camille's last name, Cookie either shrugged or told us to *shut the fuck up* and *M.Y.O.B.*! Gi told me that by the time I came along, my normally shameless mother was embarrassed that each of her kids was from a different guy. So she gave me the last name Brooks to make it appear as if fewer men had fathered us.

"Our dad's too busy for us, too," Norm said. As far as I knew, Norm couldn't remember his father. He'd left before Norm was three. I had vague, almost dreamlike memories of my father—they were sensory memories: the smell of spicy aftershave, shiny black shoes, whiskers that scratched my face when he kissed me on the cheek.

Brian and Charlie warned us to stay away from Becky.

"Sh-sh-sh-she's evil," Brian said.

"She lies like a fly with a booger in its eye!" Charlie said.

"Sh-sh-sh-she lies like a g-g-g-guy with a b-b-b-b-booger in his fly!" Brian said, and we all laughed until we heard the screeching voice of Becky from the bottom of the stairs.

"Rent-a-things! Dinner!" she shouted. I knew she'd put *thing* into action. Norm and I looked at each other. He was thinking the same thing.

Liver. After months of eating butter, saltines, and anything else Gi and Camille could get down their pants at the grocery store, the only thing I couldn't stomach was liver. Norm looked at his plate, then mine. He tilted his body so our shoulders almost touched and whispered, "We've gone hungry most of our lives. No big deal if we don't eat it." While the other kids silently forked in the gray, slimy sheets of meat, Norm and I picked at the teaspoonful of peas on our plates. Becky had cut-up apple, American cheese slices, and a pile of tater tots with ketchup on her plate. I guess she didn't eat liver either.

Mr. Callahan, our foster father, ate with his head tilted toward his plate, as if no one else was at the table. His skin was the same color and texture as the meat he put in his mouth. His hair looked wet and shiny, the color of steel cables. Mrs. Callahan and Becky chatted in louder than normal voices. It was as if they thought we needed a lesson in dinner conversation and they were going to provide it by example. I couldn't focus on what they said because I was too enraptured by the way Becky's lips flopped loosely as she spoke; and the way the nooks of Mrs. Callahan's teeth had food crammed into them like putty. Every few minutes, she stuck her finger in her mouth, cleared out the gunk, licked it off her finger and swallowed.

When it was clear that Norm and I weren't eating the liver, Becky tapped her mother on her bony elbow and nodded her salad-bowl head toward us. Mrs. Callahan slammed her fist on the table and said, "You two are disrespectin' me! Go to your room." Mr. Callahan continued to eat as if no outburst had occurred. Becky grinned, her face flushing pink as she watched us leave.

When the other kids returned to the bunkroom, there was a stiff-edged silence. I wondered if Becky or Mrs. Callahan was waiting outside the door, trying to catch one of us saying something bad about them.

Finally Jason broke the news, smiling as if he was taking joy in the message: "Mrs. Callahan says that you don't get any meals for a whole week and you better eat everything you can at school 'cause that's all you're getting."

Norm and I both laughed. After going without food, or with very little food on the weekends, school lunches were a banquet to us. We'd been living on free school lunches for years. This was something so normal for us, it didn't even register as a punishment.

Jason looked bewildered. He grinned bigger and then he said, "AND—"

We looked at him silently.

"A-a-a-a-and what?" Brian asked.

"And, you have bucket duty for the week, too," Jason said.

"S-s-s-sorry," Brian said.

"Not your fault," Norm said, and then he turned to me and said, "We'll take turns and I'll go first if you want. It won't be the worst thing we've ever done."

"I'll go first," I said. "I want to get it over with."

Jason and Brian explained to me exactly where to go and what to do with the bucket in the morning. It seemed nutty to me that anyone with running water and working toilets would use the bucket system instead.

At eight o'clock the single light bulb went out and everyone hushed. Then there was the click of a key in the doorknob lock, followed by the firm clink of a bolt lock sliding into place. The descending footsteps that followed were neither Becky's slumping waddle nor Mrs. Callahan's flat-footed slaps. They were firm, solid footsteps. The silent Mr. Callahan. I guess he knew we were there, after all, though by the look on his face at dinner, you'd think he was blind to everything but the plate in front of him.

I lay in bed and listened to the TV in the room below us. *Mork & Mindy* was on. The last time I'd seen that show I was at the home of a friend from school. We sat in the living room with her mom, dad, and twin sister. Everyone was flopped over the couch, feet up on the coffee table, a bowl of popcorn being passed from lap to lap. And we laughed. I thought then, just as I thought now, that when I grew up I'd have a family, a couch, and a TV. We'd lie around watching *Mork & Mindy* together, and everyone would be happy and warm.

The next morning, I opened the closet door with one hand, pinching my nose shut with the other. While keeping my body as far away as possible, I reached in and grabbed the metal handle of the blue plastic bucket. Like a tight-rope walker, I went slow and steady to avoid sloshing. Out of the bunkroom, then down the stairs like a bride: foot out, feet together, foot out, feet together. Becky and Mrs. Callahan didn't want the bucket carried through the kitchen so I went out the front door, through the junk car yard, around to the weedy side yard, past the stand-alone garage, past the corrugated metal junk shed (which Brian said was full of broken furniture), and into the dirt backyard to the poop hole, which was the size of a manhole cover and as deep as cellar stairs. I stood as far from the hole as possible, turned my face away so I wouldn't have to see what I'd been carrying, and upended the bucket. A shovel stood, dug into the dirt nearby. I picked up the shovel, almost as tall as I, and shoveled in a few mounds of dirt. On the way back to the house, I stopped by the shed where the hose was. The bucket was rinsed clean before being returned to the bedroom.

After doing this for a few days, I realized that if the bucket had just held pee, things might have been easier.

But one of our bunkmates was a night-pooper. Norm suspected Jason, as Charlie was a sound sleeper and had to be poked awake each morning, Hannah seemed too shy to ever poop in a bucket, and Brian shook so much there was little chance he'd be able to poop in a bucket without pooping on the floor.

One night, Norm asked the dark room: "What happens when the poop hole fills up?"

"It's an old w-w-w-well," Brian said.

"They'd probably make us dig another poop hole," Charlie said.

"Yeah," Norm said. "Then after a few years, the whole yard would be one giant poop hole."

We all laughed at the idea of slumpy Becky, flat-footed Mrs. Callahan, and liver-faced Mr. Callahan living at the crest of a giant poop hole.

There was one nice thing that happened our first week at the Callahans'. Each day when we got home from school, Norm and I found food hidden under our pillows: bits of pancake, a handful of cereal, and half an orange each. We gobbled it up quickly before the floating eyes and ears bobbed into our room and caught us.

2
The Devil We Didn't Know

O nce we were allowed to eat with the family again, we also had to take part in kitchen duty. This was almost as bad as poop duty because Mrs. Callahan and Becky sat at the kitchen table watching while we cleaned up. Often there was a box of cereal or a plastic container of cupcakes on the counter, and I couldn't help but stare at them as I washed and dried the dishes.

"Don't you be getting' any ideas about that food," Mrs. Callahan often said. Or, "If them eyes could talk they'd say, 'I want some that,' wouldn't they?" Becky laughed while her mother taunted me. And when I stood on my tippy-toes, carefully putting away the dishes I'd just washed, they would point and clap their hands as if it were a clown show. It was hard to get those glasses up onto the first shelf of the top cupboards with no footstool or chair to stand on. I could only get each glass to the edge of the shelf and so had to use subsequent glasses to push back the ones I'd already placed. When I dropped a glass (an unfortunate consequence of not being tall yet), I got the same punishment as when Mrs. Callahan didn't think I cleaned the pans or stove top well enough: a beating with a wooden spoon. Of course Mrs. Callahan went straight for my head, standing over me like a machine, rhythmically whacking my crown over and over again. Sometimes she'd turn to Becky and say, "You have a go now." Open-mouthed Becky loved nothing better than beating my head. She was taller than I was, but not as tall as her mother and she made up for the shorter distance between her raised arm and my head by bringing the spoon down with such tremendous force, I felt each hit echoing in my stomach and my vision blurred into a foggy black. It was a feeling that was both familiar and foreign. When my mother was home, she often whacked me on the head or body—wherever she could quickly throw a fist or foot. But my sisters had been a hair-trigger barricade between my body and Cookie's. They were human bumpers who padded themselves around me as soon as the first hit was thrown. So I'd never endured a beating the way I endured them at the Callahans'. My intimate knowledge to this point had been only of a first blow.

I tried to do everything right so as to avoid the Callahans' wooden spoon, but pitfalls were everywhere. Even if I did everything the right way, there was still the behavior of my foster sibs that could summon a spoon, or worse, to my head. Jason, in particular, brought a lot of trouble to the group. He refused to do his poop bucket duty, and no matter how much we begged and cajoled him, he wouldn't relent. If the bucket wasn't out, we weren't released to meet the school bus, and if we didn't meet the school bus, we didn't go school. If we didn't go to school, we were locked in the bunkroom for the entire day until dinner.

Brian quickly became my favorite foster sib. He nicknamed me *Rosie Petals* within the first week. Each day when we gathered at the school bus for the ride home, Brian stuck out his quaking hand for me to high-five.

"R-r-r-rosie Petals!" he'd say. "How w-w-w-was school?" My sister Gi had always asked me about school and she, too, had called me by a nickname, *mia bambina*. I started to understand then that curiosity is a form of love and that words can convey a feeling far beyond their meaning.

Of course there are nicknames that aren't affectionate. Norm quickly dubbed Charlie *Charlie Brown* after he pooped in the bathtub and Norm had to clean it up.

And Jason called me a baby because I was the only one who couldn't tie my own shoes. Even Brian, whose hands darted to and fro, managed to tie his laces while mine were neatly stuffed behind the tongue of my sneakers. In addition to calling me a baby, Jason called me *Raggedy Rosie* and my brother *Raggedy Norm* because our clothes were so tattered and worn. I was switching back and forth between my fancy velour outfit and a pair of pants with holes in the knee. Norm had been alternating between two pairs of pants, although he was lucky enough to have three shirts that fit.

One Saturday afternoon when Norm and I sat on the back deck looking out at the poop hole and the hoarding shed, Mr. Callahan came outside. His metallic hair glinted in the sunlight.

"Come with me," he said. I wasn't used to hearing his voice and was surprised by how high it was.

We followed him past the living room to the hallway where there was an entrance to the basement. Mr. Callahan opened a squeaky door and motioned for us to go down. I grabbed onto my brother's back and stood there. This cellar triggered an alarm in my body. I felt like a dog at an open cage door. Norm stood firm at the top of the stairs.

"There are old clothes down there for you to pick out," Mr. Callahan said in his almost girly voice.

Norm shook his head no.

"I'll sit in the living room over there," Mr. Callahan pointed to the living room. "And you two go down and pick out some clothes."

Norm nodded yes. Neither of us moved until Mr. Callahan was sitting in his chair facing the television. I stepped in first and then Norm followed and pulled the squeaky door shut behind himself.

"We'll have a little bit of warning if he comes down," Norm said, motioning with his head toward the door.

The basement floor was half cracked cement and half dirt. It smelled like a cave and there were mold spots on the walls like bruises on an old woman's legs. Green crickets leapt across the floor, jumping out of the way of our feet. Against the back, bruisy wall were a washer and dryer. Next to the washer and dryer was an old nubby couch on top of which sat three cardboard boxes full of clothes. None of the clothes were folded. My sister Gi would have dumped the boxes and folded everything before deciding what to take. Norm found three pairs of pants and a blue striped sweater. I found two pairs of pants, a dress, and three cap-sleeved T-shirts that I knew would fit.

"Do we take it all?" I asked Norm. I didn't want to be greedy, but it would be nice to have it all.

"Not sure," Norm said. He scrunched up his mouth

and stared at the clothes as if they would give him an answer.

"What if we take one top and one pair of pants each?" I said. I really wanted the dress. After my bath when I lived with my sisters, Gi would comb my hair and put me in a pretty dress. I'd never worn a dress to school. Any nice dresses we found in the trash bin, or in the bags dropped off at the Salvation Army after hours, were reserved for when I was so clean my skin squeaked if you slid a finger across my arm.

"Yeah, one outfit each," Norm said, and he put back everything but one pair of jeans and the sweater. I kept the red cap-sleeved shirt and a pair of brown corduroy pants because I figured it would be easy to hide dirt on the dark colors.

When we came up the basement stairs, Mr. Callahan was waiting on the other side of the door.

"Thank you," I said, still too scared to make eye contact.

"Thank you, sir," Norm said, and he stuck out his hand to shake Mr. Callahan's, then quickly pulled it away and tucked it into his pocket when Mr. Callahan didn't respond.

By the time we'd put our new clothes away in the room, the other kids had gathered on the back deck. It had turned out Mrs. Brady was wrong and there were no board games, or any games, at this house. The only thing the kids did was stand on the back deck and talk about the Callahans (if they weren't within hearing distance), make jokes about the poop hole, or laugh about something one of the kids had done in the night (Charlie fell out of bed regularly, Brian sometimes spasmed so fiercely his limbs hit the underside of Charlie's bed, and Hannah, once, spoke).

I suggested a talent show, or a singing competition—something my sister Gi often organized when the five of us were together. Everyone agreed this was a great idea. Jason went into the house and came back moments later with Becky's boom box, a box of tapes and, unfortunately, Becky. We could use her music, she said, as long as she could perform first.

After she finished singing "Paper Roses" along with Marie Osmond, Becky slumped into the house. She had no interest in seeing anyone else do their song.

Norm flipped through Becky's tapes and picked out a Meat Loaf duet, "Paradise by the Dashboard Light." Norm held his fist microphone close to his mouth and sang all the guy parts, which was most of the song. I didn't mind; Gi liked this song, so I liked it, too. When it was time for the girl to sing, I lifted my fist microphone to my mouth, shut my eyes and belted out the words. In the song I asked if I would be loved forever.

I imagined I was singing this song to my sisters. The three of them would answer me with *Yes, of course we'll love you forever!*

Sometimes when we sat across from each other at dinner, or on the bus ride home from school, Hannah would lift her eyes and look at me intently. I imagined we were silently communicating, commiserating about the state of things at the Callahan house. I even heard her words in my head: *Why does Becky get to eat hot dogs when we get split-pea soup?*

After school one day, Hannah paused on the stairs leading to the bunkroom, turned, and gave me her look. I was right behind her, Norm behind me, Jason behind Norm, and Charlie Brown catching up from the bottom. Brian had stayed home that day as he'd had a fever the night before.

"What?" I said.

Hannah cupped her palm around her ear and leaned toward the top of the steps and we all did the same. It was moments like this when I connected the idea of being a foster kid with the idea of being an abused pet. We were cordoned off in rooms, sent to beds, and locked in at the owner's convenience; we had a continuing growling hunger that had no correlation to whether we were fed or not; we were always grateful for the smallest scratch on the back, the tiniest morsel of food; and we continually feared the hobnailed boot to the sides of our heads. Like dogs and cats, instinct was the driving force that helped us survive. And instinct was directing us now as we silently lined up on the stairs and listened.

Jason started to speak, and I turned back and shushed him. There was a soft whimpering coming from the bunkroom. Hannah looked at me. Her yellow-brown eyes were the shape of lemons and when she actually made eye contact, they seemed huge and vibrating.

"Brian," I said, and we all ran up the steps, Norm passing me on the way.

"They tied him up!" Norm said when we filed into the room.

Brian's hands were bound in white sweat socks around which an extension cord had been circled many times. The extension cord led to the bottom of his bed.

Charlie dropped onto the ground and scooted under the bed.

"It's tied to the springs," he said.

"D-d-d-don't touch it," Brian said.

"We have to untie you." Norm dropped to the ground below Charlie.

"N-n-n-no!" Brian said. Charlie and Norm scooted out from the below the bed and looked at Brian.

"They'll b-b-b-b-beat you if you un-t-t-t-t-tie me."
Brian swallowed like he was trying not cry. And then
he smiled.

"Do you want another pillow?" I asked, and I
grabbed mine from my bunk and went to stack it on
Brian's flat pillow, which looked dirty and wet, probably from him crying on it.

Norm and I then sat on the floor near Brian, Charlie
hung over the bunk, Jason lay on his bed, and Hannah
lay on hers as Brian told us what had happened. That
day, when his fever broke, Mrs. Callahan asked Brian
to bring the folded laundry up from the basement. He
made it down to the basement, but couldn't make it up
the stairs without the pile of clothes scattering out of
his flailing arms. Mrs. Callahan immediately dragged
him up to the bunkroom and tied him to the bed. She
told him to think about what he'd done wrong so that
he wouldn't repeat the same mistake of messing up her
folded laundry.

"Does it hurt being tied down like that?" I asked. I'd
seen my sister Gi tied to the hanging bar in the closet.
But because Gi wouldn't let Cookie get close enough
to tie me up, I'd been able to avoid my mother's worst
tortures.

"I'm k-k-k-kinda used to it," Brian said.

"How?" Norm asked. He went to Brian's wrist and

played with the cords, trying to loosen them. Brian jerked like a fish hanging on a hook.

"The l-l-l-last t-t-t-time I stayed home s-s-s-sick, they t-t-t-t-tied me up," Brian said. Usually we didn't have the patience to wait for Brian to finish a sentence and one or the other of us would jump in and finish it for him. But that afternoon, we all sat quietly and waited through Brian's stuttering as he told us about the various tortures he'd received at the many homes he'd been in. The worst was the house where the foster mother was convinced that the reason Brian twitched was because the devil was inside him. With a cross nailed to the bed above him, and his arms and legs bound to the rails of the bed, the foster mother thumped Brian on the head with a bible while saying prayers and incantations to draw the devil out of him.

"Did it work?" Norm asked.

"N-n-n-nope." Brian said. "I'm still t-t-t-twitching!" We laughed as if that was the funniest thing we'd ever heard.

With Brian tied up—the brutality directly in front of us—there was more of an openness in our conversation that night. Eventually we each listed the other foster homes we had lived in. For all of us, each stop had been transitory and rarely felt like a home where we belonged.

"Our two oldest sisters had to rescue Rosie from one home because she sat in a rocking chair all day and wouldn't talk or eat." Norm and I both glanced back at Hannah, whose head was dropped toward her toes. I knew what it was like to be silent like that. I remembered the terrifying aloneness I'd felt—aloneness as an impenetrable tangle of nerves in my body. When I opened my mouth there was no space for words to escape. Only my sisters could untangle me and clear the way for me to speak. The social workers had called it "failure to thrive."

"Sometimes I have nightmares that I'm in that rocking chair again, all alone," I said. "And I always wake up hungry." Everyone laughed. It was then, when I remembered the feeling of hunger, that I recalled the food that had been tucked behind my and Norm's pillows the week Mrs. Callahan decided we wouldn't be fed. "Hey, were you the one who put that food behind our pillows?" I asked Brian.

"Yes," Brian said. I had noticed that Brian never stuttered when he said yes. But he always got caught on no.

"You gave them food?" Jason asked. "Where'd you get food?"

Brian explained that with all his spasms it was easy to stuff food in his pockets. When his hands jerked under the table, everyone thought he was just twitching as usual.

"Thanks, dude," Norm said, and he gave Brian a high five on his bound hands.

"Thanks," I said, and I high-fived him, too. I don't know why I wanted to cry just then, but I did. Maybe it's because sometimes the small things could feel so huge. It was as if these gestures of kindness were pieces of wood I was gathering and—slowly, over time—I knew I'd eventually have enough materials to make a life raft and paddle away.

Brian had to stay tied to his bed during dinner. I tried my hardest to slip a bit of meat loaf under my shirt but Becky must have sensed something was going on as she had her pinpoint eyes trained on me the whole meal.

Back in the bunkroom after supper, Hannah produced a roll from under her shirt. Too shy to hand it to Brian, she gave it to me. I fed Brian while everyone was changing and getting ready for bed.

Norm came in from brushing his teeth and started singing Three Dog Night's "Joy to the World." Brian had recently told us that that was his favorite song. I started singing along, and then the other kids jumped in. We got louder and louder with each verse until we were deliriously belting it out off key. Even Hannah played along, moving her lips as she mouthed the words. I think we all knew that the Callahans wouldn't come up and tell us to quiet down. If they did, they'd have to look at us while looking at Brian bound to his bed. It was one thing to torture a kid, it was a whole other thing to be bold enough to face your witnesses.

When the song was over, I taught everyone something I'd learned at school a few days earlier.

"Count to ten, but put the letter D in front of every word," I said.

Everyone began in unison: "Done, doo, dree, door, dive, dicks—" We broke apart laughing.

"D-d-d-dicks!" Brian shouted again, and we laughed even harder.

In the middle of that night I awoke to Brian whisper-shouting my name.

"R-r-r-rosie P-p-p-petals!"

I got out of bed and went to him; he was still bound by his wrists. "You okay?" I whispered.

"I have to p-p-p-pee." Brian rarely used the bucket at night but he'd been tied like that since late afternoon.

I tapped on my brother's leg. He startled awake as if someone was attacking him. Then he calmed and leaned over the bed and looked at me and Brian.

"Brian has to pee," I said.

Norm hopped off his bunk and the two of us scooted under Brian's bed and felt around in the thick blackness for the cords tying him to the springs. After several minutes we were able to untie him and free his hands. We both edged Brian out of bed and then Norm helped him get to the closet. Brian was shaking more than usual and his stiff legs kept folding like a broken lawn chair. Norm stayed with Brian at the closet to make sure he got everything into the bucket, and then he walked him back to bed.

"You n-n-n-need to t-t-t-t-tie me up," Brian said. "You'll get in t-t-t-t-t—"

"No way," Norm said. "I'm not gonna do that."

"No one will tell that we untied you," I said.

"I d-d-d-don't want you to get b-b-b-beat," Brian said.

"I'd rather be beat than tie you up," Norm said.

None of us spoke again, but I thought I heard sniffing from Brian's bed, as if maybe he was crying.

It was a relief to be at school, immersed in books, studying, and jumping rope on the playground. In sharp contrast to that relief was the dread I felt when the school bus stopped in front of the Callahans' in the afternoon. The day after we'd found Brian tied up, Mrs. Callahan was waiting for our bus on the sidewalk. When I saw her out the window, the usual dread turned to cement bricks that dropped to the bottom of my stomach.

Jason shouted with a big Cheshire cat grin on his face, "Look out, someone's in trouble!"

The foster gang filed off the bus, five of us pausing nervously in front of Mrs. Callahan. Jason waltzed right past our foster mother, straight into the house. Becky spastically skipped behind him.

"Thing One and Thing Two!" Mrs. Callahan pointed at Norm and then clasped her hand around my ponytail. "In the kitchen. Now." We marched off, Norm in front with Mrs. Callahan dragging me in by my hair.

The wooden spoon was on the table. Mrs. Callahan dropped my ponytail, lifted the spoon, and whacked Norm on the top of the head many times in succession. When I watched, it was like I was being hit, too. I felt a ringing down my spine. Norm winced and his eyes teared up, but he didn't make a sound.

"That," Mrs. Callahan said, waving the spoon in front of Norm's nose, "is for untying Brian before he was good and ready! Now say you're sorry!"

"Sorry," Norm said.

"You know I do that for his own good," Mrs. Callahan said. "That boy needs to get a little muscle control is all and I'm tryin' to help him out and you're up there undoing all the good I do!"

"Sorry," Norm said again.

Mrs. Callahan lifted the spoon and came down once, right where I imagined a tender purple lump had already formed on Norm's head. His body rocked back from the blow.

"That's for calling Charlie *Charlie Brown*." Mrs. Callahan pushed her sharp voice into a whiney singsong when she said *Charlie Brown*.

"Sorry," Norm said. His eyes were shut and quivering as if they were stuck that way and he really wanted to open them.

Mrs. Callahan lifted her spoon and came down once more on the same spot. Norm made a little half-choking, half-coughing sound.

"And that's for saying that my yard is full of poop! You yourself have stood out there horsin' around in the dirt like the animal you are, so you oughta know that ain't a yard full of poop!" Mrs. Callahan was starting to wheeze as she spoke. It seemed the effort of the spoon beating along with her enthusiastic explanations was too much for her lungs.

"Yes, ma'am," Norm said. He blinked his eyes open; his eyelashes were shining wet.

"Say it's not a poop yard!" Mrs. Callahan lifted the spoon above Norm's head.

"It's not a poop yard," Norm said. He scrunched up his eyes waiting for the blow. Mrs. Callahan smiled. She lifted the spoon higher and I had to scrunch up my eyes, too. And then she came down and tapped him. Lightly. Just once. Like it was a magic wand. Mrs. Callahan laughed, her lungs making violin sounds, as Norm gasped with relief.

"Now git outta here and don't you be causin' me any more trouble or you'll end up lookin' like Brian did last night!"

Norm looked back at me, his eyes wild and darting. He was scared for me, but there was nothing he could do, so he ran out. Mrs. Callahan smiled at me as if I were a piece of steak she was about to eat.

"You untied him, too, didn't ya?"

I nodded.

"And you stole a roll from my dinner table and fed it to him, didn't ya?" The violin sounds of her wheezing lungs started to pick up a second note. Now it was more of an accordion playing inside her.

I nodded again. There was no way I was going to tell her that Hannah stole the roll. The way Hannah curled up in silence every night, it was pretty clear she'd already received enough beatings for a lifetime.

"You know what you are?" Mrs. Callahan held the spoon above my head. "You're a dumb little doo-doo-head."

I shut my eyes and braced myself for the blow.

"Say it," Mrs. Callahan said. Her accordion lungs played a few wheezy notes.

I opened my eyes and looked at her imploringly. I didn't know what I was supposed to say.

"Say it!" Mrs. Callahan said.

"Say *I'm sorry?*" I asked.

"Say *I'm a dumb little doo-doo-head.*" She laughed, and the accordion wheeze played faster.

"I'm a dumb little doo-doo-head," I said.

"How dare you get fresh like that in my kitchen!"

And there it was. The hammer game. Over and over again she pounded the center of my skull with the wooden spoon. I didn't have the resolve and strength of my brother and I yowled in pain.

"I want my sisters!" I cried when she was done.

"Yeah, some help they are." Mrs. Callahan wheeze-laughed. "Now tell me about that little game you taught everyone."

I sniffed and took several stuttering breaths.

"The talent show?" I asked.

"No, the game. The counting game." The accordion wheeze was transitioning into a donkey's hee-haw with every thick inhale.

"With the letter D?" I asked.

"Yeah. With the letter D." *Heeee haaaw.*

"You count and you put the letter D before each number," I said. Snot and tears fell down my face. I wanted to take the hem of my shirt and wipe my nose but I was afraid to move.

"Do it," Mrs. Callahan said. "Count like that for me."

"Done, doo, dree," I paused, and Mrs. Callahan raised the spoon higher and took a giant noisy breath.

"Say it, keep countin'," she said.

"Done, doo, dree, door, dive, dicks," I said, and I shut my eyes waiting for the blow.

"What did you say?" Mrs. Callahan put the spoon on the table and looked at me, her mouth gaping, head tilted to one side.

"Done, doo—"

"No, say the last one you said, say"—she wheezed a few times as if to catch enough breath to finish her sentence—"the word for six."

"Dicks?" My body clenched, waiting for something to happen. Surely she wasn't going to stand there and listen to me say a dirty word.

"Again." *Wheeze, wheeze.*

"Dicks." I didn't understand why she wasn't hitting me. Was Becky going to burst into the kitchen and tackle me to the linoleum floor?

"Once more and hold it this time. Like you're singin'

it." Mrs. Callahan picked up the Holly Hobby dishrag from the counter and wrapped it around her left hand as if she were about to enter a boxing ring.

"Diiiiii—" I started and Mrs. Callahan bridged the towel-wrapped hand over my lower teeth and pushed down so that I couldn't bite her as she shoved three fingers deep into my throat. I grabbed her wrists but couldn't pull her away from me. It felt like there was a two-hundred-pound man at my throat, a thirty-pound weight holding my jaw open. When I stepped back away from her, she stepped forward until we had done some terrible dance—me backward and her forward—across the kitchen so I was now pressed against the back door, gagging but unable to cough.

"I don't ever want to hear them dirty words coming out of a little doo-doo-head like you! You hear?" The wheezing was almost as loud as her voice. From violin to accordion to donkey, it now sounded like a group of tiny people in her body, screaming to cheer her on as she continued to fill my throat with her hand.

Mrs. Callahan swirled her fingers as if she were clearing a drain. I couldn't get enough air to make any noise. My throat was on fire and my jaw felt as if it might snap loose from the pressure. Her fingers felt as if they were made of bottle brushes. I continued to pull at her arms, but she didn't seem to feel it as she leaned into me, her hand going deeper down my throat.

"You got it? Dumb little doo-doo-head!" Mrs. Callahan pumped her hand now, the motion of plunging a toilet. My eyes went black and my stomach lurched and spasmed, ready to churn up the pizza I'd had for lunch at school. She plunged again and it brought forth a tornado spinning in my head and lungs. It was about to wipe me out, cast me down, choke me into oblivion.

And then Mrs. Callahan pulled her hands away and the tornado was gone. I coughed and gasped, and now I was wheezing just as she was. Face to face, we were both bent over our knees, each of us swallowing in huge gulps of noisy air—even then as young as I was I sensed the perverse intimacy in an act of one-on-one violence. A yin-yang of torturer and torturee.

Mrs. Callahan stood first. She went to the sink, washed her hands, and then leaned her scraggly head over the faucet and lapped up water. When she was done, she looked back over her shoulder and said, "If I ever catch you using nasty words like that again, I'll rip your lungs straight outta ya."

I stood up straight and nodded. That cool water had looked so soothing, it was all I wanted. My single desire.

"Now get outta here before I stick that spoon down your throat and really make you cry." She picked up the spoon and started coughing. I was out the kitchen door before she could take a step in my direction.

In the upstairs bathroom, I leaned over the running faucet and gulped at the water just like Mrs. Callahan had done. It ran down my throat, over my chin, down my neck. When I couldn't take any more, I turned off the faucet and stared at myself in the mirror. The brown of my eyes nested in a veiny red pool. The skin surrounding my eyes was puffed up like miniature life preservers. My nostrils were red and the corners of my mouth looked ripped and swollen. I splashed water on my face, refixed my ponytail, and went to the bunkroom. Everyone was in a circle on the floor playing gin rummy. The game paused, and they all looked up at me.

"R-r-r-rosie P-p-p-petals," Brian said. "You O-k-k-k-kay?"

"Yeah." My voice was raspy.

"You sure?" Norm asked.

"Deal me in," I said. Half my words were swallowed by air. Just talking made it feel like there was an emery board filing my throat.

Hannah scooted over so I could sit between her and Norm. Jason dealt me into the next hand. While Jason talked on and on about a kid at school who pooped his pants, Norm leaned into me and whispered in my ear, "We got a snitch."

That night as we listened in the dark to *Mork & Mindy* on the TV in the living room, we all knew who the snitch was. Jason wasn't in his bed. And we could hear his laughter chugging up to us each time Mork did something particularly funny.

In second grade, after reading *Charlotte's Web*, my teacher, Mrs. Evans, said that we should feel sorry for the people who mistreat us because they were miserable wretched souls who were trying to spread their misery into us. If we let them get to us, she'd said, then they'd win: we'd be sad wretched souls, too. I tried real hard to feel bad for Jason as he watched TV while I lay in bed with the top of my head pounding, my jaw aching, and my throat pulsing so hard that currents of pain radiated down to my feet. But I couldn't do it. All I could do was hate Jason. Hate him and take joy in the fact that everyone in that room, even Hannah, I'd bet, was hating him, too.

3

Out of the Poop Hole

I thought about my sisters constantly, and I rarely thought about my mother. Yet Cookie was the one for whom the social worker had arranged regular supervised visits. Before the first two visits, Mrs. Callahan took Norm and me into the kitchen, fed us Oreo cookies and said, "If you tell anyone anything about what goes on in the privacy of this here home, I will shove my hand down your throats and rip your little lungs out."

For the visits, Cookie was escorted to the Callahans' by the Mrs. Brady caseworker. Mrs. Brady sat at the kitchen table, stooped over paperwork, ignoring us. We ate the sandwiches and bags of Lays potato chips Cookie had brought and listened to her talk about the people she'd met at her court-ordered Alcoholics Anonymous meetings. Usually she made fun of them because they cried or did something she thought was particularly stupid. Norm laughed at Cookie's stories, and I listened quietly and ate as much as I could, as quickly as I could, before the food was gone. When Cookie fed us like that, chatting in the voice she usually used with men who were giving her things such as liquor, cigarettes, affection, or an empty house to store her kids, I could almost convince myself she was a good mother. Once Cookie had left, Norm would talk about how much he missed Cookie and how great everything would be if we were with her again. After living at the Callahans', I almost missed her, too. At least with Cookie I knew exactly what to expect.

The day Norm and I waited in the kitchen for Mrs. Brady to bring our mother for her third visit, Mrs. Callahan said, "One word about what happens here and you two foster things get the wooden spoon on your head." Then she smiled, shoved the Oreo package toward me first, then toward Norm, and added, "In fact, all your little bunkmates will get the spoon, too!" Norm and I looked at each other and I was sure we were having the same thought: all but Jason, the real eyes and ears that reported to Mrs. Callahan.

For this visit, because Cookie had been sober for four weeks straight, Mrs. Brady stayed in her car in the driveway. Cookie made a big show of hugging us and kissing us when she first came in. Mrs. Callahan stood watching, a corkscrew of gray and brown hair spiraled up from the center of her head. It occurred to me then that in Cookie, Mrs. Callahan had met her equal. Visually they were misaligned: Cookie's hair was a luxurious dyed black, her lips were the color of fresh blood, and she wore clothes that emphasized her massive breasts. Mrs. Callahan wore oversize sweatshirts with teddy bears on them, and her face and hair presented a coarse desert with no variation in color. Her eyes were as gray as her nearly invisible eyebrows and pencil-line lips. But they both knew who their audience was, and each had two distinct personalities according to who was present: the nice, kind mother or the abusive dictator who fed off brutalizing little children.

"Make yourself at home," Mrs. Callahan said, holding the kitchen door open. She pulled her lips back in an approximation of a smile. We sat at the kitchen table and ate the bologna sandwiches and Frito chips Cookie had brought. As usual, Becky and Mrs. Callahan were flitting in and out.

"If I stay sober the next few weeks, I get to have you two come home for Christmas," Cookie said.

"Will our sisters be there?" All I wanted for Christmas was to see my sisters. Period. I wouldn't even consider wishing for a Teddy Ruxpin or a Lite Brite, or a pretty dress with a matching headband. As I'd never had a proper Christmas with a tree and presents brought by Santa Claus, those things seemed as likely as wishing I could be the first eight-year-old president of the world.

"Up to them," Cookie said.

Norm upended the nearly empty bag of Fritos into his mouth.

"You don't look so excited," Cookie said to Norm. "Don't you want to be with your mommy at Christmas? You'll get presents. And candy. And did I mention presents?" When Cookie smiled, her face was almost unrecognizable. Her eyes turned into crescent moons and her lips stretched out like thin red rubber bands.

"We're just tired," Norm said. "But we're excited." He rubbed the top of his head where Mrs. Callahan had beaten him the night before. She'd gone at my head, too. Our crime this time: not emptying the poop bucket for Jason when he refused to take his turn.

"Do you have lice?" Cookie said. "Are these people dirty?" Cookie stood and leaned over Norm's head. She pushed aside his short hair. He cringed when she touched the raised purple lump. "What the fuck happened here?!" Now Cookie looked angry. It was the face that usually preceded tossed beer bottles and sharp-heeled pumps to the thigh.

Norm shrugged.

"You tell your mommy who hurt you!"

"No one," Norm mumbled.

"Tell me who hurt you!" Cookie's fury was growing, but it wasn't directed at us. It was odd to be on our mother's side of the anger, to be aligned with her.

Before Norm could answer, Becky shuffled into the room and went to the cupboard. Cookie sat down, and we watched as Becky opened a box of Ding Dongs and took out three that she held against her slopey chest as she slumped out of the kitchen again.

"Was it her?" Cookie whispered.

"It was—" I started.

Norm put his finger on his lips to shush me. He nodded his head toward the kitchen door. I didn't want to risk our foster sibs being beaten, particularly Brian and Hannah. But the words were coming out of me with a force I couldn't suppress. I was sore and exhausted. And, mostly, I was scared. More scared of the Callahans than I'd ever been of Cookie. In the Callahan house there was no Gi or Camille or Cherie to fight back for me.

"Mrs. Callahan," I said.

"But it's worse than that!" Norm said. Once I'd cracked open the reveal, he couldn't stop himself from ~ing too. With tag-team sentences, we whispered everything: Brian being tied up; the wooden spoon on our heads; the fingers down my throat; the bunkroom door locked at eight p.m.; the poop bucket; Jason who would never empty the bucket; the withholding of meals as punishment; the fact that even when we were fed, it was from a menu far inferior to what was handed the princess of the house, open-mouth-breathing Becky; and the injustice of having had to take my favorite games out of the Hefty bag when we left home only to find that there was not a single game here.

Cookie gasped, cursed, and dragged her sharp red-nailed fingers along the bottoms of her eyes to wipe away black mascara tears. She scraped back the kitchen chair and hugged Norm, kissing him all over his head. Then she went to me and kissed my cheeks and the top of my head, murmuring, "My sweet babies, my sweet little babies . . ." It was such an odd display. All I wanted was to be loved and here she was loving me. But it didn't feel any more real than Mrs. Callahan's stiff, stretched smile. How strange, I thought, that it took another person beating the daylights out of us for Cookie to be horrified by her children being hurt.

Cookie sat and blew her nose into a paper towel. Mrs. Callahan came into the kitchen, took a bag of beef jerky from the cupboard, and then used her small teeth to rip open the package.

"Ya want some?" She held the open bag toward the three of us. Norm stuck in his hand and took a tiny, shriveled piece.

"Oh, take some more," Mrs. Callahan shook the bag. "Take as much as you want." Norm took a larger strip and handed it off to Cookie. Then one more that he handed to me. I immediately ripped it in half with my teeth and chewed the leathery piece like a wad of gum.

"I taught them not to be greedy," Cookie said to Mrs. Callahan in her seduction voice.

"Looks like you did a good job all right," Mrs. Callahan said, and she left with the jerky bag.

Cookie leaned over the table, and Norm and I leaned toward her. I was still working on my first bite of jerky.

"I promise, I will break you out of this shithole as soon as I can!" My mother knew as well as Norm and I that nothing good would come of a confrontation with Mrs. Callahan. We'd been removed from Cookie because she was an alcoholic who abused us. In a credibility battle between our mother and Mrs. Callahan, our mother would come out the loser. Cookie had never been sober long enough to get away with things the way Mrs. Callahan did.

Just get me back to Gi, I thought. *Gi will take care of me.*

The Sunday before Christmas, Mrs. Brady fetched Norm and me from the Callahans' house. We had been granted a two-hour Christmas visit alone with our mother at her new apartment.

"R-r-r-rosie P-p-p-petals," Brian shouted from the top of the stairs just before I walked out the door. "S-s-s-see ya on the f-f-f-flip side!"

"See ya!" I shouted. "If I get candy in my stocking, I'll save some for you!" I knew there would be no Christmas stocking, but if my sister Gi was there, she'd probably have a sweet for me that I could share with Brian.

"We need to get a move on," Mrs. Brady said, and she put her firm hand on my back and scooted me out the door to Norm, who was already waiting by Mrs. Brady's car.

"Are my sisters there?" I asked as I fastened my seatbelt.

Mrs. Brady didn't answer and instead slid on a pair of black sunglasses like the ones I'd seen on movie posters for *The Blues Brothers*. She backed out of the driveway and then put the car in gear. I looked out the back window and watched the Callahan house recede in the distance. Other than Brian, there was nothing in that house I'd miss if I never returned.

"Are my sisters there already?" I asked again.

"No," Mrs. Brady said. "They're—"

"How long is the ride?" I asked.

"Fifteen minutes," Mrs. Brady said.

"Does the fifteen minutes of the drive count as part of our two hours?" I didn't want the commute to cut into my time with Gi and Camille, and Cherie if she could get there too.

"No," Mrs. Brady said. "Now let me drive."

"If my sisters show up late, can we stay for two hours starting when they get there?" I asked.

"Rosie," Mrs. Brady said, "your sisters won't be there. But they'll meet you at the Callahans' when you get home from your mother's apartment."

"Wait! They're going to be at the Callahans'? Do they know what time we'll be back?"

"Yes. They're bringing presents."

"Can I wait for them at the Callahans'?" I flipped around to look out the back window. The Callahan house was long gone. Two hours with Cookie seemed like a torture I'd have to endure to get to my sisters.

"We're going to see our mom!" Norm said. "Stop asking questions!"

I shut my eyes and thumped my back against the seat. I wanted time to accelerate like a fast-motion film.

And then, once I was with my sisters again, I wanted it to slow to a dragging tenor hum.

I hoped my sisters would be allowed to visit for more than two hours. After all, they hadn't beaten or starved us. All they'd done was steal food to feed us, wash us in cold water so we'd always be clean, and love us so much they'd take a wooden-heeled shoe in the face just to keep us safe.

Mrs. Brady stopped the car in front of a chipped stucco building surrounded by disheveled, slouchy duplexes. Half the front porch sloped off into the weedy front yard. There was a black-barred front door, making it look it like the entrance to a jail cell. Cookie stood at the end of the walkway in black spandex pants and a white blouse that ruffled down the front, giving her the look of the Looney Tunes Tasmanian Devil.

Norm rushed out of the car and wrapped himself around Cookie's sturdy body. I stood on the sidewalk watching as Cookie kissed the top of Norm's head and stroked his chocolate brown hair down behind his ears.

"I'll be here at three sharp," Mrs. Brady said. "If all goes well, we can do a visit like this every two weeks."

"I'm sober as a judge," Cookie said, and she gave Mrs. Brady that stretched-rubber-band smile that looked like it was about to snap and break.

We stood on the walkway with Norm reaching around Cookie and Cookie's red-clawed fingers grasping my shoulder as we watched Mrs. Brady drive away. Once she'd turned the corner, Cookie peeled Norm off her, grabbed each of our hands and quickly walked us down the sidewalk, past the apartment building.

"Where are we going?" Norm asked. We both trotted to keep up with Cookie. She was yanking my arm so hard, I thought it might break off and then I'd look like the one-armed Barbie Camille once found for me in the Salvation Army Dumpster.

We stopped a block away, alongside a long brown station wagon with peeling fake-wood paneling. It was parked in front of a fire hydrant. Three tickets were tucked below the windshield, flapping in the icy breeze. I had been so anxious and worried about making it back in time for my sisters that I hadn't noticed how cold it was outside until this very moment.

"Is this our new car?" Norm asked. He didn't appear to be cold, though, like me, he didn't have a jacket. Last week, the temperature had significantly dropped. I borrowed a big down coat with a fur-trimmed hood—probably a fifth-grader's—from the lost and found at school and wore it home to the Callahans'. I got four days in that coat until a large girl with hair as orange as fire stopped me in the hallway and asked if it was hers.

I shrugged my shoulders up and down. She reached her freckled hand into the collar and turned the tag out. On the back was her last name, O'Brien. My face burned with embarrassment as I took off the coat and handed it over to her. She took it without a word and tied it around her waist with the arms. She didn't even put it on as she walked out of the building.

"This is our getaway car!" Cookie raised her eyebrows and grinned. She opened the back door and told us to get in. There were clothes, shoes, dusty blankets, mud-encrusted boots, old grease-stained McDonald's and Wendy's bags, empty beer cans, and the noisy foil and paper wrappers of Sno Balls and Mounds bars filling the backseat. It smelled like the clothing we got from garbage bins: the stench of used gym socks, fried grease, and cigarette smoke.

"Can we sit on your clothes?" I asked. Our mother was the opposite of my sisters in this way. While Cherie, Camille, and Gi pulled lint off sweaters and sprinkled water on wrinkled clothes and hung them up to dry with, hopefully, fewer wrinkles, Cookie treated her clothes, the only clothes in the family that were actually purchased at stores, like balled-up used Kleenex.

"No!" Cookie said. "Get on the floor, under the clothes. Pile everything on top of yourselves."

Cookie stood at the open door and watched as Norm

and I burrowed like a couple of hamsters. She leaned in and arranged more clothing on our backs. I heard the clinking of empty beer cans over my head as she piled those on, too.

"Norm, you're the man now. You're in charge, got it?"

"Got it," Norm said, his voice muffled.

"You take care of your sister and keep her hidden until I get back."

"Got it," Norm said again.

"And don't come out no matter what, you hear?"

"Got it," Norm said firmly.

The door clicked shut, and then Cookie was gone.

Norm shook me awake, his hand under the pile of clothes that covered me. I tented a sour-smelling sweatshirt over my and Norm's heads. He put his finger to his mouth in the *shhh* gesture. Outside the car I could hear Cookie yelling and screaming. And then I heard Mrs. Brady's voice.

"Norman! Rosanne! It's okay to come out!" Mrs. Brady called.

"Don't move," Norm whispered.

Mrs. Brady and Cookie stopped just outside our car. Cookie was crying as she talked, but it didn't sound like there were any tears involved.

"And they had to shit in a bucket!" Cookie wailed. "A bucket! Now tell me, do you think it's civilized in this day and age to shit in a plastic bucket?!"

"I promise you, we'll find them and we won't return them to—"

"Find my children now!" Cookie screamed. The conversation faded as Cookie and Mrs. Brady walked away from the car. Every now and then, one or the other of them would shout out, "Norman! Rosanne! Come out! You won't go back to the Callahans'!"

Eventually there was quiet, and then the sound of a car slowly driving past us. Ninety seconds later, Cookie opened the squeaking front door. The car shifted to the left as she sat.

"Kids," she said as she started up the engine. "Keep your heads covered. We're making a break for it." The tires screamed as we pulled away from the curb. Cookie lit up a cigarette; menthol filled the car and mixed with the other pungent odors.

"What about the visit from our sisters?" I whispered to Norm. "They're bringing us presents!"

Norm shook his head, and I started to cry. I didn't want to live at the Callahans', but I didn't want to live with my mother, either. I just wanted my sisters. I wanted Gi and Camille and Cherie.

"Mom!" I popped up from the rubbish pile like

Oscar the Grouch coming out of his trash can. "Can we pick up our sisters?"

"Keep your head down for fucksakes!" Cookie shouted. She tossed her cigarette out the window and then shoved in a cassette and sang "Coward of the County" along with Kenny Rogers.

I burrowed deeper under the clothes, shut my wet eyes, and sent a message out to Gi that I hoped she would magically hear: *Mom's kidnapped us from the Callahans'. Come get us as soon as you can!*

4

Before the Storm

"Stop signs are optional," Cookie shouted back to us over the Kenny Rogers cassette. Cars honked, presumably at us. I had no idea how fast we were going, but there was a sense of high speed by the way the floor vibrated and rumbled.

"Red lights are optional, too, when you've got precious cargo in the back!" Cookie shouted. There was more honking.

"Whoops!" Cookie said, and the brakes screeched and trembled as we jolted to a stop. I was so padded in by trash, I barely felt it. "OUTTA THE WAY, YOU STUPID FUCKS!" Cookie shouted, and we were off again.

I pushed the clothing and beer cans off my head to get to the smoky air. Norm did the same. His face looked like a doll head peering out from a trash can. I laughed.

"What you laughing about?!" Cookie turned down the music.

"Nothing," I said.

"You still hiding?"

"Yes," Norm and I both said, and he winked at me.

"You know when Kenny says his name it sounds like Kinny," Cookie said.

"That your new boyfriend?" Norm asked.

"Ha! I wish!" Cookie laughed. I heard the click of the lighter, and the smell of fresh menthol soon drifted over me. "I'm talking about Kenny Rogers. The singer."

"I bet if you met him, he would be your boyfriend," Norm said. He always knew the right way to talk to Cookie. Flattery got you everywhere.

"I bet you're right," Cookie said. "Kenny and me, we'd make a good couple. You know, I used to love Frank Sinatra and Elvis. But Elvis is dead and Frank is old, old, old. I sang backup for a few bands, you know? When I wasn't go-go dancing."

"Uh-huh," Norm said. We'd heard about go-go dancing and backup singing many times. Everyone believed the dancing part. But Gi liked to point out that Cookie could barely carry a tune. Who would hire her for backup singing?

"I'm all about the future now. Zooming ahead. Living in the here and now. You get me?"

"Yup," Norm said.

"And Kenny Rogers, he's the future. He's where it's at."

Cookie turned up the music and belted it out along with "The Gambler." When the song was over, she turned down the music again.

"Remember Jeff?" Cookie asked, but she didn't wait for an answer. "He's that tall sexy cop—or retired cop—and he's gonna make sure I get custody of you kids."

"That's great," Norm said.

"Great," I said with less enthusiasm. Of course I remembered Jeff. I'd never met him but Cookie had been living with him the four months she'd abandoned me, Norm, Gi, and Camille in the Toad House. The night she returned she told us she'd had to stay with Jeff because his wife had died of cancer and there was no one to take care of his daughter, Candice. Gi's face had turned dark and she blinked her eyes hard when Cookie had told us how terrible she felt for Candice and how much that girl needed a mother figure around. Later, Gi whispered to me and Camille that she was disgusted that Cookie would take care of someone else's kid but not her own. It wasn't until I saw how outraged

Gi was that I understood the senseless misdirection of Cookie's affections.

The road beneath us changed from bumpy and grinding to soft and quiet. We slowed and there was no longer the sound of cars passing. Soon we jerked to a stop and Cookie killed the engine. There was a click-clicking as the car cooled down. My mother reached into the glove compartment, pulled out a bottle of Jontue, and sprayed her chest and the back of her neck. The car now smelled of musk, cigarettes, beer, and fast food.

"You kids wait here," Cookie said. Her door made a loud squawk. Then there was the sound of a house door opening and shutting again. A minute later Cookie was back at the car. She opened the back door and looked at us, buried to our shoulders in old clothes and garbage.

"Can we get out?" Norm asked.

"Yup. We're staying here now, but you two have to share a pull-out bed in the den." Cookie turned and walked back to the house as Norm and I pushed our way up and out, sending several beer cans clattering to the ground. The December air stung my face, and I wondered if in all that trash there was a coat or hat that might fit me.

Cookie sauntered into the house, her big hips swinging like a pendulum. We followed her straight into the living room, which was tidy and symmetrical. There was nubby brown wall-to-wall carpet and two brown couches. A peach floral throw pillow sat angled at the arms of each couch. The walls were the same peach color, and a peach shag rug sat like a pond between the couches.

"A rug on a rug," I whispered to Norm. I'd never seen anything like that.

"Sit here," Cookie said, and she pointed to a couch before leaving the room. Norm and I sat side by side, our hands on our laps. We were each in our outfit we'd picked out of the Callahans' basement. I'd been wearing mine for three days and I'd been sleeping in it, too, because I didn't own any pajamas.

Cookie returned with the very tall Jeff, whose eyes looked as plastic and hollow as a Ken doll's. I wondered if he was still sad about his dead wife. His mouth was a dash above his chin. His nose was a perfect triangle. His daughter, Candice, stood beside him. She was about the height of Gi and had dark hair like Gi's, only Candice's hair was as straight as a ruler. Gi always wanted her hair to be straight like that. Once she went to sleep with a wool beanie on her wet head and a scarf bound around the hair that hung below the beanie in an attempt to tame her wild locks. In the morning, when she unraveled the scarf and removed the hat, her hair was a plastered smooth bullet on top and frizzed open like an umbrella from her ears down. She quickly rinsed her head under the cold kitchen tap to erase what she'd done in the night.

When I stared at Candice, I wished I could stick my whole self under the kitchen tap and erase everything about me. Candice wore Jordache jeans like the rich girls at school. Her top was shimmering purple with feathery ruffles at each shoulder. Over the bottoms of her jeans were glittery purple leg warmers and below those were suede boots with purple laces. Nothing looked used. Or old. Or slept in.

"This is Norman," Cookie stood behind Norm and put her hands on his shoulders. "And this is Rosanne." She reached out one arm and shook my shoulder.

"Hey," Candice said. She dropped her head a little and smiled. Jeff kept his empty eyes and hard face on Cookie.

"This is a glorious night!" Cookie said, and she clapped her hands together. "Our first night as a complete family!"

"Cool," Norm said.

"Cool," I said, and I couldn't help but wonder why we'd call ourselves a family if we'd just met, and how this family could be complete without my sisters.

The next morning, Jeff drove Candice to school, leaving Cookie, Norm, and me alone at the white kitchen table. There was a platter of bagels and cream cheese on the table. I was on my third bagel, my stomach hurting and distended. I didn't trust that this wouldn't be our last meal for days.

"Jeff has invited us to live with him forever!" Cookie said. I put down my unfinished bagel. Cookie's forever wasn't a forever I could believe in, but it did mean there were probably a few more meals coming my way.

"Can we go to school?" I asked. School was the only reliable refuge in an unreliable life.

"Not until I get the heat off my back," Cookie said. She got up from the table, leaned in front of the silver toaster and applied a coat of red lipstick. "Jeff's getting me a job. He's got connections."

"What kinda job?" I asked.

"An executive secretary," Cookie said. "That's a fancy job."

"Are you going there today?" I asked.

"I'm going to talk to them today." My mother played with her thin hair that had been fluffed up into a helmet, still looking at herself in the toaster.

"Can I come?" I asked.

Cookie turned toward me. "No! Not with the heat on my ass. If they catch us, it's off to the big house for me and the little house of horrors for you two." She laughed.

Cookie picked up her big silver purse from the counter and hoisted it onto her shoulder. She kissed us each on the top of the head. "You're the man in charge, Norm." She ruffled his hair and then rhythmically scratched the back of his neck with her flittering nails. Norm shut his eyes. I thought of dogs being scratched in just the right place and wondered if Norm would start kicking his leg in bliss.

Once Cookie had left, Norm said, "You think there's any chance Jeff would let me be the man in charge?"

"No way!" Jeff only spoke to, or looked at, Candice and Cookie. How could Norm be in charge if Jeff didn't even see that he was in the room?

"I hope she gets that job," Norm said. He picked up my half-eaten bagel and took a bite. There was a slug of cream cheese at the corner of his mouth.

"Who's *the heat*?" I asked Norm.

"The police," he said, chewing.

"Why are they called *the heat*?"

"I dunno." Norm shoved the remainder of the bagel in his mouth.

"So, isn't Jeff *the heat*?"

"I guess." Norm's words were dulled from the giant chunk of bagel he was chewing. "But he's not after her to arrest her. He's after her so he can touch her."

"Gross," I said, and Norm just laughed, revealing great smears of cream cheese across his teeth.

Before she left for school, Candice had given Norm and me a pink satin bathrobe and a white satin nightgown, both of which had belonged to her mother. These were to wear while we washed our clothes.

"I would give you my clothes," Candice said to me, "but there's no way they'd fit." I had a feeling she was glad about this and wondered if she'd really let me wear her clothes if they did fit. I'd have loved nothing more than to put on something purple, sparkly, and feathery like the outfit Candice was wearing when we met.

Norm put on the robe and I put on the nightgown. The bottom dragged on the ground behind me and tripped me when I walked up the basement stairs after loading our dirty clothes in the washing machine. We spent the day in the peach and brown living room watching reruns of *The Jeffersons* and *The Love Boat* along with all the daytime game shows.

"You think Mrs. Callahan beat Brian and the other kids because we left?" I asked Norm. A commercial for Golden Dream Barbie was on. I'd love to have had

Golden Dream Barbie with her stiff, white hair that could be styled using the tiny plastic curling iron that was included in her box.

"Mom told the social worker everything that went on in that house. I guarantee no one's gonna spend another night there."

"You sure?" I asked.

"Trust me!" Norm said. "I'm the man of the house and I know this stuff."

I wondered why Cookie wanted Norm to be the man of the house. What about me? Couldn't I be in charge, too? Still, I believed what Norm said. Believing that my foster sibs would be okay allowed me to enjoy the luxury of a satin nightgown, food in the refrigerator, and *The Twenty-Thousand Dollar Pyramid.*

"Will our sisters be able to find us here?" I asked at the next commercial break.

"Mom doesn't want them to see us," Norm said.

"Why not?"

"She's thinks they'll call Social Services, or the heat, and turn her in."

"No, they won't! They have presents for us! They just want to visit!"

"She doesn't trust them," Norm said. "Now be quiet." The commercial was over, and Norm was focused on the TV. I could no longer see what was on the screen. My head was fizzing and my body felt electric. I wanted Camille and her soft cheeks that folded into little apples when she smiled. I wanted Cherie, who was so grown up there was nothing she couldn't do. And I wanted Gi. I was her *bambina,* the one she loved. *Je t'aime,* I whispered, hoping my sisters would feel the message, wherever they were.

After a five thirty dinner of hamburgers and tater tots—all made by Jeff and served by Cookie—Jeff went down to the basement and came up with a sparkly white plastic tree. Christmas was only three days away. Jeff sat on the couch, his long legs spreading out wide, and Cookie pushed her round body against him, giggling, as the two of them watched us three kids decorate the tree. Every ornament was either silver or peach colored. When it was time to put the big silver star on the top of the tree, Jeff slowly got off the couch, reached his large arm up and jammed the star downward once, quickly, onto the shiny white peak. His mouth was weighted into an angry frown, and I wondered why this beautiful tree didn't make him smile. Cookie turned off the lights in the living room, and Jeff plugged in the tree lights. It was my first Christmas tree; I wished that my sisters could be there to see it.

"Isn't this perfect!" Cookie said. She went to Jeff, wrapped her arms around him, and pushed her breasts into him as if they were dancing. Jeff stood still and solid as a telephone pole. But I could tell he liked it by the way he kept one arm firm on her hip. Cookie was always like this when she had a man: grabby and doting as if the man would evaporate if she diverted her attention from him for even one second.

"It's a great tree," Norm said. He had one hand on each hip, like a superhero about to take off, and was staring at it, up and down.

"A beautiful tree for this beautiful family," Cookie said, her face alighting on Jeff. I still didn't understand why she called us a family.

"I miss my mom," Candice whispered to me.

"I miss my sisters," I whispered back.

"This is going to be the best Christmas ever!" Norm said.

It wasn't. Candice had a purple fake-fur Christmas stocking hanging from a gold hook on the windowsill. It was heaped and overflowing with chocolate Santas, malted milk balls, peanut butter cups, Butterfinger bars, Bottle Caps candies, and three little cardboard boxes, each of which had a pair of earrings in them. Cookie had taken a pair of Jeff's large gym socks and written my name on one and Norm's on the other. They were folded over the back of one couch. In our socks there was one chocolate Santa each (surely taken from Candice's abundance), a peanut butter cracker snack pack (there was a case of them in the cupboard, and Candice put one in her lunch each day), a Twinkie (Candice's lunchbox loot, too), an orange, a toothbrush, a comb (in Norm's sock), and a hairbrush (in my sock). Norm ate all the food in about thirty seconds, then sat like a puppy next to Candice watching her slowly open a Butterfinger and bite off splintery chunks of it that she swirled around in her mouth without chewing. Later, when everyone was in the kitchen having breakfast, Norm stole a package of peanut butter cups and a package of malted milk balls from Candice's stocking. He flashed them to me under the Christmas tablecloth on the kitchen table. I smiled and didn't feel bad that he'd taken them. We both knew she had so much candy in there she wouldn't even notice they were missing.

After scrambled eggs and sausages, made by Jeff, we returned to the living room for presents. Candice opened box after box, gifts from her dad, her aunts and uncles, her grandparents on both sides of the family. There was even a present from the mailman that had been placed under the tree, and Candice was the one who got to open it. Norm and I got one gift each. The tag said, "Love, Mom and Jeff." For Norm, a brown snorkel jacket. For me, a pink snorkel jacket. Candice got a purple snorkel jacket from Cookie and Jeff, too.

It turned out my first Christmas with a tree and presents didn't feel any more wonderful than all the Christmases I'd spent watching people on TV with a tree and presents. In fact, without my sisters around, it was far worse.

In January, my mother started her new office job. Norm and I still couldn't go to school because Cookie was worried the heat would find out where she was and take her to jail. She explained one morning that she had multiple warrants out for her arrest ranging from shoplifting to hit-and-run to drunk driving to speeding tickets. I had a feeling she was almost proud of this list, of the number of things she'd gotten away with.

Norm and I stayed home and watched TV or played board games. If it was sunny out, we'd wander around the snow-covered backyard where there was no poop hole and no hoarding shed. I thought of my sisters every single day. In my head, I composed letters to Gi, telling her what I was watching on TV, or how pretty and tidy Jeff's house was, or how Cookie loved Jeff so much she looked only at him when he was in the room. I never wrote the letters because I didn't know where to send them. Cookie said she had no idea where my sisters were and that if they really loved me, they'd come to me. Every time she said this, I shut my eyes and remembered Gi saying *Je t'aime*. How could someone say that and not mean it?

Once Cookie was collecting a paycheck, she started going out after work, usually coming home after Norm and I were already in bed. One night there was knocking on the window of the first-floor den where we slept. Norm got up and opened the curtains. Cookie's face was splatted against the glass. She was laughing and drooling.

"Open the fron' door," she slurred.

Norm and I tiptoed to the front door, unlocked it, and let our mother in. She smelled like beer, cigarettes, and sweat. Her blouse was misbuttoned, the left side hanging down like a pointed tail at her crotch. In one hand was the pair of suntan pantyhose she'd been wearing when she left the house. In her other hand were her white pumps.

"I los' my purse," Cookie said. "An' my keys."

"How'd you get home?" Norm asked.

"Where's the car?" I asked.

"The car?" Cookie tilted her head like she was trying to remember. "Who the fuck cares!"

"Did you lose your wallet?" Norm asked.

"Mommy don' have credit cards, honey—" Cookie dropped the pantyhose and shoes. She squeezed Norm's cheeks, like she was about to kiss him.

Norm pulled his face from her hand. "How much cash did you lose?"

"Don't you worry," Cookie singsonged. "Mommy's got it all unner control." Cookie zigzagged toward the stairs. She went up one step, then back down again. Once more she tried: up one step, back down again. Norm went to our mother and pushed on her back.

"Help!" he whispered. I took Cookie's hand; it felt sweaty, hot, and unfamiliar. I realized then that'd I'd never held my mother's hand. I'd held my sisters' hands—it was a rule, I had to have a hand when I crossed a street. But this lump of flesh was as foreign to me as if it were Jeff's hand.

"Do you like the Bee Gees?" Cookie asked as we worked our way up the steps.

"Yeah," I said.

"They're good as Kenny Rogers. Kinny. Call 'em Kinny. No more Elvis! No more Ol' Blue Eyes!" Cookie laughed. "One day I'm gonna fuck tha' man. I'm gonna fuck Kinny Rogers. Right, Norm?" Norm didn't answer. I had heard Cookie use the F word many times, but she'd never used it like this. My guess was that when Cookie said she was going to *fuck Kinny Rogers* she meant she was going to feed him. I imagined Cookie taking a silver fork cocooned in saucy red spaghetti noodles and jamming it into Kenny Rogers's mouth. The idea made me smile.

When we got to the upstairs landing, Norm opened Jeff's bedroom door and I pulled Cookie inside. At the sound of Jeff's voice, Norm and I ran down the stairs and back into the den. We could hear Jeff yelling on the floor above us. Cookie was mostly silent. Eventually his voice lowered to a murmur. And then we couldn't hear them at all.

By February Jeff had had enough. We were at the breakfast table when he told Cookie she had one week to get out. Candice stopped eating her cereal, her spoon poised in the air. She looked from me to Norm to me. Once she saw our impassive faces, she got up from the table, dumped her bowl in the sink, and left the kitchen. She was probably relieved to be getting her father back to herself.

Cookie dragged her long red fingernails from Jeff's knee to his crotch. "Sweetie. You're not serious now, are you?" she purred.

"One week," Jeff said. He removed her hand and then stood and left the kitchen, too.

"WELL FUCK YOU, YOU UPTIGHT FUCK-WAD!" Cookie threw her napkin on the ground and then swept her arm across the breakfast table, sending the box of Life, my and Norm's bowls, and her and Jeff's coffee cups sailing to the ground. "I'm not staying in this shithole another motherfucking minute," she said, and then she left the kitchen as if nothing had happened.

5
The Devil We Knew

By lunchtime that same day, we'd landed at a hotel off the expressway. It was shaped like a white farmhouse with a steep, sloping tin roof. The parking lot cars all had New York license plates, but there were two trucks parked there, too. One from California and one from Florida. I'd never left Suffolk County, New York, in my life, and though I remained there now, the out-of-state plates made the hotel seem farther than it was from all the other places I'd lived.

"This sure as hell ain't the Hotel California." Cookie started singing the song. Norm and I sang along with her. When we sang together like this, I felt like we were a regular family, normal people. And I liked my mother when she sang: even though she barely carried a tune, she was happy, her voice didn't have its saw-tooth edges. She wasn't angry.

Cookie was still belting it out as she turned the rear-view mirror toward herself and applied a fresh coat of red lipstick and a few coats of black mascara. She fluffed her hair with her lacquered nails, then reached into her front-button blouse and pulled each of her breasts up higher in her bra before spraying her cleavage with Jontue.

"Showtime!" Cookie interrupted our song and waggled her fingers around either side of her face. She turned to us in the backseat and said firmly, "Wait here." I wished we could go back in time, just forty seconds, so we could be singing again.

A few minutes later, Cookie returned to the car. She'd secured a highly discounted second-floor room and a job as the hotel barmaid. She'd be paid in tips, but she could drink for free. "Good enough for me," Cookie said.

"Me too," Norm said. He was picking out his clothes from the piles of garbage in the backseat. After our time with Jeff, we had more than one outfit each. And we had our Christmas jackets.

"You know a hot-sheets hotel like this usually only gets customers for a few hours, not for a few weeks,"

Cookie said. "So they really appreciate a nice family like us classing up the joint."

I wasn't sure what my mother meant by a *hot-sheets hotel*, but I sensed it was somewhere my sisters wouldn't want us to stay. "Can Gi, Camille, and Cherie visit us here?" I asked.

"Absolutely not!" Cookie said. "Those bitches will complain to Social Services about me, and then the gig is up."

"But what could they complain about?" I asked. "You have a job. We have a place to sleep. We have clothes—" I picked up the pair of purple leggings Candice had given me.

"They're lying twats!" Cookie said. "All of them! They'll do anything to destroy this family. You watch!"

I knew if I started crying, Cookie would turn on me. I had to hide my love for my sisters from her or I'd be recategorized into a lying twat too. Whatever that was.

The hotel room had a queen-size bed, a daybed, and a cot. Cookie claimed the bed, Norm took the daybed, and I happily took the cot as it was on the far side of the room, away from the window and so away from the sound of drunken bar patrons wandering out into the street.

Other than the fact that Cookie wouldn't enroll us

in school, I didn't mind living in the hotel. I felt safe as there were plenty of people around and always someone awake at the front desk. It was sort of like having a doorman or a butler. Once Cookie was making enough tips to pay for a second room, she moved in next door. I kept my place on the cot and Norm took the bed. This time, I was trying to stay away from the sounds that floated through the wall: Cookie in her happy singsong, adoring a man for a night or sometimes a few nights. If they lasted more than a week, she said it was love and called the group of us a family. When they left, Cookie blamed us.

"Clean yourselves up so you don't drive 'em away!" she said one night, her wobbling body flopped against a wall. "No one wants a woman who passed two ratty lil' terriers outta her twat!" I was starting to understand what *twat* meant and I immediately wanted to correct her. There were five of us. My mother had passed five of us out of her twat.

Most days Cookie watched TV until she had to go to work at night. When Norm and I were hungry, we knocked on her door. She'd reach into her bra and pull up a bill that was always slightly sticky and warm. If she handed us a twenty, we'd eat in the restaurant at the bar, ordering enough food to keep us full the whole day. It was fun to look at the other people eating there:

lots of pretty ladies with glittery short skirts, heels as high as a steak knife on end, and eyelashes that were so long they looked like black butterflies. If Cookie handed us a ten or five, we'd walk along the busy road to the market about a mile away and buy what Norm always called the biggest bang for the buck. My brother's single concern was quantity, not quality, and so our diet consisted mostly of giant bags of beef jerky and Circus Peanuts, which we could get for less than one dollar.

One day that winter, we turned into the neighborhood near the market. There were little detached houses, snow-covered lawns that didn't have cars or bikes or broken toys popping out like junkyard tombstones, and curbside mailboxes where people had their name painted in cursive or with colorful doughy print. At the end of one street we found a library. This was almost as good as finding free food. No matter where we lived, my sisters had taken us to the library when we weren't in school. There was heat in libraries, bathrooms with abundant toilet paper, and hot water if you wanted to wash your face. No one yelled at you or hurt you in a library, and there were books, of course. So many books that you could never, ever run out.

Norm started running, and I quickly caught up with him, almost slipping on the icy front steps. When we got inside, we walked a circle in each section until we'd found the areas where we wanted to park ourselves. Norm was near the comic books and graphic novels. He loved anything with robots, or monsters, or evil forces that threatened to destroy the world. I liked Judy Blume books about interesting girls who had a lot to think about and much to say. Every now and then, I'd stop reading, close my eyes, and imagine that I was one of the characters. My favorite was Sheila Tubman from *Otherwise Known as Sheila the Great*. Sheila's afraid of everything: dogs, swimming, thunder. But she gets herself through it all. I wanted to be Sheila the Great and live a life where thunder was the scariest thing around.

By spring, the librarians knew us and let us check out more than the limit of five books each. And because we were living in a hotel room, it was easy to find our books to return them when they were due. The farthest anything could hide was under Norm's bed where the maids, who only came when they felt like it, never cleaned. I always hoped the maids would be our friends, or stand-ins for my sisters. They were young and pretty, like my sisters, and I wanted them to bring us candy, brush my hair, and put on talent shows with us. Instead, they ignored us, like a couple of forgotten pet goldfish in a murky-water bowl.

Sometime after Norm's thirteenth birthday that summer, Cookie started taking daily trips out of the hotel. She'd return an hour or so later with a brown paper grocery bag filled with goods. There were lavender towels one day. A Mr. Coffee coffeemaker another day. Pillows and sheets. A radio. And purple sparkly rainboots for me that were about five sizes too big.

When she came into our room with a boom box and a shoebox of cassette tapes, Norm finally asked where she was getting this stuff. Cookie said, "It's mine. Stuff I had in storage."

I pawed through the tapes. "*Saturday Night Fever!*" I said. I'd never seen the movie, but every person in my family loved the songs when they came on the radio, especially Cookie. Camille had learned some of the dances at school and had taught me how to do them. She tried to teach Norm, but he was always going left when you were supposed to go right, and he tripped over his feet as if he were wearing his shoes on the wrong foot.

"Oh, let's dance!" Cookie said.

When Cookie drank, each drink changed her, like layering a cake with different flavored frostings. After the first drink, she was still mean and angry. By the second drink, she'd quieted down a little. Following the third, she was fun—she'd dance, sing songs; she might put makeup on me or finger some gel into Norm's hair. At the fourth drink, she started to get mean. And by the fifth, you didn't want to be nearby if she was around because something terrible would soon be pounding down on you. (And if there was a first drink, there was always a fifth one.) But this day, the day she'd brought home the box of tapes, Cookie wanted to dance, and she seemed completely sober.

I put on the first song of the A side, "Stayin' Alive." Cookie clapped her hands, and we danced together across the flat-carpeted floor. Her butt bounced at its own rhythm when she moved, but she was a good dancer. Better than me, and almost as good as Camille, whose friends had called her the Dancing Queen. Norm sat on the bed and sang along in a perfect falsetto.

When the song was done, Cookie sat on the bed, panting. "If I hadn't blown it by having you fucking kids I coulda kept it up as a go-go dancer." And that was it. The moment was over.

The morning Cookie walked into our room carrying a large wooden jewelry box—its velvet-lined drawers crammed with silver and gold, diamonds and other stones—was the day she was arrested. Norm and I were out at the library when it happened. The front-desk clerk, a man with shiny strings of hair that looked glued to his forehead, told us the guy Mom was stealing from had confronted her in the parking lot. She went nuts and started punching and kicking him. That's when the cops showed up and arrested her for theft and assault. The desk clerk's thin lips formed an unmistakable smile when he said, "She fought hard against those handcuffs."

My own hands went to my wrists and I felt sad and embarrassed for my mother. Norm had known all along, but he didn't tell me until we'd returned to our room that the stuff Cookie had been bringing home belonged to Jeff. Cookie still had the key to his house.

Norm and I waited in the hotel room while Cookie was in jail. We didn't know when she'd be coming back or if Social Services would turn up to collect us. Norm wanted to walk to the convenience store—he had eighty cents he'd gathered from pay phone change slots over the past week. But I refused to leave in case my sisters came to claim us. All day long, I sent Gi mental messages, quoting the directions from the one-page brochure at the front desk: *One minute off the LIE! We're the old white farmhouse with the new-found feel!*

Cookie returned the next day. She'd called Cherie to bail her out.

"Is she going to come visit us?" I asked. "Did she tell Gi and Camille where we are?"

"Are you fucking kidding me?" Cookie said. "Your dumb bitch sister told Social Services on me! Those girls don't give a shit about you and they don't give two shits about me. They're never coming to visit!"

I didn't believe her. I was Gi's *bambina*. If she knew where I was, she'd show up.

The social worker we thought of as Mrs. Brady came to the hotel later that morning. Cookie put on the good-mother act. She stroked my hair and held Norm's hand as she promised that she was still going to AA and calling her sponsor every single day. "I'm seeking therapy," Cookie said. "I *want* to be a better person!"

Now that Norm was thirteen, Mrs. Brady was fine with us being alone when Cookie worked at night. If Cookie stayed sober and continued to go to meetings, Mrs. Brady said, she would work on getting Cookie official custody.

Norm whispered in my ear that the only reason we were being left with our mother was that Mrs. Brady was overworked and didn't have the help she needed to deal with two kids kidnapped from an abusive foster home. I sensed that my brother was right. Cookie was obviously lying about going to AA—she worked as a barmaid! Leaving us with our mother was probably easier than having us in the system. Fine by me, of course. I didn't want to return to the Callahans'. And I was thrilled to learn that now that the heat knew where Cookie was, we no longer had to hide from them. Norm and I could enroll in school.

Cookie watched out the window as Mrs. Brady drove away. "Dumb bitch doesn't know her own twat from the hole in her ass!" Cookie laughed and pulled a pack of menthol Virginia Slims from her cleavage.

"Twat's the place where babies come out, right?" I needed to have my instincts confirmed. I wanted to know for sure.

"Ha!" Cookie said, but she wasn't laughing. "It's your pussy, your cunt, your gash, your hole." My mother lit a cigarette.

Norm put his hands over his ears and shut his eyes. "Stop," he whispered.

"It's the only thing any man ever wants. Other than your tits!" Cookie cackled with laughter, smoke coming out of her mouth as if she were half dragon.

I watched my hooting, smoking mother and wondered why she couldn't just answer my question. When I asked my sisters what a word meant, they explained it clearly, precisely. Gi liked to look up words in the dictionary at the library. She'd hold me on her knee, and we'd flip through the pages until we found the word.

Then she'd read the word aloud, pronouncing it just right, before reading the definition. The next time I saw Gi, I'd ask her to look up *twat* with me. Gi was always happy to look up words. I shut my eyes and called to my sister again, *One minute off the LIE! We're the old white farmhouse with the new-found feel!*

Like magic, Gi and Camille showed up that evening. When Cherie had bailed our mother out, it was in exchange for Cookie telling her where we were staying.

"MIA BAMBINA!" Gi shouted, and I jumped into her arms. Norm was leaning into Camille, letting her kiss the top of his head. We switched and Camille hugged me and Gi hugged Norm.

They brought us baseball hats from a trip to Disneyland they had gone on with their foster parents.

"Can you imagine the Callahans taking us to Disneyland?" Norm asked. We both laughed.

Just as Gi let go of Norm, Cookie was jabbing her finger into the top of Gi's chest and accusing my sister of turning Norm and me against her.

Camille nervously turned on the TV and gathered Norm and me to sit with her on the floor, our backs against the end of the bed. "Don't listen to them," she said, and she put an arm around each of us and began telling us how much we were missed and how Cherie would have been there, but she had to work.

I could barely follow what she was saying as Cookie and Gi were both yelling. And then screaming. And then Cookie told Gi and Camille to *Get the fuck out.*

I hugged Camille close and started crying. She let go of me and hugged Norm. Soon, Gi was on her knees crying as she hugged me. "Don't go," I said.

"*Mia bambina,*" Gi whispered, "*je t'aime and don't you forget it.*"

"Get the fuck out NOW!" Cookie roared, and my sisters got up and hurried out of the room, pulling the door shut so hard that the windows shook.

"FUCK YOU!" Cookie gave her middle finger to the back of the door. "Fucking uppity piece of shit bitches." She looked down at me and Norm and added, "I shoulda aborted every single one of you."

That fall I awoke to someone in our room. Who could it be except Cookie? But even in the dark I could tell this person was tall and thin—the shape of the number one, as opposed to Cookie who was a solid number eight. I wanted to get Norm's attention, but no words would come out. I just started screaming. The figure ducked down so he was hiding beside Norm's bed. Norm awoke, saw him, and screamed too. Together we made an incredible racket. The tall skinny figure jumped up from the bedside and ran out without ever showing his face. Norm hurried to the door and locked it, then slumped down with his back against the door. I was still screaming.

"Stop!" Norm said. "He's gone now."

I got out of bed and sat beside my brother, leaning against the locked door. We heard footsteps in the hall. And then there was knocking.

"Go away!" Norm shouted.

A man said, "You okay in there? You need help?"

Norm and I looked at each other. How could we know that the man who was now offering to help wasn't the man who had just left?

"Who are you?" Norm asked.

"I'm staying in the room next door. I heard screaming."

"Are you the guy who just broke into our room?" Norm asked.

More voices accumulated in the hall. The man who was at the door explained the situation to the others. A woman's voice, whispery-sweet, spoke into the door, "Are you kids okay? Do you need some help?"

"Should we unlock the door?" I whispered to Norm. He violently shook his head no.

"Did the man hurt you?" the woman asked, and Norm and I looked at each other again. It never occurred to me that he came there to hurt us. It didn't seem to have occurred to Norm either.

"No. I think he wanted to steal stuff," Norm said. If he was a common burglar, he picked the wrong place. The most valuable thing around was the TV, which belonged to the hotel and hardly worked because of the pink lines on the screen.

"What did he look like?" a new voice asked.

Norm looked at me. I answered: "Tall and skinny. A grown-up."

There was more mumbling and consulting among the adults. Some of the men ran off to search for the intruder.

"Where are your parents?" the woman asked.

"Our mother works in the bar here," Norm said.

A man's voice: "Cookie? Is Cookie your mom?"

"Yes," Norm said. "We're fine now, but if you could tell her to come up here, that would be great."

I heard the footsteps of the hallway crowd leaving. Hopefully to get Cookie.

"Sweethearts," the woman said, "do you want me to come in and sit with you until your mother shows up?"

"No thank you," Norm said firmly. It would be years, decades even, before either Norm or I could trust a stranger. We'd been in the hands of so many strangers already and though some were genuinely kind, the few who hurt us changed the way we responded to a smile. An offer. A voice. After all, even our own mother could talk with the sweetness of a sit-com mom while acting with the darkness of a cinematic villain.

"Well, my boyfriend and I are going to sit right outside this door until your mother returns," the woman said.

"We're right here," the man said, and I could hear the two of them shifting down to the floor. I imagined I felt the heat from their backs, the four of us like bookends on a single book.

Twenty minutes later, I heard Cookie's cackling laugh in the hallway. Norm and I stood and unlocked the door. Cookie was being held up by two men, one on each arm. Her head lolled, and lipstick was smeared down her chin.

"He shoulda jus' took 'em," she said, eyeing me and Norm. "Woulda made my life soooo much easier if he took 'em!" She laughed so hard, she snorted. And then she laughed even harder. The man and woman who had been sitting outside our door helped the other two get Cookie to the bed. Norm and I, along with the four adult strangers, stood by the bed waiting for Cookie to settle down. She rolled from her stomach to her back and then kicked up her feet so that her strappy shoes flew off.

"Alrighty then," said one of the men who had carried her up, and he and the other man left the room.

"You gonna be okay?" the woman who had sat outside the door asked me. She was in a shirt that was so short the bottoms of her breasts hung out. "You wanna stay in my room?"

"Or do you want us to stay until you fall back asleep?" her boyfriend asked. He was in a red nylon jogging suit.

I shook my head no. "We're fine," Norm said, and he took my arm and pulled me away from them and closer to him.

Two hours later, when the sun was fully up and Cookie was still drunk and snoring, the hotel owner knocked on our door.

"It's Benny. I need to talk to Cookie," he said. Norm let him in while I tried to wake our mother. She smelled sour and unsanitary, like beer that had spilled on a bathroom floor.

"Wha—" Cookie slapped my hands away.

"Benny's here," I said, looking back and forth between Benny, who was now standing at the end of the bed, and Cookie, who was pushing me away.

"Cookie, sit up." Benny was a thin, short man with a demanding voice. He was bald and had so much hair on his chin and lip that I always thought he should trim it off and paste it to his head.

"I'm sleeping," Cookie said.

"Sit up," Benny said. "We need to talk."

"Sit up, Mom," Norm said. He scooted behind her on the bed and pushed her into a sitting position. Cookie burped and then giggled. Norm and I looked at each other, embarrassed.

"Benny!" Cookie said, as if she'd just noticed him.

"I need you to pack up the kids and leave by the weekend."

"Why?" Cookie folded up her brow and swirled her head around, as if it was astonishing that anyone would ask her to leave any place.

"You need to take better care of your kids." Benny looked from me to Norm, then back at Cookie, who seemed to be more awake.

"The fuck you talking about?" Cookie scooted to the edge of the bed and stood. She wobbled for a second and then righted herself.

"I'm talking about you leaving these kids alone in this room while you're off drinking and cavorting with patrons. It's wrong, and I won't have it in my establishment."

"Am I *cavorting*, Benny? Is that what I'm doing? *Cavorting* with *patrons*?" Cookie laughed and stepped closer to Benny. His lip quivered a little and I thought he was about to speak, but he didn't. "I don't think you have any right to tell me I can't CAVORT!" Cookie started laughing.

"I've called Social Services," Benny said, and he turned and left the room.

Cookie ran after him. She stood in the hallway and hollered as he walked away. "YOU'RE RUNNING A FUCKING BROTHEL HERE AND YOU'RE POINTING A FINGER AT ME FOR CAVORTING?! FUCKING CAVORTING?! FUCK YOU!" Cookie stepped back into the room, then turned and went out to the hall again. "AND FUCK YOUR UGLY WIFE, TOO!"

When she returned to the room this time, she was laughing and panting from the effort of having yelled.

"Should we pack our things?" Norm asked.

"Yeah," Cookie said, and she took a few hard breaths. "But not because he's kicking us out. No one kicks out Cookie!"

"Then why are we leaving?" I asked, and Cookie glared at me.

"We're leaving, little Miss Smarty Pants, because we don't wanna be here. We don't wanna *cavort* with such low-class clientele!"

6
No Safe Haven

In the few months we'd lived in the hotel, we'd accumulated what seemed like a lot of stuff: most of it clothing left behind in unlocked rooms that Cookie would rummage through after her shift before the maids came in for the morning cleaning. With the exception of a few cassette tapes, the stuff she stole from Jeff had all been returned.

"Where are we going now?" Norm asked. We'd just gone through the drive-thru at McDonald's. Cookie was driving with a can of Schlitz wedged between her thighs, a box of large fries sitting between the neck of the beer and her belly, and a Big Mac in her hand. I was leaning over the front seat, taking fries from Norm's box. There hadn't been enough money for us each to get our own box, so Norm and I had to share.

"We're going where we end up," Cookie said. She popped a cassette into the player while still holding her Big Mac. A pickle slipped out and landed on the seat between Cookie and Norm, but she just ignored it and then started belting out "Looks Like We Made It" along with Barry Manilow.

"How will our sisters find us?" I asked Norm. He shrugged his shoulders and then shoved a huge handful of fries into his mouth. My brother was never as concerned about my sisters as I was. But I understood. He'd always been more independent, playing with other kids or even alone out on the street until someone went out and got him. And they couldn't carry him around and baby him the way they'd done with me. Norm wasn't Gi's *bambina;* that was reserved solely for me.

"Pit stop!" Cookie said, and she turned down the music. We'd gone about a mile up the road and were stopped in front of a small brick building covered in neon signs that said Miller, Bud Light, and Schlitz. Norm looked back at me and rolled his eyes.

"We'll wait here," Norm said.

"No you won't," Cookie said. She cranked down her window, picked up the McDonald's wrappers and trash, and dropped them out onto the pavement. I never understood why my mother didn't make use of public trash cans. Like toilets with toilet paper, trash cans were something I thought we should utilize whenever one was available.

"Please, can we stay here?" Norm asked.

"Please, can we stay heeeeeere!" Cookie laughed. She leaned over Norm and flipped open the glove box where she kept her perfume. After three quick sprays—cleavage, cleavage, neck—Cookie tossed the perfume on the floor of the car and then opened her squeaky door. She hoisted herself out slowly and then stood there waiting for me and Norm to get out, too. My guess was that the only reason she wanted us in the bar was just to prove to Norm that he wasn't the boss of her.

Norm found us an empty booth in the corner. It had torn red vinyl cushions and a good view of Cookie at the bar. We sat quietly, picking at the white stuffing coming out of the seat, and watching our mother chat with the people around her.

"I thought that Mrs. Brady lady said she's not allowed to drink," I said.

"No, duh," Norm said.

"And Camile told me once that it's against the law for her to take us to bars."

"Just ignore it," Norm said.

My head ticked back and forth between my mother and the front door. If the police came I wanted to run out of there and hide. After the Callahans, I'd rather live in the Oscar the Grouch station wagon with Cookie than go to another foster home.

When her second drink was gone, Cookie leaned over the bar and kissed the bartender on the cheek. He made a show of it, acting like he'd just been kissed by a movie star. If you didn't know Cookie was a mother of five kids, three gone and two currently hiding in a nearby booth; if you didn't know that all of these children had been removed from her care because she beat and starved them; if you didn't know that she would spend every dollar she had on Virginia Slims Menthol 100s and a case of Schlitz before she'd feed even one of her children; if you didn't know that when she met a man she liked, she abandoned her children and left them without money, clothes, food, heat, or hot water; if you didn't know any of this, you might see her smiling with her newfound friends at the bar and think, *Now there's a nice woman! What a load of fun she is!*

Once the third drink was down, Cookie brought to our booth a Coke for Norm and a Shirley Temple for me.

"That's an expensive drink," Norm said, pointing at my pink Shirley Temple.

"Wait, there's more!" Cookie said, and she sashayed back to the bar, then returned with a bowl of peanuts. "Dessert!" she said before she returned to her pals.

Sometime around Cookie's fourth drink, a short redheaded man came into the bar and sat beside my mother. They talked for a minute and then they kissed on the lips. When they pulled their faces apart, Cookie pointed to me and Norm. The man waved and then approached us. Close up, he looked just like Richie Cunningham from *Happy Days*. He even smiled like Richie.

"You must be Norm and Rosanne," he said and put out his hand for Norm to shake. "I'm Ricky." He smiled at me.

"Hi," I said and ate the cherry out of my drink.

"You hungry?" Ricky asked.

"Yes," I said. I wasn't really, but my instinct was always to eat when I could, just in case the food ran out.

"Be right back," Ricky said.

Norm and I watched Ricky at the bar. He had one arm around Cookie's thick waist, and he was talking to the bartender. A few minutes later he returned to us with a red plastic basket full of french fries.

"Your mama says you all need somewhere to sleep tonight, that right?"

"I guess," Norm said.

"Well, I've got a little place to hang my hat right up the road. It's close quarters, so it'll be a bit cozy, but I don't mind if you don't." Ricky looked at me and clicked his eye into a wink. Unlike most of Cookie's boyfriends, this one didn't pretend we were invisible.

"It's up to my mom," Norm said.

"I think she'd like it better than the car tonight," Ricky said. "And if you want, you can ride over there in my tow truck."

"You got a tow truck?" Norm asked.

"Yup. I drive a tow truck. It's my own business. And you know how many employees I have?"

"How many?" Norm asked.

"One! Me!" Ricky laughed, and Norm finally smiled.

The booth made a comfortable bed in spite of the cheesy smell of the cushion. I stayed on my back so my face wouldn't touch the vinyl and slept soundly until Cookie woke me up. It was after two and the bar had just closed.

"We're goin' to Ricky's." Cookie's lips hung loose as she talked, as if she didn't have the strength to control her mouth.

Norm and I scooted out of the booth and followed our mother to the door. Ricky held it open while we three filed out, Cookie staggering in front. "Can we ride in the tow truck?" Norm asked.

"Ab-so-lu-ly not," Cookie said.

"I told them they could ride with me," Ricky said. He was holding Cookie up by the waist. Norm and I followed them to the station wagon. The air felt cold and damp, and I wished I had a sweater. The Christmas coat was somewhere in the back with the empty beer cans.

"Yeah," Norm said. "He said we could ride with him."

"What if you try an' steal my kids?!" Cookie said to Ricky. She pulled away from him and opened the squeaky station wagon door.

I whispered to Norm, "Didn't she just tell the people in the hotel that she wished the robber had stolen us?"

"Shhh!" Norm said.

"GET IN THE CAR!" Cookie yelled, and Norm hurried into the front seat while I took my place in the back. Ricky climbed into his tow truck a couple of parking spaces away. I hated waking up in the night like this and almost wished we were staying in the car so I could go straight back to sleep.

Ricky pulled the tow truck alongside us; his window was down.

"Follow close," he said. "It's just up the road."

Cookie pulled the car out of the lot and immediately turned the wrong way.

"Left!" Norm shouted. "He went left!"

"Fine, fine, fine." Cookie turned the car around and accelerated so that I was thrown back in the seat.

"LIGHT!" Norm yelled, and Cookie slammed the brakes. The car bumped and skidded, and I tumbled into the back of the front seat.

"It's hard to follow when you can't see," Cookie said.

"I'll see for you," Norm said. "Go. Now! It's green!"

This wasn't the first time one of her kids had dictated the drive to Cookie. Usually it was the job of the oldest. But with my sisters gone, Norm was the new copilot.

Cookie missed the driveway and straddled the curb as she followed Ricky to the back of a red brick apartment complex. There were bars on every window.

"Get your jammies," Cookie sang. She killed the engine and stumbled out of the car, leaving the squeaky door open.

"Get your jammies!" I said to Norm, and we both laughed. We'd never had pajamas. The few times I'd been invited to a sleepover at a school friend's house, I pretended that I'd left my nightgown or pajamas at home. The girls I was staying with always offered to lend me a pair of their pajamas. Putting on fresh, clean pajamas felt so good I would compulsively stroke my arms and legs just to feel the cotton against my skin.

Norm ran around to Cookie's side and shut her door.

I got out, and we followed our mother and Ricky into the building and then up two flights of metal stairs.

Ricky's living room had a window that looked into an airshaft. There was a big fat TV on the floor below the window and two worn green couches facing each other.

"Pick a couch, and I'll get you blankets and sheets," Ricky said, and he ruffled Norm's hair and left the room. Cookie had already gone into the bedroom.

"Riiiiiiickeeeeee," she called in her sweetest voice. "I have something juicy and special for yooooou!"

Ricky rushed into the living room and handed us each a pile of sheets and blankets.

"Something wet and delicious is waiting for yoooooou," Cookie called.

"You want help setting up?" Ricky asked. I could tell by the drooling-dog look on his face that he just wanted to go into the bedroom and be with Cookie.

"We can do it," I said, and Ricky was gone.

"Sleep on your side and then cover the other ear with your hand," Norm said. He threw the sheets on the floor, lay down on the couch, and pulled the blanket over himself. I did the same.

It was October sixth, my ninth birthday, and we were still living at Ricky's. Norm and I hadn't been to school for over three weeks, since we'd left the hotel. Most days we drove around in the tow truck with Ricky. It was better than staying home and taking care of Cookie, who liked to lie in Ricky's bed and have us bring her things: food, coffee, beer, cigarettes.

When we got home from towing cars with Ricky that evening, Cookie was sitting at the kitchen table with a six-pack of Schlitz and a Baskin-Robbins ice cream cake.

"Today is a wonderful day," she said. I stared at that cake and couldn't wait to tear into it. I hoped I'd be allowed to eat half of it all by myself.

"Why's that?" Ricky asked. I hadn't told him it was my birthday, and Norm seemed to have forgotten. My sisters never would have forgotten. Gi liked to make an event of everyone's birthday, singing songs or doing hand-claps. If we had no money or food stamps, she and Camille would go into a grocery store wearing sweatpants or two pairs of pants, the outer one particularly large, and they would shove a plastic container of cupcakes down their pants. A cake was too hard to get out of a store, and a cake mix, without all the ingredients, was useless. We often didn't have electricity or gas for a stove anyway. Before we could eat the cupcakes, Gi would wash my hair and braid it or put it in a fancy bun. If we had a special outfit we'd scavenged, she'd put it on me and I'd be real careful to keep it clean and not get any cupcake frosting on it.

I couldn't remember having spent a birthday with Cookie, although chances are she was around for one or two of them.

"It's my birthday today!" I said. Cookie's face flashed with surprise and then she stretched her mouth into a huge, strained smile. Was the cake a coincidence or had she really remembered? If she'd forgotten, I didn't want to know.

"That's right, it's Rosanne's birthday today," she said. "And—" Cookie paused to open a Schlitz that she passed to Ricky. She opened another one for herself and took a sip. "The Fair Hearing judge gave me full custody of you little rodents today."

"Cool," Norm said.

"You're no longer kidnapped!" Cookie laughed.

"Congratulations." Ricky leaned over Cookie and gave her a thick, wet smooch.

"Can we eat the cake now?" I asked.

"*Can we eat the cake now?*" Cookie whined in a baby voice that I didn't think sounded like me, and then she took a slug of beer.

"Can we?" Norm asked. We were both standing beside the table staring at the cake.

"First you clean the house. Then you get cake."

Cookie chugged her beer and then dropped the empty can on the table.

"I have to clean the house on my birthday?" I asked.

Cookie tilted her head to the side and said, "*I have to clean the house on my birthday?*" She pulled another Schlitz off the plastic ring.

"I kinda agree with Rosie," Ricky said. "House don't need to be cleaned anyway."

"Social Services is coming tomorrow to make sure the house is decent enough for these two. You'd think I was raising the next king and queen of England!" Cookie laughed, and then Ricky laughed too

"Can I please have my cake before I clean the house?" I knew the house would pass inspection—we'd lived in far worse and Social Services never seemed bothered by it.

"No, you can't have your fucking cake before you clean the house! You don't get to live a life of leisure just 'cause you happen to have been born on this day nine years ago. I'm the one who should get the cake! I'm the one who sat around all night screaming my ass off as I pushed your big block head out of my twat!" Cookie stared me down until I dropped my head.

"Give her the cake, Cookie." Ricky pushed the box toward me and opened it. There were forks on the table. He handed me one. "Don't mind your mom, kid. Dig in."

I did. And then Norm and I cleaned the house.

On Thanksgiving morning, Ricky slept in. His jeans were on the floor of the kitchen where he'd removed them when he and Cookie came home last night, loaded. Cookie dug through his pockets, pulled out a twenty-dollar bill, and then hustled my brother and me out of the apartment before we could put on our coats. We had the Macy's parade on TV, and the announcer had just said it was twenty-nine degrees out, the coldest day this month. Cookie wanted to buy a turkey for half price before they all sold out or the store closed. Either was a possibility as the store was closing at noon and it was after eleven already.

Our first stop was at a deli, where Cookie bought two cases of Schlitz beer.

"Is there gonna be enough money for the turkey?" Norm asked. He was carrying one case, and Cookie was hauling the other.

"Yes! Everything's on sale, goddammit! Quit worrying about your turkey!" Cookie opened the passenger door of the station wagon, and Norm put his case of beer on the floor. Cookie put hers on the seat. "Get in the back," she said to Norm.

I pushed aside the trash and clothes, and Norm squeezed in next to me. Cookie opened a beer and had chugged it before we pulled out of the parking lot onto the road. She threw the empty can over the seat toward us, then opened another beer. We'd gone barely a mile when the station wagon fishtailed on the ice down a hill.

Norm and I laughed at the back-and-forth motion of the car, and Cookie laughed, too. When I caught her face smiling in the rearview mirror, I could see why men were drawn to her. There was a lusciousness to my mother that only came out when she was happy. A rare moment.

"Good thing no one's on the road," Cookie said. Of course Cookie's driving was no more dangerous and swervy on the icy road than it was any other night or day she was driving.

"Can I drive?" Norm asked. He'd been wanting to learn so he could take over the wheel when Cookie couldn't see straight.

"Yeah, I'll teach you soon," Cookie said. It was the first time she'd agreed to this.

"Hey, I've got an idea," I said. I wanted to capitalize on Cookie's current good mood.

"What's that?" Cookie popped the lighter and lit a cigarette. She had one hand on the wheel and the beer and the cigarette in the other.

"Why don't we invite Cheri, Gi, and Camille to Thanksgiving—"

"Stop," Cookie said and took a sip of beer. She still didn't seem as angry as she usually was when I brought up my sisters. I tried again.

"Well, if they brought all the food—"

"Enough!" Cookie threw her beer over the seat at me. It sloshed down my shirt and then rolled to the trash-filled floor. I picked it up and handed it back to her.

"Sorry," I said.

"If you think there's any fucking way I'm having those lying whores in my house, then you're fucking crazier than they are." Cookie wasn't angry as much as irritated. It gave me hope. Maybe she was softening. She took another sip of beer and singed her hair with the lit cigarette. The rubbery smell was familiar. My mother frequently fell asleep, or passed out, with a burning cigarette in her mouth and had singed bits of hair all over her head. She also left behind tiny burn-hole craters wherever she landed: chairs, sofas, carpets, and the seats of cars.

Cookie turned on the radio and started singing along with Willie Nelson. It was a song about mamas and babies and not letting your daughters marry cowboys. I wondered if Cookie ever thought about the person I might marry when I grew up. Cherie's marriage didn't seem to interest my mother at all. Probably because Cookie claimed to still be looking for a husband herself.

"What if I married Brian?" I said to Norm.

"He can barely walk," Norm said.

"But he's not a cowboy," I said.

"It's just a song," Norm said. "It's not real advice you have to follow."

There was enough money for a small turkey and a box of Stove Top stuffing, but nothing left for dessert or a can of string beans. I didn't care. I'd been watching the Stove Top commercials all week and couldn't wait to taste it. The turkey and stuffing were put in the backseat, piled onto the trash and clothes with Norm and me; the liquor remained in the front. Once, after Norm had won the fight over the front seat, he turned to me and said, "The one who's most important goes up front." It seemed to me that this was entirely true now that the Schlitz was up there.

Cookie was on her fifth beer when the car slid across the nearly empty road and tumbled over an embankment, nose down. It happened so unexpectedly that by the time I thought to be scared, or scream, we'd already stopped moving. The trash and clothes cushioned Norm and me, but Cookie had slammed into the steering wheel and hit her head against the windshield, which now had a crack through it that looked like a cartoon lightning bolt.

"My tits!" Cookie hollered. "I smashed my fucking tits!"

None of us had been wearing a seat belt.

Norm and I stumbled out of the car, and then Norm helped Cookie out. I reached back in and grabbed an old blanket to wrap around myself.

"Grab me a beer," Cookie said, and then she yelled, "GODDAMMIT MY TITS HURT!"

I got Cookie a beer before hurrying to catch up to her and Norm, who were already headed toward the road. Cookie opened the beer and chugged it as we walked. When she was done, she tossed the can to the side of the road.

It wasn't too far along when we hit a gas station with a phone booth. Cookie made a collect call to Ricky. "Hurry the fuck up!" she said to him. "I got a fuck-load of warrants out for my arrest and if the cops show, there's no pussy for you tonight!"

Pussy was a word I didn't have to look up. Cookie had used it so often, so explicitly, that it was like understanding the word *table* or *chair*.

Ricky was there in less than five minutes. At first I thought he'd rushed for the promise of "pussy." But when he ran to me and Norm first—checking our heads for lumps, our eyes for mismatched pupils, and then checking out Cookie to make sure she was all right—I realized he'd hurried because he'd been worried about us. And though I wasn't happy we'd gotten in a car accident, I was happy to see that there was someone besides my sisters who cared about our well-being.

We looted the station wagon for anything of value—Cookie's Jontue, a carton of Virginia Slims menthol, the cases of beer, turkey, stuffing, and a few other items—leaving all the trash and some of the dirtier blankets and clothes. Ricky took off the license plates and threw them onto the floor of the tow truck. We drove away from the station wagon and never saw it again.

Cookie was too smashed to make the turkey, and no one else knew how. Norm and I made the stuffing, however, and it was delicious. We didn't offer any to Cookie and Ricky. They were hiding out in the bedroom for the rest of day anyway. Seemed they had everything they needed.

The next day, I went with Ricky to the tow yard to find a new car for Cookie. He'd been instructed to "bring home a fucking boat." The tow truck didn't have any seatbelts, and I bounced around the cab as we drove down the icy potholed road.

"My sister Gi likes to take me to the library," I said, as if we were in the middle of a conversation.

"What?" Ricky looked over at me. "You have a sister?"

"I have three sisters."

"Your mother never mentioned them."

"That's 'cause she doesn't like them."

"Why doesn't she like them?"

"'Hmm." I thought about it for a second. "Maybe because they told Social Services about her. But maybe because they're so pretty and smart and it's hard for my mom to be the boss of them."

Ricky laughed. "Well, where are they?"

"Cherie's married, and Gi and Camille are in a foster home, but my mom won't tell me where it is." My heart fluttered at the thought of my sisters. I knew Ricky would love them if he met them.

"Your mom works in mysterious ways." Ricky laughed, then looked over and winked at me.

"Can we get a pink car?" I imagined Ricky and me in a pink car, driving to Camille and Gi's foster home so I could visit them.

"If there's a pink car available, then it's all yours!" Ricky reached his hand over to pat my head and the next thing I knew, there was the horrible sound of smashing steel as we drove into the car ahead of us.

My head slammed into the dashboard and back again. I was crying, but I couldn't feel crying. I could only feel a giant drum banging out a rhythm in my forehead.

My right eye felt wet, wetter than tears. And I couldn't see out of it. I reached up to wipe away the wetness and saw that my hand was covered in blood. Ricky was crying. I'd seen Norm cry, but I'd never seen a grown-up man cry. It was so startling that I stopped crying. Ricky got out of the truck and walked around to my side. He opened the door and carried me out, mumbling about how sorry he was. The banging in my head continued as my stomach swirled.

"I feel like I'm gonna throw up," I said, and Ricky cried even harder.

A tiny black-haired woman got out of the car we'd hit. She was pointing and hollering at Ricky, Cookie style. In front of her was another car that she had hit. It was a three-car pileup, and we were at the end of the train.

"I have a little girl here," Ricky said to the screaming woman, "so you just calm yourself down." He rocked me in his arms as if I were a baby. Everything inside me still hurt, but the rocking did make it feel better. Being held like that made everything okay.

Ricky's truck could still drive, so after exchanging information with the drivers of the other two cars, he took me to the hospital. We were in the waiting area of the emergency room when he called Cookie from a pay phone. She was yelling so loud, Ricky held the phone away from his ear, and I could hear everything she said.

"I mean, that's fucking impossible! Impossible!" Cookie yelled. "How does a little shit like her get in two car accidents in two days! It's fucking impossible!"

"Well, it's not impossible because it just happened. If you take a cab down here, I'll pay him when you get here."

"Are you out of your fucking mind! If you were in an accident, the heat will be there any minute! I fucking skipped bail on those last fucking theft charges! You are FUCKED UP if you think I'm going anywhere near . . ." Cookie went on. Ricky eventually put the phone to his chest so we both couldn't hear her very well. Then he gently told her we'd be home soon.

Three hours later, with a pink bandage on my forehead and the word *concussion* floating in my head, Ricky carried me into his apartment. Cookie was wearing spike-heeled black shoes, a black lace bra, and black satin underwear. She was behind a low-standing ironing board, pressing a burgundy silky blouse. Her pale belly jutted out, a gelatin-like awning over her crotch. Norm was on a couch. The TV was on, and they were watching *Days of Our Lives*. Norm glanced up at me.

"I've got a concussion," I said.

"No big deal," Norm said, and he looked back at the TV. I thought he was jealous because he'd never had a concussion.

Cookie turned her head from the TV and watched Ricky set me down on the couch and then tuck a blanket around me. She was tapping her foot. There was a burning cigarette in an ashtray poised at the end of the ironing board.

"What took you so long?" Cookie unplugged the iron by yanking the cord over and over again until it finally unhooked from the wall.

"A lot of people in the emergency room." Ricky pulled my hair out from under the blanket around me. He stroked my head. "We've got to wake her up every hour tonight to make sure she's okay."

We saw the flying iron at the same time. I screamed. Ricky dove over my face so that he took the iron in the back.

"WHAT THE FUCK IS WRONG WITH YOU?!" Ricky grabbed the iron from the floor, went to the ironing board, and slammed it down. "What the fuck?!"

Cookie picked up her cigarette and took a hit. She tapped out an ash using her pointer finger and then took another hit. I could tell she was breathing hard the way her stomach moved up and down. There were shimmery stripes from her navel down. Stretch marks. She'd always blamed me for them, *fifth one drags your body through the shits and it's all fucking over,* she'd said more than once.

"You like little girls, huh?" Cookie was so calm that I knew it was only the lead-in.

"What?" Ricky looked back at me as if he wasn't sure I was the little girl to whom she was referring. At nine years old I fully understood what Ricky didn't: Cookie could create a crime and a criminal out of any innocent circumstance and with any innocent person. It was what she continually did to my sisters—insisting they'd done terrible things to harm her.

"You like little girls. You fucking pervert!" Cookie reached for the iron, but Ricky grabbed it first. He held it up in the air away from himself. Norm and I watched from our separate couches. I started to say something, and Norm put his fingers to his lips and shushed me. I knew he was telling me that Ricky was a grown man. There was no way Cookie could do to him what she'd done to my sisters.

"I don't know what the fuck you're talking about," Ricky said. "Your daughter smashed her head on my dashboard. She actually dented a dashboard with her bean! She was in the hospital, and she has a concussion.

I'm sorry you couldn't get your shit together to show up—"

"She is a whoring, conniving slut just like her sisters!" Cookie smashed out the cigarette and stepped around to the front of the ironing board so she was face-to-face with Ricky. With her spikey high heels she was almost as tall as he was, and certainly wider.

"I have no fucking idea what you're even saying here. I just learned about her sisters today!"

"You like little girls, don't you? You like the young whores, right? Never pushed a baby out." She was speaking so softly that I started to wonder if this time, with this invented crime, she was just joking. Soon, she might start laughing.

"Get a grip, Cookie! She's nine! I took her to the hospital!"

"Mom," I said, "we just went to the hospital, I swear." I hoped that confirmation of our activities would put an end to this, whether she was joking or not.

Norm looked at me with his eyes bugged out and again said, "Shhh!"

"You wanna fuck her?!" Now Cookie was yelling. She definitely was not kidding. "FUCK HER! You can have her, she's yours!" Cookie pulled the blouse off the ironing board and jammed one arm into the sleeve.

"Fuck you, you crazy bitch." Ricky walked out with the iron, the long cord dragging behind him. He went into the bedroom and slammed the door.

"Mom, nothing happened. He just took me to the hospital," I said.

Cookie rushed at me, her blouse hanging from one arm. She slapped me across the face and hissed: "You want him? That what you want? Dangling old man meat?!" She slapped me again and I pulled the blanket over my face.

"Mom!" Norm said. "Stop!"

"Nothing happened!" I said, stuttering through tears.

"WHORE!" Cookie grabbed my hair and pulled me off the couch. I screamed when I landed on the floor. My hands went over my head and I turned facedown as Cookie kicked me, jamming her heel into my back, my ribs, my legs, my arms. It sounded like the screaming was coming from someone else, but I knew it was me. Inside my head all I could hear was my heart beating, my lungs expanding and contracting, my blood swooshing through my veins.

Norm was trying to pull Cookie away. I looked up in time to see her backhand him with a fist. Ricky returned to the living room, hollering at Cookie. It sounded far away and hollow. The magnified sounds inside my body now raged above the noise.

It was a hard battle between Cookie and Ricky. She was able to land a few more stomping kicks before he finally wrested her away from me. They were both huffing and panting. Norm was curled up on the floor by the couch.

"You touch that kid again, and I'm calling the cops," Ricky said. A trail of sweat glinted at his red hairline.

Cookie looked down at Norm and went to him. She tried to pull him against her chest. Norm pushed her away and crawled across the floor to sit by me.

"Honey, I'm so sorry I hurt you." Cookie kneeled beside Norm and kissed the top of his head. He covered his face with his hands and ignored her. Finally Cookie let go of Norm and sat on the floor beside him. My mother's legs stuck straight out in front of her; her belly sat like a bag of laundry on her lap. She stared at the TV, but I didn't believe she was really watching it.

Ricky helped me up. He craned his head around to examine me. I could tell he didn't want to lift my shirt or look at any of my bare flesh and set Cookie off again. He helped me back onto the couch, covered me up, and then went into the kitchen. When he returned, he handed me a bag of frozen peas and a bag of frozen corn.

"You want me to make you some peas and corn?" I asked, and Ricky laughed in a way that could have been crying.

"Put those on the places it hurts most," Ricky said. He turned to Cookie, who was still on the floor with Norm, and said in a powerful, cutting voice that I'd never before heard him use, "I'm serious about the cops. I don't care how many fucking warrants you have, or if you jumped fucking bail—you touch that kid again and I'm calling."

Ricky woke me every hour. He asked my name, age, and where I was, just to make sure I knew. The last time he woke me before morning, he said, "Don't worry, kid. As long as I'm around, you'll be safe from your mother's tantrums."

"Okay," I said, and I knew I was smiling as I drifted back to sleep.

7

Swirling Winds

The day Ricky bought Cookie a used Chevy Vega was the day we left him. I was still swollen, bruised, and sore from Cookie's beating. The pink bandage from the car crash remained on my forehead, the edges black and curling.

When we drove away from Ricky's apartment, Cookie chanted, "We were here, but not to stay, we didn't like it anyway!" Norm joined her, and they said it over again a few times while I started crying. At the first red light, Cookie reached back and smacked me across the face, right where my cheek was most tender. "Quit crying over that dumb asshole!" she said.

This was the beginning of almost a year of living in and out of the car, and in and out of strangers' homes, along the streets of Long Island. Cookie quickly named the car Green Spermy. Norm and I called it The Veg.

While we lived in The Veg, most days were spent sitting in the car while Cookie slept off her hangover. Nights were spent either waiting in the car while Cookie drank in a bar or sometimes going into the bar with her. If the right people were around, Cookie found that two sad-looking little kids brought enough sympathy that men would buy her drinks.

Once a month when Cookie picked up her check from the welfare office, we drove to a video arcade where they had lanes of standing yellow Pac-Man machines. Cookie loved Pac-Man almost as much as she loved Kenny Rogers. And Norm and I were just as hooked on the game as she was. We started out three in a row, a roll of quarters in Cookie's purse. If I finished my game first, I stood and watched until my mother finished hers. Then she'd reach into her purse and give me another quarter. Cookie never played too long—she loved alcohol more than Pac-Man and Kenny Rogers put together. Before she left, she'd hand Norm a roll or half roll of quarters and tell him he was the man of the house, so he was in charge of the money. I always wondered what house he was the man of, considering we lived in the car.

Usually, my brother and I were the last people at the arcade when it closed. We'd sit on the curb and wait for our mother to drive up or we'd walk from one to the other until we found Cookie. Norm would get the keys to The Veg from our mother and then we'd wait for her in the car. If Cookie didn't go home with a man, she'd leave the bar between two and three in the morning depending on what time they kicked her out. Many bars let her hang around until the employees themselves left—who knows what she did to earn that time. Post bar time, my mother drove The Veg like a bobsled, caroming around the empty roads. We parked behind grocery stores or little markets where early-morning baked goods came in. Norm and I would rouse our snoring mother when the noise of the delivery truck woke us. We'd watch the man load a metal cart and roll it through the back door that some early-morning employee had just opened for him. In the chilly predawn air, we ran out of the car to grab whatever food we could from the open truck: loaves of bread, boxes of donuts and, once, five cases of giant cinnamon buns. The three of us tore into the food as my mother made a getaway. With Cookie at the wheel, driving while eating donuts was just as dangerous as driving while drunk. It was hard to taste the first donut or slice of bread, which I ate as quickly as possible trying to fill the clanging hunger hole in my belly. I often felt like a boa constrictor squeezing down the latest catch as giant lumps of dough caught in my throat. Cookie washed down her meals with whatever bottle she had in the car. It didn't matter if it was vodka or beer, she drank it like water. Every now and then, Norm would take a sip from Cookie's bottle to ease down the food he too was shoveling in.

Our mother would repark at a different parking lot and conk out again to sleep through the morning. When she woke up, she rolled down the window and threw out any trash she hadn't heaved over to the backseat: liquor bottles, bakery boxes, food wrappers, and bloody rags when she had her period. Each time we drove away, there was a little pile of garbage left behind—evidence of our existence.

When Cookie wasn't with us for the night, Norm slept across the backseat and I slept in the front bucket passenger seat, reclined so it almost hit Norm's legs. If Cookie slept in the car, she took the backseat, Norm took the fully reclined passenger seat, and I was in the half-reclined driver's seat. When it was warm out, Norm opened the roomy trunk and slept on the junk accumulated there, giving me the reclined passenger seat. If Cookie was angry at us, or if she had picked up a guy who lived with a wife or girlfriend and could only spend time with her in our car, Norm and I were banished from The Veg and would pass the night sitting on curbs in bar parking lots, or lying in nearby patches of grass and weeds. On cold nights, we huddled together, too miserable to talk. My bones hurt and my muscles ached from shaking as I tried to stay warm. Nothing ever exhausted me as much as simply being cold.

There were the many nights when Norm and I would start out sleeping in the car while Cookie was in the bar, only to be awoken by Cookie, the car driven and newly parked at whatever home or apartment belonged to her boyfriend for the night. "Get your jammies," she always said, and Norm would reply, "That's so funny I forgot to laugh."

In these strangers' homes, Norm and I slept on couches, in guest rooms, in easy chairs, on wooden floors, on carpeted floors, on tiled floors, in bathtubs filled with towels for cushioning, under dining room tables, on back lawns, on back decks, on front porches, on closet floors more times than one would imagine, in kitchens with cockroaches and mice, with dogs in a mudroom, and with cats who padded over our bodies and explored our faces.

If the surface was flat enough, we slept on it. This wasn't particularly a gift or a luxury, as we had acclimated well to The Veg. But the use of a proper toilet—an appreciation that never left after the poop bucket—a shower when we could get one in, and a heated room were things for which we would have slept just about anywhere.

The nights Cookie didn't meet a man at the bar, she blamed me. "You've fucked up my life!" she'd say. With her body wedged between the bucket seats in front, my mother would reach into the backseat and hit me with the wooden handle of her hairbrush, over and over again on the head, or on my ear, or on my back and legs when I dove my head under blankets or trash. The hairbrush had grown to be Cookie's preferred tool of torture. When she wasn't hitting me with the brush, she liked to yank it through the tangled knots gathered at the nape of my neck. Later, she'd run her sharp nails along the rows of bristles and remove the pads of hair from the brush, dropping tiny hair nests wherever she sat.

On the rare days Cookie was sober, we were treated to a version of her that made my heart ache for love. Those days made alternate lives, alternate childhoods, seem possible. Once she took us to J.C. Penney and bought me a pair of shoes and a new shirt. Once she bought Norm a battery-operated hand-held Pac-Man game. And often, we drove to a deli where we'd eat corned beef sandwiches that were as big as a brick and drink cream soda out of a glass bottle. My mother talked differently on those sober days: long monologues about love and family and how we needed to stay together because we were all each of us had in life. Norm would drop his head onto Cookie's shoulder, and she'd scratch the nape of his neck. And she'd kiss us both and tell us how much she loved us. Norm always said, *I love you, too,* and I wondered if he really meant it.

Norm had the gift of being able to live completely in the moment. Once Cookie was being nice, he let everything that came before then slip away. But I could never be in the present without remembering the past. If family was so important, I wanted to ask my mother, why weren't my sisters with us?

On my tenth birthday, in 1982, Cookie bought another ice cream cake. The open cake box teetered on The Veg's emergency brake; we ate using plastic spoons from Baskin-Robbins. Cookie and Norm were in the front seats, I leaned up from the back.

It was a Wednesday in October and unseasonably warm, something I appreciated since I'd outgrown my coat. The cake, the weather, and the fact that Cookie appeared to be sober were adding up to make this a pretty good birthday.

Until Cookie said we were leaving New York.

"What about my sisters?" I asked.

"What the fuck about them?" Cookie scowled as if she'd just bitten into a lemon seed.

"How will I see them if we leave New York?"

"You don't fucking see them anyway." My mother shoved a big corner of icing into her mouth.

"We don't have a home," Norm said. "There's no place for them to see us."

I shot Gi a mental message: *Hurry! We're in the Baskin-Robbins parking lot. But soon we're leaving the state!*

"Anyway," Cookie said, "we have to leave or I'll be put in the slammer."

"What's the slammer?" I asked.

"Jail, dummy!" Norm said. And then he looked at Cookie and asked why.

"The usual. Tickets, skipping bail, DUI—" Cookie took another big bite.

"If it's the usual, can't we just stay?" I'd lost my appetite and put my spoon down on the open lid of the box.

"Nah." Cookie had a smear of frosting on her lower lip. "Now they're saying I hit a kid on a bike in Mastic." She shrugged and took another bite.

"Did you?" I asked.

"It don't fucking matter whether I did or not, little

Miss Legal Aid. If they pull me in, there's so much other stuff—" She took another bite. "Did you know I was supposed to go to jail for forging checks right after Cherie was born?"

"No," Norm said. I shook my head.

"I was. But then I was pregnant with Camille already and no one wants to put a pregnant lady with two babies in jail so—" Cookie shoved another huge bite of cake in her mouth.

"So I guess having so many kids was good for something," I said.

"Fuck no!" Cookie said. "My go-go dancer body got fucked into this!" My mother put down her fork and grabbed a roll of her stomach and lifted it up and down. "I used to be slender. I was perky!" She dropped her belly and took another bite of cake. "Thank god men like big ol' tits."

"Can we call my sisters and tell them where we're going?" I asked.

"I didn't even tell *you* where we're going," Cookie said.

"Where are we going?" Norm asked.

"Idaho," Cookie said.

"Why Idaho?" Norm asked.

"To see my friend Jackie. Then we'll work our way to Arizona."

"Why Arizona?" Norm asked.

"This one's dad"—my mother pointed her cake-smeared fork at me—"bought up some land at Lake Havasu before he was rubbed out."

"What's rubbed out?" I asked, and Cookie turned the fork toward her temple as if it were a gun and then knocked her head to one side—a pantomime of having been shot.

Cookie went on to explain that Vito, my father, had purchased the land around the time I was born. Cookie and Vito had gone out there together and brought home matching T-shirts for all of us. Wherever Gi went, she kept with her a picture of the five of us, Norm and Gi in the T-shirts, everyone smiling. Vito must have taken the picture, developed the film, and given us the snapshot. Other than that photo, the only picture I'd seen of myself was my first grade school photo. My sisters pooled their babysitting money to pay for the package. It was a luxury that happened only once.

I imagined those few months with my father before he went to prison as glorious. According to Cookie, Vito was charismatic, a natural-born leader, and smart as anything. I decided that if Vito was as great as Cookie claimed, he would have adored any child of his the way my sisters adored me. Believing my father had loved me gave me a warm, centered feeling in my stomach. Vito was gone, but the connection remained.

"It'll be no problem transferring that land to you," Cookie said. "They'll recognize you as one of their own."

"Who will recognize me?" I asked.

"Vito's family. The Mothers and Fathers Italian Association," she said. "You look just like them." It was nice to think of having a family who might recognize me.

"Did my dad ever buy any land?" Norm asked.

"Hell, no!" Cookie said. "Your motherfucking dad never even bought underwear."

I could tell by the way Norm started quickly eating cake that he wished it was his father who had bought land. His father who had been rubbed out.

8

Into Idaho

Norm and I leaned against the wall on the second floor open-air hallway of a roadside motel. It was the night after my birthday and Cookie was in the room with a man named Mack. He had a long, gray, scraggly beard and a giant belly that jutted out over his pants. He barely spoke, but he smoked a lot of cigarettes and drank just as much as Cookie. When he started kissing Cookie's neck while unbuckling his belt, we fled the room.

It was getting cold out. I wanted to go back in and watch TV.

"Five more minutes," Norm said. He had an uncanny intuition about how long these things would take. Or maybe he just listened more carefully to the sounds coming out of the room: groans and periodic howling from Cookie.

"Okay," Norm said when he sensed they were done.

Cookie and Mack were in one bed. He was already asleep, his mouth hanging open like a corpse from a movie. Cookie had the covers pulled up under her bare armpits and was watching *Knots Landing* on TV, a beer in one hand, a cigarette in the other. She looked relaxed. Happy almost. Norm went straight to the bathroom and started a shower.

"Are we leaving for Idaho tomorrow?" I sat on the edge of the bed, as far from Mack as I could get. There were empty beer cans scattered on the floor.

"Yup." Cookie took a sip of beer, keeping her eyes on the TV.

"Can we call my sisters before we leave?"

"Why would you wanna call those dumb bitches?" Her voice didn't have its angry edge. She was drunk, half-asleep, maybe content even with the bloated Mack snoring beside her.

"To say good-bye," I said.

Cookie turned her head toward me. She studied me—as if she was deciding what to do. "Okay," my mother said. "You call them, you tell them good-bye from me, too. Good-bye forever! From all of us!"

Cookie laughed and her eyes closed up into slits of half-moons. I could tell she was about three sips from unconsciousness. That was probably the only reason she was agreeing to this call.

"How do we get their phone numbers?" I asked.

"In that zipper pocket inside my purse is the number for the bitch's house that's guarding your sisters . . . now stop botherin' me." Cookie turned to her side, pushing her rump against Mack.

My throat throbbed and tears rushed to my eyes. All this time she'd had the number. I could have been calling my sisters at their foster home every week. Every day. Every time I was near a phone! I opened my mother's big white purse and found the scrap of paper with a number on it. There was no name or any other information.

"How do I use this phone?" I was at the desk, holding the receiver in my hand. There was a row of square buttons.

"Fuck if I know." Cookie's eyes were closed.

I studied the phone. In typed words it said, "Dial 9 for an outside line." But there was no dial. I pushed 9 and got a dial tone. And then I punched in the numbers from the piece of paper.

A calm and cheery-sounding woman answered.

"Can I speak to Regina or Camille?" I asked, my voice shaking.

When Gi came to the phone, I started crying. "We're moving to Idaho tomorrow!"

"*Mia bambina*!" Gi said. "You can't move to Idaho! How will I ever find you in Idaho?!"

"I don't know," I cried.

"*Bambina*." Gi's voice was rushed, urgent. "This is crazy. Tell me where you are right now and I'll come get you."

"I'm in a motel," I sniffed.

"What motel? Where?!"

"It's a yellow motel off the expressway—"

"What's the name of the motel? What street is it on?!"

Cookie hoisted herself out of bed and wobbled toward me, naked. Her face tightened and her eyes darkened.

I looked at the phone, at the brochures and pieces of paper on the table, trying to find something with the motel's name on it. In the drawer there was a small white pad of paper with a drawing of the motel and the name printed above in a loopy cursive that was hard to read. "It's called the—"

Cookie placed her finger on the plastic triangular

wedge and disconnected the call. Then she picked up the piece of paper with Gi's number on it and ripped it into tiny, fuzzy pieces that she threw in the air like confetti.

Norm was out of the shower now. He wore sweatpants and a T-shirt; his hair was wet. He climbed into bed without even glancing toward our naked mother.

Tears slid down my face. My throat felt closed. If I opened my mouth again, I'd be wailing.

"So much for good-byes," Cookie said slowly. My mother walked back to the bed, her bare bottom rippling like something that lived underwater. She lifted the covers and scooted in close to snoring Mack.

I went to the bathroom, turned on the bathtub shower, took off my clothes, and stepped in. I sat on the floor of the tub, my back curled like a shell around my knees and the water raining down on me. I cried so hard it felt like I'd been turned inside out and all of me had been washed down the drain.

The next afternoon, we took everything we needed from The Veg and put it in the trunk of Mack's four-door Chrysler. The body of Mack's car was the color of a raspberry Popsicle, and the roof was white and looked like it was made of plastic. There was plenty of room for Norm and me to stretch out on the cushy seats in the back.

"We're traveling in luxury now," Cookie said, and she sprayed herself with Jontue, filling the car with a sickly thick stench of musk. Norm and I watched Mack out the window. He was crouched at the back of The Veg, his belly draped over his pants, removing the license plate. Cookie watched too as he tossed each plate, Frisbee-style, into the litter-strewn lot behind the motel. She clapped her hands. "Say bye-bye to Green Spermy!"

"See ya, wouldn't wanna be ya," Norm said.

Mack got into the car and started the engine, and we pulled away from the motel. Cookie chanted her departure refrain, "We were here, but not to stay, we didn't like it anyway!" Norm and I didn't join in, and Mack grunted and pointed at the radio, which Cookie turned on. Crystal Gayle was singing about her blue eyes.

"Where is Idaho?" I asked.

"You'll find out soon enough," Cookie said.

"Who's your friend Jackie?" Norm asked.

"Jackie is Jackie!" Cookie said. "You know Jackie!" Our mother had been so sporadically in our lives that Norm and I didn't know if she had friends outside of the people with whom she sat in bars.

"Oh yeah. Jackie." Norm smiled at me and rolled his eyes.

"7-Eleven!" My mother slapped Mack's upper arm and had him pull over so she could get road supplies: beer, potato chips, sandwiches, and Mountain Dew for Norm. Mack paid for it all, and Cookie repaid him by leaning into him and stroking his leg as he drove.

While we were eating our road food, Cookie informed us that since Mack was driving, and it was Mack's car, Mack got to pick the music we listened to. It later became clear that this arrangement was encumbered by the fact that Mack didn't use words to string together sentences. Instead, he grunted one-word answers or commands. Playing the music Mack wanted entailed Cookie dialing the radio until he made a noise; or Cookie picking up each 8-track tape, reading what it was, and waiting for Mack to respond. Sometimes Cookie pretended to take a no for a yes and just put in whatever tape she wanted to hear, which was usually Kenny Rogers, Willie Nelson, Waylon Jennings, or Linda Ronstadt.

Waylon Jennings was singing "I've Always Been Crazy" as we drove into Manhattan. As far I knew, I'd never been there even though it was only an hour from Suffolk County, where I'd lived my whole life. I rolled down my window, stuck my head out, and looked up at the high buildings. I'd never seen anything like it—it was beautiful and mystifying. I couldn't understand how things that high and skinny could stand still without falling over.

"Make a wish!" I told Norm as we drove through the Lincoln Tunnel. A girl in a book I'd read made a wish and held her breath each time she drove through a tunnel. This tunnel was so long, it was impossible to hold my breath. But I got two good wishes in: that my sisters would find me, and that we would be warm in Idaho.

When we exited the tunnel, Cookie rolled down the window and stuck her heavy upper body outside. She jabbed both middle fingers into the air and shouted, "FUCK YOU, NEW YORK! FUCK YOU, COPS! FUCK YOU, SOCIAL WORKERS! HURRICANE COOKIE IS OVER AND OUTTA HERE!"

Cookie slapped my face to wake me. I sat up, stunned; my palm went to the hot spot on my cheek. It was the middle of the night, and we were parked amid rows and rows of trucks.

"Wake your brother," Cookie said, and I did. Norm sat up, his brown eyes were half closed and unfocused, his hair popped straight up. He reminded me of Scooby-Doo after he'd been bonked in the head by a ghost. I forgot about my stinging cheek and laughed at Norm's befuddled face.

"Mack needs a coffee," Cookie said, and she handed Norm a dollar bill.

"What time is it?" Norm asked.

"Four in the morning. Now go! And take your time!"

Norm and I scooted out of the car and stood staring at the massive trucks surrounding us. It felt like we'd walked into a cement field of sleeping steel dinosaurs.

"Shut the goddamned door!" Cookie shouted.

Norm glanced behind himself and shut the door. We walked past the trucks toward a cinderblock building with the lights on. Inside was a diner. There were a few men at center-pole stools at the bar and more men in booths. Most of them were drinking coffee. Half of them had giant plates of food in front of them. As hungry as I'd been in my life, it was hard to imagine eating a dripping hamburger and a plate of shiny fries in the middle of the night. Many of the men turned and stared at us. It was like we were aliens, or naked, or . . . well, I guess we were the only kids around and so maybe that seemed as strange as if we'd been naked.

A waitress leaned over the counter, knocked on it with her fist to get our attention and then said, "You kids need something?"

"Bathroom and a cup of coffee to go," Norm said.

"Bathrooms are over there—" She pointed with her long red nail and smiled at us. "Coffee'll be waiting for you when you come out."

I held the back of Norm's shirt as we walked to the bathroom. A few men whipped their heads around and watched us.

"I'm going into the ladies' room with you," Norm said. "I don't trust those guys."

I went in one stall, Norm went in the other. We met at the sink where we washed our hands. I looked at the two of us in the mirror, our eyes puffy from sleep, Norm's hair sticking up like fur, mine growing longer in spite of the fact that Cookie had ripped out so much of it with the hairbrush.

"Do you think I'm pretty?" I asked my brother. My sisters were beautiful, each of them with thick dark hair: Gi with her romantic almond-shaped eyes; Camille with round cheeks and big, bright eyes; Cherie with a perfect button nose and a wide, white smile. But I had no idea what I looked like. If this face was pretty or not.

"No duh," Norm said. "That's why Mom hates you so much. If you weren't pretty, she wouldn't pick on you."

"Like Snow White's stepmother." I looked at myself again and smiled. I wanted to see what Gi saw when she called me *bambina*. "I hope I'm as pretty as my sisters."

"You are," Norm said. "Let's go." He pulled my arm, and we left the bathroom.

When we returned to the car with the coffee, the doors were locked and there was a horizon of fog at the bottoms of the windows. The car bounced up and down, and I immediately stepped back. I didn't want to see what was going on.

We didn't have coats and it was cold out. Norm and I sat on the curb outside the truck stop, leaning into each other. We took turns holding the hot coffee cup to warm our hands.

"You think the guys in the trucks next to them are watching?" I asked.

"Probably," Norm said. "Grown men are gross that way."

"How do you know?" I asked.

"'Cause I'm a half-grown man," he said, and we both laughed at this idea.

"I'm still just a girl," I said. Though the longer I was without my sisters, the quicker I felt myself growing up. They'd babied me for so many years, I had never known a fraction of what was going on. Now, with Cookie around, it was hard to hide from the gritty life she gave us.

"I think they're done now," Norm said.

When we reached the car, Mack was standing outside, zipping and buttoning his pants. Cookie sat in the front seat, pulling a sweater on over her bra. Her hair was a wild mess of black waves. Norm waited for Mack to buckle his belt and then handed him the coffee and the fifty cents change. Mack made a sound that sounded half like *thanks* and half like a burp.

"It's time for Willie," Cookie sang, once we'd left the truck stop. She slid the book-size tape into the 8-track player and she, Norm, and I belted out "On the Road Again" along with Willie Nelson. It was our theme song and when we sang it together, we were—for those brief few minutes—perfectly and happily in sync.

The next few days more or less followed the pattern of the first day and night. Norm and I passed the time by playing on his Pac-Man game, counting train cars as they went by, punching each other in the arm and saying *punch-buggy* every time we passed a VW Bug, and playing the color game where one person would name a color and the other person had to shout out everything they saw in that color. A teacher once told me that no word rhymes with purple. On this trip I also found that few things on Route 80 across America are purple.

Early every evening, I had a moment when I thought

about my sisters and how hard it would be for them to find us again. I couldn't help but cry. Norm ignored me, Mack never seemed to notice, and Cookie reached over her seat and slapped me in the face.

"Shut the fuck up!" she'd say. She rarely asked why I was crying, and when she did, I told her I had a stomachache. I knew it would do no good to bring up my sisters.

The only way to get myself out of the crying was to imagine one of my sisters in a bubble hovering over my head telling me she'd find me and everything would be okay.

"I'll see you soon," I'd whisper in response to their imaginary promises. Then I sniffed up my sadness and buried it again.

Mack pulled over and slept in the car once a day from around six a.m. until one or two in the afternoon. He took his second break around three or four in the morning. As on the first trip, Norm and I were sent out of the car during these middle-of-the-night breaks while Mack and Cookie spent time alone. Once, as Norm and I sat on a hill looking down at the car, Norm said to me, "It's gonna be quick this time."

"Do you know 'cause you're a half-grown man?" I asked.

"No, 'cause they're doing this—" Norm lifted his

fist toward his mouth and pumped it back and forth as
he poked out his cheek with his tongue.

"They're doing that?" I did it, and wondered why
two people would kick a couple of kids out of the car,
take off all their clothes, and then sit there and pump
their fists in front of their faces while pushing out their
cheeks with their tongues.

"Mack likes it," Norm said.

"Well, Mack's dumb," I said.

A few nights before we hit Idaho, when there were
few other cars on the road and Mack was going well
past the speed limit, Cookie told us about wearing a
blue plaid uniform to school. My mother was, according to herself, a good, chaste, Catholic girl. And then
she added, "If your sisters had worn uniforms instead of those tight Jordache jeans, they wouldn't have
turned out to be such whores."

I wanted to point out that if Cookie had actually bought them clothes, they wouldn't have worn
Dumpster-found, or sometimes stolen, jeans. I also
wanted to mention that the Catholic uniform certainly
hadn't kept Cookie on the straight and narrow: she was
a woman with five kids from five different men. And
there were easily over a hundred men before, during,
and after our fathers.

The Catholic uniform she'd once worn also didn't stop Cookie from doing what she did early the next morning. It was particularly cold out, we'd run short on cash, and we were desperately needing showers. Mack was snoring in the backseat. The inside of the car smelled sour and mulchy, the way I imagined Mack's beard smelled if you got close enough to it. My mother, brother, and I had moved to the open trunk, where Norm and I often slept. I was cocooned in a dirty blanket. Norm had put on one of our mother's red sweatshirts. Cookie stood near the bumper and pulled her breasts up high in her bra so that they flowed out her open shirt. She sprayed Jontue on her cleavage and then handed me the bottle.

"If go-go dancing taught me one thing," Cookie said, "it was how to make a buck in a time of need." My mother had decided we needed a motel room and showers.

Norm and I watched from the trunk, our feet resting on the bumper, as Cookie climbed into the cab of a truck.

"How long do we have to wait for the room?" I asked Norm.

"It'll be quick," Norm said, and he did the fist and tongue thing again.

I could see the trucker's boxy head in the window

as my mother's head ducked out of view. And suddenly I understood the gesture Norm had been making. It seemed odd, but clearly not impossible, that anyone would ever want to do that. Nonetheless, our mother must have been good at it, for the trucker bought us a motel room and even gave Cookie money to get us some food.

The changing landscape during the drive stunned me as much as the towering buildings in Manhattan had. I'd never seen so much open space, so much broad, shining sky as I did in Ohio, Indiana, Illinois, and Iowa. In Nebraska the hills amazed me. They lifted and fell, dipped and curved, and I wanted so badly to jump out of the car, climb to the top of a hill and roll down with my arms tucked at my sides, nothing to stop me but air and grass. When we entered Wyoming, I gasped at the high, solid mountains. They filled the horizon like giant buffalo shouldering each other to block out the sky. And I loved the animal sightings as we crossed the country: cows grazing, horses hanging their long necks over the tops of wooden fences, lambs in flocks, geese in formation, crows on telephone wires, and, once, a herd of llamas.

In Utah, when I saw an enchanted-looking castle, I gasped and pointed out the window. "OZ!" I shouted

"Shut the fuck up!" Cookie said. She reached back and slapped me across the face. She and Norm had both been sleeping. My brother remained conked out.

"But look!" I held my throbbing cheek with one hand and pointed at the beautiful multispired white castle with the other. I wondered if I should wake Norm so he could see it, too, but decided against it. Norm often wasn't impressed with the things that amazed me.

"Mormons," Mack grunted.

"What?" I leaned up over the seats. I needed to know exactly what this fairy-tale looking building was.

"It's a Mormon temple, you dumbass," Cookie said.

"What's that?" We were passing it now. I turned to look at it out the back window.

"It's a religion." Cookie lit a cigarette. "They don't drink, they don't smoke, they don't even have coffee or Coca-Cola, so there's no way I'm ever turnin' Mormon!"

Mack grumbled something and Cookie laughed.

"What'd he say?" I asked.

"He said they should be called *Morons*, 'cause what's the point in living if you can't drink?" Cookie laughed harder. Other than their moments alone in the car, alcohol appeared to be the bonding force between my mother and Mack.

If Mack didn't like the Mormons, then I was going

to like them with all my heart. How could anyone who built something as beautiful as that temple be all that bad? "They look nice to me," I said.

"Well, you don't know shit about shit." My mother rolled down her window and threw out three beer cans that must have accumulated on her lap. Earlier in the day she had thrown Norm's Pac-Man game out the window because the noise was driving her batty. Cookie had never tossed out as much stuff as she had on this trip with Mack. Unlike my mother, Mack couldn't abide any trash or clutter in the car—so most things eventually landed on the road.

Sometimes I imagined the aerial view of Mack's raspberry-colored car driving across the country. There would be a line of garbage that had been heaved from the window. Like Hansel and Gretel, we were marking our path.

When we crossed the border into Idaho, Cookie and Mack clinked beers to toast that we'd made it so far. Outside the window was farmland. There were bales of hay stacked in a way that created long, low straw walls. Silos and barns dotted the rolling hills. Each view framed by the car window looked like something from a picture book.

When I saw a waterway meandering though a field of wheat, I pointed out the window and said, "Look at that river!"

"That's an irrigation canal," Mack mumbled, and Norm and I elbowed each other, trying not to laugh. It was the most he'd said in five days.

Cookie wanted us to pee and brush our teeth and hair before we got to her friend Jackie's house. Jackie had found herself a good husband, according to my mother, and we needed to look nice for him. His name was Kenny and his family was from Idaho. Jackie and Kenny had two kids, Tina and Sam, who were from Jackie's last marriage.

We all got out of the car near a field of horses. There wasn't a single other vehicle on the road. Cookie pulled down her black spandex pants and squatted on the road, right behind the bumper. I walked out into the field a little ways and tried to hide behind some tall grass. Norm said he didn't have to pee, and Mack stood near Cookie, his hands on his forward-tilted hips as he peed on the road, too.

When I returned to the car, Cookie handed me a toothbrush. Norm was already brushing his teeth. I brushed and brushed and then spit the foam out onto the road where my brother had spit foam.

"I need water," I said. The toothpaste was spicy in my mouth.

"Use this," Cookie handed me her Schlitz. I looked at the beer, shook my head, and just swallowed the toothpaste. Norm stuck out his hand and I gave him the beer. He took a giant slug, gargled, and then spit it out. Cookie laughed. Norm took another sip of beer, swallowing this time. Cookie took the beer back and then handed Norm her cigarette.

Mack barked a word that sounded like *nay*. Norm looked at him and returned the cigarette to Cookie without having taken a puff.

Back in the car Mack and Cookie both smoked. I rolled down my window and let the cold air blow in. Cookie read Mack directions to Caldwell, Idaho, that she had written down on the back of a takeout menu. Soon we were off the empty highway and driving through a town with neighborhoods, convenience stores, super-markets, dollar stores, and liquor stores. Caldwell looked a lot like Long Island where we'd started.

"Let's stop and get a bottle of something to cel-ebrate." Cookie pointed out the window at a liquor store. Mack ignored her and drove right past it.

"Salvation Army!" I shouted. "Let's get new clothes!"

Mack grunted something that sounded like a cross between the word *trash* and the word *tray*. He accelerated past the Salvation Army.

"Don't be puttin' down the Salvation Army," Cookie said. "They have plenty of nice clothes and the money goes to help drunk old men like you!" My mother laughed so hard she started coughing.

My mother didn't tell Mack that we had never bought Salvation Army clothes; we couldn't afford them. During the times when Cookie lived with all five of us, we'd pile into her car, and she would pull up as close as possible to a Salvation Army Dumpster. Gi was always practicing to be a gymnast, so she was the one who had to stand on the open window ledge of the car and hoist herself over the edge of the Dumpster where she'd pike in. Norm and I would stand on the seat and hold her ankles while she tossed out clothes. Camille and Cherie sorted through the flying clothes until they'd found at least a couple of new outfits for each of us.

A few minutes later we were at Jackie's house. It was the shape of a child's drawing of a house: a blue square with a triangle roof. There was a window on either side of the door and a window above the door, under the peak of the roof. All the windows and the door had bars on them. There was a short driveway, but Mack parked the car on the street instead.

"This looks scary," I said. Though we'd lived in many run-down and ramshackle houses, none of them had ever had bars on the front door.

"Relax," Cookie said. "It's not the fucking Amityville house."

"That would be so cool if it was," Norm said. "I'd go in there and kick some ghost butt!"

My mother once worked at a deli near *The Amityville Horror* house on Long Island. One night she told me, my sisters, and Norm stories about the possessed house. When she was done, she said, "See! Things could have been much worse for you all!" Norm might have agreed, but my sisters and I surely believed that a house with ghosts in it seemed much more manageable than a house with Cookie and her dangerous shoes and flying fists.

Cookie leaned on the horn and honked it over and over again. Mack leaned back in his seat with his hands in the air, like he was in a stick-up.

"Always good to announce yourself," Cookie said, and she got out of the car. Norm and I followed and stood with our mother on the sidewalk.

"Come on," Cookie waved her arm at Mack who sat in the car.

"Cig," Mack said, and he leaned back and lit another one.

The three of us walked up the front steps and stood at the barred door. There was a small triangular overhang above us. The underside of it looked black and rotting in places. Cookie pushed the doorbell, in and out, in and out. I could hear it ringing inside the house.

Moments later the door opened. A girl about Gi's size stood there. She had the same dark eyes and skin as my sister. Her hair was as straight and shiny as wet nail polish. I remembered her. She had been Gi's friend in school. Cookie must have known her mother through Gi and this girl.

"Tina!" Cookie said, and she stepped in and hugged Tina in a way she had never hugged me. I wondered what Gi would think if she saw this display. The whole family soon gathered in the entrance hall: Jackie, who was a grown-up version of her daughter; Sam, a tall skinny boy who was the male version of Tina; and Kenny, Jackie's blond husband who didn't look anything like the rest of them.

Jackie gave me and Norm a hug that didn't quite allow her body to touch ours. We'd showered in the motel room Cookie got from the trucker, but maybe after another couple of days in the car with cigarettes and fast food, we'd started to stink again. Or it could have been that my clothes stank. For five days I hadn't changed out of my knee-bare cords and the

white-and-pink baseball shirt Cookie had bought me
on one of her good days when we were living in The
Veg. The "white" was now the color of a water spot
on a ceiling.

We moved through the living room into the kitchen
where every flat surface was covered with food or
dishes. I saw Norm eyeing a bowl of half-eaten mac
and cheese and knew just what he was thinking. I was
thinking it, too, and hoped we'd move into another
room soon, so I could sneak back into the kitchen and
take a couple of bites.

Jackie wanted everyone to sit around the big, round
kitchen table. Kenny gave Cookie a beer.

"We gotta celebrate this reunion," Cookie said. "Let
me treat you all to some vodka!" Cookie turned and
looked at the back of the chair as if she were searching
for something. "Rosie, my purse is in the car. Go out
there and tell Mack to take money out of my wallet and
get a nice big bottle of the best vodka."

"Okay," I mumbled. I didn't know how much vodka
cost, but I figured Cookie had a little money left from
the trucker as the only thing she'd bought with the
food money he gave her was a box of Kentucky Fried
Chicken that Norm and I had to share with Mack, who
devoured most of it. Norm and I suspected that Cookie
had had her own box of chicken when she was in the

restaurant ordering for us. While the three of us ate in the car, Cookie claimed she was forgoing a meal so her children could eat. But from the way she smoked her cigarette and smacked her oily lips from time to time, I could tell that she was nice and full.

I went to the car where Mack still sat at the wheel. The engine was running now, and the radio was on. Mack was listening to a baseball game.

When I approached the driver's side door, Mack rolled down the window.

"Huh," he grunted.

"My mom said you should buy really good vodka to celebrate that we're here." I pointed to Cookie's white purse that sat on the floor in front of the passenger seat. "She said to take money from her wallet."

"Yup," Mack said.

"Will you get me a candy bar, too? Something with two parts that I can split with Norm. Like, a Reese's Peanut Butter Cup? Or a Kit-Kat bar so we can give one to Sam and Tina, too?" I'd never asked Mack for anything, but now seemed as good a time as any.

"Hmmum," Mack said.

"That mean yes?" I asked. He was staring straight ahead over the wheel, so I couldn't see his face to read his expression.

"Yup," Mack said, and he started to pull out before

I'd stepped away. I jumped back and Mack zoomed forward and down the street.

When I returned to the kitchen, Sam and Tina were standing with Norm, who stared at his feet. His eyes lifted and he looked at me, that Scooby-Doo expression again. "Jackie wants us to shower," he mumbled.

"You kids go clean up," Jackie said. "And give me your clothes and I'll throw them in the wash."

"You know Kenny Rogers pronounces his name Kinny, like with an I," Cookie said to Kenny. Her head was down and her thin hair was falling over one eye. Also, her breasts were popping out, like they'd been for the trucker.

"What do we put on when we get out of the shower?" I asked Jackie.

"I didn't know that about Kenny," Kenny said to Cookie. "But I do love his music."

"You and I have something in common then," Cookie said, and she winked at Kenny.

"When you get out of the shower, you put on your other clothes," Jackie said.

"I think we have more in common than that," Kenny said to Cookie.

"Our other clothes are in the car, and the car's with Mack at the liquor store," I said.

"It'll only take him ten minutes to get there, buy a

bottle, and get back," Jackie said. "Go on, it's time to clean up." Jackie moved us out of the kitchen, waving her open hands at us, like she was going to push on our rumps. Sam and Tina shuffled along. They took us to the bathroom that was across the hall from Kenny and Jackie's room. Their door was open and I could see that the bed was made, the orange bedspread pulled taut. I wondered if they'd made the bed for our arrival, or it was always like that. When we had beds, my sisters made them. I'd never seen Cookie make a bed.

"You go first," Norm said, and I stepped alone into the bathroom.

Tina waited outside the door for me to hand her my dirty clothes.

"I'll bring you your new clothes when your stepdad comes back," she said, and then I heard her walking away.

There was no lock on the door and the paper shade on the window had a diamond-shaped hole in the middle. I looked out through the shade. There was mostly dirt in the backyard, with a couple of trees and a big chicken coop. Beyond the coop was a wooden fence with half the slats missing. It reminded me of a long-toothed jack-o'-lantern, gaps here and there. There was a broad dirt road on the other side of the fence and though I couldn't see the tracks from where I stood, I could see the train as it rolled in just then, tooting its harmonica-sounding whistle. I was mesmerized by the way the black, yellow, and orange train cars cut through the landscape, breaking up the monotony of brown, green, and beige.

Once the train had passed, I took one of the two towels from the towel bar and threw it up toward the roller shade, missing several times. Finally the towel hooked over the shade and covered about half the diamond.

In the shower there was Clairol Herbal Essences shampoo that smelled so good I wanted to eat it. I did take a sip, just to see. It was bitter and sharp. I spit it out and rinsed my mouth with the spray.

When I was out of the shower and wrapped in a towel, I opened the bathroom door and waited for someone to get me, or tell me where to go or what to do. The conversation in the kitchen floated down the hall to me. Cookie was telling Jackie and Kenny that Gi was a terrible, dishonest person. According to my mother, Gi had called Social Services and made up awful stories about Cookie just so she and Camille could be sent to a fancy foster home where they took the kids to Disneyland. "That lying whore doesn't give two shits about the kids," Cookie said. "While she and her sister were luxuriating in the suburbs, those two little ones were gettin' the shit beaten outta them by some crazy woman who kept deformed kids in her house."

"Brian's not deformed," I whispered to no one.

"Well, where were you?" Kenny asked.

"Oh, Kenny," Cookie sighed. "You know I had to take care of this little girl whose mother just died of cancer or I wouldn't have left Gi and Camille in charge. But I thought they were up to the task—"

"Well, that's a lot of work for two teenaged girls," Kenny said.

"It was a babysitting job, short term, and those two sluts turned it into a giant party, screwing around with every cut of cheap meat . . ."

Norm came down the hall.

"There's a clean towel hanging on the window," I said. "Where are my clothes?"

"Mack's not back," Norm said. He paused before entering the bathroom. We stood silently together and listened to Cookie.

". . . you know I love those children more than anything in world, anything! But that Rosie's making it hard on me. She's turning out to be every bit the slut her sisters are."

I wondered if my mother believed everything she

said. Or did she make these things up so she'd have an excuse to be angry, to fight, to throw her fists?

Jackie said, "Oh, come on, she's a little girl!"

"You shoulda seen her with my last boyfriend, Ricky!" she lied.

"Wasn't Ricky about fifteen boyfriends ago?" Norm said, and we both laughed.

Jackie ordered pizza over the phone, and Kenny and Cookie went out to pick it up. Also, they were going to look for Mack, who had yet to show up. My mother worried he'd gotten drunk at a bar and forgotten how to get back to Jackie and Kenny's.

I was in Tina's pink bathrobe and Norm wore a Van Halen shirt and a pair of giant elastic waist shorts that belonged to Sam. The oversized clothes made Norm look even smaller than he already was. I wondered if Norm would be as big as Sam if he'd been regularly fed his whole life. They were only a couple of months apart in age. We watched TV in the living room that had orange wall-to-wall shag carpeting and framed prints of chickens and roosters on the wall. Sam and Tina barely talked at the commercials, but I kept catching Tina staring at me and smiling. "I remember when you were so little," she finally said. "You were like a little doll that Regina and I played with." It was nice that she remembered me; it seemed like there was more of me when I was carried in other people's minds.

When the food finally arrived, everyone sat in the living room and ate off paper plates. The grown-ups drank beer and the kids drank Coke. Cookie laughed at everything that came out of Kenny's mouth. She appeared to find him the most fascinating man in the world.

By the next morning, Cookie and Jackie decided that Mack was never coming back. All our stuff was gone. We four kids sat at the kitchen table. Kenny had already left for work, and Jackie was at the stove making pancakes. Cookie leaned against the counter making a dramatic show of being upset that Mack had *all* her travel money, her credit cards, and her driver's license.

"How am I going to pay for the trip to Arizona?!" Cookie stopped talking and picked up a pancake from the plate Jackie was bringing to the table. She dangled it over her mouth like a cartoon cat with a fish and took a giant bite. "That asshole took every dollar I had! Every last dollar!"

I knew my mother had no credit cards, and I don't think she'd ever had a valid driver's license. As for cash, she could only have had the unspent food money given to her by the trucker. It was probably less than ten bucks.

I watched Jackie to see if she was buying the drama and if she'd give Cookie the money she was angling for. Jackie seemed unmoved as she served us pancakes. When she returned to the stove to make another batch, Cookie gave up and went off to shower.

"Sorry about your stepfather," Tina said. Her hair was pulled back into a bouncy ponytail, and she wore a pink sweater with puffy cap sleeves. Norm and I were barefoot and still in the bathrobe and shorts we'd been loaned after our showers. We'd slept in these outfits on a fold-out couch in the basement den that separated Tina's and Sam's rooms. Cookie had slept on the living room couch.

"He wasn't our stepfather," Norm said.

"He was just a guy our mom picked up to drive us to Lake Havasu, Arizona, where my dad bought some land that his family's gonna give to me." I rarely bragged as I'd never had anything to brag about. But the land in Arizona felt like a big deal, and I wanted to say it aloud.

"You own land?" Sam said.

"Her dad bought it," Norm said. "Before he was rubbed out."

"Killed?" Sam asked.

"Yeah." I swirled some pancake in syrup. And then I tried to adjust my face to look like I was sad about it since it seemed like a girl whose dad had been killed should be sad.

"How'd they kill him?" Sam asked.

"They shot him in the head," I said. I didn't really know if it was the head or not. But I remembered Cookie pointing the cake-smeared fork at her temple and imitating a bullet going in.

"Whoa," Sam said.

"That's scary," Tina said.

Jackie turned from the stove and looked back at us, smiling. "You two have quite the imagination." And then she added, "Just like your mother."

Unlike Cookie's boyfriends, Jackie could not be seduced into giving up money, a car, or any other resources. Including her husband. When Kenny got home from work that evening, Cookie ran to him crying real tears. The ten or so bucks that Mack had stolen was now thousands in hundred dollar bills, which my mother claimed she'd been saving for years. She also cried over her lost credit cards, and the lost driver's license. I watched Jackie eye Kenny over Cookie's shoulder. It was a quick, cutting look that prompted Kenny to remove my mother from his chest. Jackie hustled Cookie away from Kenny and asked me to come with her, too.

We settled in Tina's room where Jackie searched her daughter's drawers for clothes that might fit me, while telling Cookie the requirements for our residency in Jackie and Kenny's home. Cookie had to look for a job, apply for food stamps, and apply for housing vouchers. Also, she'd have to enroll me and Norm in school.

"I dunno about all that," Cookie said. She was lying on Tina's bed, her mud-heeled shoes plopped on the bedspread. A Sean Cassidy poster was tacked to the yellow wall over the bed. "I don't have the kids' records, and I don't want to be on any records here myself."

"What are you running from?" Jackie asked. I looked at my mother to see if she'd list her multiple warrants.

"Oh, just a couple of DUIs," Cookie said. "No big deal."

"A couple of DUIs and you still have a driver's license?" Jackie seemed skilled at managing people like Cookie.

"Oh yeah," my mother said. "They were little DUIs, you know, bumpin' up on the curb, that sorta thing."

"Well, unless you killed someone, your little DUIs aren't gonna follow you to Idaho," Jackie said.

I decided that if my mother never applied for food

stamps and refused to enroll us in school, it would mean that she had actually killed someone. Probably the person she hit on the bike in Mastic, New York. Or maybe she was the one who shot my father the day he got out of prison. Though that was unlikely since she'd never complained about Vito. The man she'd always said she'd kill, if she ever had the opportunity, was Gi's dad. No one knew exactly what happened with him; my mother never explained herself or her feelings. Even when she was sober.

9
Safe from the Storm

The Monday after we showed up at Jackie and Kenny's, I was enrolled in the fifth grade at Caldwell's elementary school. Norm was in enrolled in the ninth grade at the high school. My brother walked to school with Sam and Tina, and Jackie drove me to the elementary school, pointing out the roads I'd take to walk home that afternoon. She said I could go to a friend's house and play after school if I wanted. I just needed to be home by five thirty for dinner.

There were twenty-five kids in my homeroom, and they all looked clean and tidy with fresh clothes and crisp haircuts. I was in Tina's purple velour elastic-wrist top and green corduroy pants. Nothing matched and I hated my outfit until Tina caught me before leaving home and put a gold braided headband across my forehead. When she fixed my hair like that, I missed my sisters more than ever. Gi was the one who usually got me ready for school, always fixing my hair before we walked out the door. I scanned the classroom to find the girls who might be my friends. Gi had always told me to find kids at school who would take me home with them so I could see how happy people lived, how happy families loved. This is how she had learned to be a good sister to me, Gi had told me; she had modeled herself after the best moms in the happiest homes.

My teacher, Mrs. Roahr, introduced me to the class as Rosanne Brooks. There were many students with the same first name in the class, so everyone, including the teachers, called the students by their last name. I was Brooks.

I was happy to be back in school, to have my days organized and occupied, to have things to think about and projects to work on. And I was particularly happy to have access to books again. Mrs. Roahr said I could check out as many books as I wanted from the classroom library or the school library. And so on my first day of school, I checked out seven books. Four were by Judy Blume, and one of them I'd started the last time I was in school but wasn't able to finish before we'd moved again. The other books were Nancy Drew mysteries.

The next day at school, when I went to the library to return *Are You There God? It's Me, Margaret*, I made my first friend: Flavia Feliciano. Flavia had tumbling, wavy black hair, like my sister Gi. Like me, she liked to read and went to the library after lunch, after school, and sometimes before school. By day three, Flavia was my best friend. This is when I learned that it only took a connection with a single person for me to feel okay. When I didn't have that person, I internally returned to being the girl who sat silent for weeks, rocking herself in a wooden chair at the foster home. Brian had been my connection at the Callahans'. Norm had been my connection there, too. My sisters, when they were near, always made me feel connected. And now I had Flavia at the new school. When we sat together in a library beanbag chair, each of us holding one side of the same book that we'd read together, I felt a perfect, peaceful contentedness.

Flavia introduced me to a playground that was midway between the trailer park where she lived and Jackie and Kenny's house. At the playground, there were giant tires in ascending sizes buried halfway in the dirt. Flavia and I liked to leap from one tire to the next, like an obstacle course. If there were enough kids at the playground, we'd start a hide-and-seek game. The two of us could always find each other as we both loved to hide in the tires. If there were no other kids around, Flavia and I nested together in a tire and read or just talked.

On the weekends, if I wasn't with Flavia, I read books on the couch in the den where Norm and I slept. Tina told me I could hang out in her room if I wanted, but I never did. I felt like an interloper already, wearing her castoff clothes and sleeping just on the other side of her door.

When it wasn't too cold or snowy out, I put on the enormous puffy coat Jackie gave me (it had been hers, but she bought herself a new one) and trampled across the backyard. I'd pass the chicken coop, pausing to say hello to the chickens, and then scoot between broken slats in the fence. For hours, I sat with my back against the fence, reading. When the trains ran through, a rush of cold wind blew past me and it felt like the ground was shaking. I always looked up from my book and watched. Once, I counted fifty-five cars including the engine. I tried to imagine what each car held, where they came from, and where they were going.

Sometimes I put pennies down on the tracks. I collected them after the train had passed. The pennies were hot, flat, and shiny as river rocks. When I came in from watching the train, I always had questions for Jackie: *Do trains run on coal? Does the conductor steer the train? Are those the exact same tracks that were laid when the railroad lines were first built? What year were the railroad lines built?* And once, *Do you like the sound of the train in the backyard, 'cause I sure do!*

Cookie started a job as a bartender the week after we arrived in Idaho. She claimed everyone in town loved her New York accent—an accent I'd never noticed until we'd left the state.

The job was good for all of us, as it kept my mother out of the house and away from the constant string of questions that were plaguing me that year. I think my mother didn't like my questions because she didn't want me to know more than she did. Cookie seemed to prefer it when we weren't in school. And in some ways, she was happiest when we lived in the car. The smaller our world, the tighter her control over it. And over us. But Jackie wasn't like that. She answered every question she could. And the day I listed for her the letters on the cars (UP, GATX, FURX, NATX . . .) each set memorized, Jackie laughed and said I better get myself to the library and read about trains because now I was digging into stuff she knew nothing about.

Mrs. Connor, the librarian, helped me find books to read about the Union Pacific Railroad. She even ordered a couple of new train books and let me check them out first, when they were brand new and the pages smelled like plastic. At the atlas, as I fingered out the route of the Union Pacific Railroad, Mrs. Connor looked over my shoulder, rested her hand on mine, and pointed out where the state universities were along the route. "Some day you'll go to college there," she said. "Or maybe there." It gave me a hopeful feeling to think that I might go to college. Gi had talked about college before; she had said it seemed like it was only for rich kids and she wondered how we'd ever be able to go.

I spent so much time in the library that Mrs. Connor gave me a job sorting and stacking books. Right away, it seemed like the greatest job I could ever have. No one complained when I paused and read. And there were so many great books around; I'd start one, put it back, and then pull it out again every day or so to get in another few pages. There was a blue-eyed, black-haired boy, David Collins, who also helped Mrs. Connor stack books in the library. I thought he was handsome and imagined that he was a genius and that's why he hung out in the library. But I was too scared to talk to him, and he never said a word to me. We'd look at each other bashfully across the stacks. Or we'd stand together, our elbows knocking as we silently sorted books by their call letters and then alphabetically. In my imagination I had long conversations with Collins about Cookie, or about Norm, who never had time for me now that he had friends and was at a different school, or about Tina, who was so nice to me that it hurt in my heart because she reminded me of my sisters. Together, we were a library nerd version of Popeye and Olive Oyl, or Donald and Daisy Duck. Me in Tina's castoff clothes, usually with a headband across my forehead, and Collins with his blue eyes and thick black eyelashes and his head dropped down.

One afternoon when I was thinking about my sisters, I remembered Gi telling me about the love notes she had exchanged with a boy in fifth grade. If she could do it, I thought, I could, too. I took a piece of scrap paper from the checkout counter and I wrote on it, *Hi! From Brooks.* Then I went to the shelved book Collins had been reading when we were filing during recess and slipped the note inside. The next day, when I pulled out *From the Mixed-Up Files of Mrs. Basil E. Frankweiler,* which I had been reading in the stacks, I found a note that said, *Hi. From Collins.* There were notes every day after that, always limited to one or two sentences. We talked about the gross school lunches, the kid who barfed in the hallway, the spelling bee we were both studying for. This was the beginning of a nonverbal relationship that lasted for months.

Flavia approved of this relationship. And so did her mother. Just like Gi said, when I went to Flavia's house, I saw how happy, loving families acted. Flavia lived in the Paradise Homes Trailer Park with her parents and her little brother, Luis. After school, Mrs. Feliciano sat us down on the bench seats at the tiny table, fed us homemade tamales made with hand-pressed tortillas, and asked us questions about school, about teachers, about boys. She thought Flavia and I were funny, and she laughed when we imitated the principal making announcements on the school's PA system. Unlike Cookie, Mrs. Feliciano was never angry, but every now and then she'd pretend to be angry. Mrs. Feliciano would start speaking in Spanish so fast that even Flavia had a hard time following her. And then she'd laugh and pat the tops of our heads, or kiss Flavia in the middle of her smooth, broad forehead.

Jackie and her family went to the First Assembly of God church, which everyone in town called The Domes because of the two white domes that made up either side of the apse. From a distance, as you walked toward the church, it looked like two giant golf balls shoved into the earth. Cookie told Kenny and Jackie that she was a good Christian and had raised us as good Christians, too. We'd all been baptized, except Gi. The reason Gi hadn't been baptized, according to my mother, was because her father was the devil, and as the child of the devil, Gi couldn't enter a church or it might burst into flames. I'd had the biggest baptism of all; it was an event my sisters had told me about many times. I wore a long lacy dress and had two god-fathers who stood by Vito's and Cookie's sides at the baptismal font. What my sister Cherie remembered most about my baptism was how many men in suits wore sunglasses inside the dark church.

Every Sunday Jackie invited the three of us to go to services with her. I happily accepted the invitation. Norm usually grunted, then ran outside and met up with his neighborhood friends. Cookie always claimed that she *would* go, she *wanted* to go, but she really needed to stay home and clean the house. She promised she'd do some praying while she vacuumed.

"You're home-churched," I said to my mother one day, and Kenny and Jackie thought that was hilarious.

"Home-churched," Kenny repeated. "I like that."

With Tina's too-big dresses on, and a headband across my forehead, I marched off to church with the family. Like school, there was a wonderful order in church, a calmness. I loved knowing what we'd do next, when to stand, when to sit, when to sing. And I never felt alone at church. When I belted out "The Lord's Prayer" with the congregation, I felt just as connected to Jackie, Kenny, Tina, and Sam, as I did sitting in the library with Flavia.

The house was never vacuumed when we got home. Cookie came up with a new excuse every week: she fell ill, she got an important phone call from my Italian family about my land, and, eventually, she had to tend to her boyfriend, Hal Pinkerton, a trucker she met at the bar where she worked. Like all her other boyfriends, Hal quickly became a priority that trumped all else. Cookie spent so much time with Hal that she was like a traveling salesman: someone who rarely came home and never showed up for dinner.

When she did sleep at home, she slept in until well after we kids had gone to school. Jackie woke me early, before Tina, because she knew I liked to run out to the chicken coop and gather the eggs for breakfast. When I walked into the coop, the chickens clucked and bobbed their heads while doing the chicken dance. They'd dance closer and closer, pecking the dirt around my feet. I named each of them according to their distinct personalities: Mack (after Cookie's last boyfriend) for the fat, ugly rooster who ran toward me like he wanted to attack. I'd stomp my boot in the icy dirt to get him away. Minnie for the little brown hen who looked like she was happy and fun, like Minnie Mouse. Margaret for the hen who darted around like an anxious teenager who wished she'd grow breasts (after Margaret in *Are You There God? It's Me, Margaret*). Chrissy, the dumb-seeming hen, after a character on the TV show *Three's Company*. Mindy for the tidy-looking brown hen, after Mindy from the TV show *Mork & Mindy*. Gi for the sleek black hen. Camille for the fluffy brown one whose eyes weren't as beady as the others'. Cherie for the confident hen who liked to circle the periphery of the pen, as if she were keeping everyone in line. And Flavia for the red, orange, and black hen who ran toward me and then away again, toward me and away, as if she were playing with me.

I'd stick my hand into the nesting boxes and pull out eggs that were warm and smaller than grocery store eggs. Some of them were brown. Delicately, I'd place them on the cloth napkin in the pink Easter basket that was used for egg collecting, and then carefully walk back to the house where Jackie scrambled eggs for everyone. They were the best eggs I'd ever had. Each day they tasted different than they had the day before. I imagined that I could taste whose eggs I was eating: Chrissy's being fluffier than Mindy's, Gi's being the sweetest, and so forth.

One evening, I was returning from watching the trains outside the fence when I ran into Kenny at the chicken coop.

"Hey." I stood outside the coop holding *James and the Giant Peach*.

"It's dinnertime," Kenny said. "Watch this." Kenny grabbed fluttering Chrissy and then flipped her upside down and held her by the feet. She immediately calmed. He carried her like that out of the coop to where a tree had been cut down but the stump remained. There was an axe stuck there. Kenny laid Chrissy on her side, still holding her feet while she remained calm. With one swift motion, he lifted the axe, took off Chrissy's head, then set her body on the ground where she flapped her wings and ran.

"Welcome to Idaho," Kenny said, laughing as headless Chrissy circled in erratic bee-like patterns.

My book fell from my hands. "That's Chrissy," I gasped.

Kenny whipped his head toward me. "Ah, you shouldn't have named them, Rosanne!" Kenny slapped his thigh. "It always makes it harder when you've named them." I wondered then how much worse Cookie might have been if she hadn't named us. Maybe our names were the only thing that had kept us from getting our heads chopped off.

I couldn't eat Chrissy for dinner that night. In fact, I couldn't eat chicken at Jackie and Kenny's again. Even when it was store bought. Kenny shook his head every time and said something like, "Man, I never shoulda let her see that." Nonetheless, this started an ongoing nightly dinner table discussion about where food came from. Before living with Kenny and Jackie, I'd never connected milk to cows; cereal to wheat to the farm down the road; peanut butter to peanuts to a farm in Georgia. It was hard not to think of the chickens' names when I gathered the eggs in the mornings. I'd try to turn away when they each did little dances, or cluck-songs, that were particular to them. The eggs still tasted amazing.

A few weeks before Christmas, in the evening, I found my mother sitting in the living room on the couch that was her bed, watching *Three's Company* on TV. Norm was at a friend's house, and Tina, Sam, and Kenny were out Christmas shopping. Cookie had a can of Schlitz and a cigarette in her hand. Her feet rested on the coffee table, crossed.

I reclined in Kenny's La-Z-Boy, above which hung a framed poster of a proud-looking rooster standing on a hill.

Jackie walked into the room holding a green garbage bag. She stared at Cookie.

"Cookie," she said, but my mother didn't seem to hear. "Cookie," she said again. When my mother didn't respond, Jackie moved so she was standing in front of the TV.

"Anyone ever tell you, you make a better door than a window?" Cookie said, and she laughed.

"What's this?" Jackie's voice was hard. She lifted the garbage bag up and down. I could see shapes pushing out the way toys push out of Santa's bag in picture books and cartoons.

"Trash?" Cookie said.

"No," Jackie said. "It's a bag I found under the couch with your things." My mother's "things" were the clothes and trinkets she'd bought since we moved in. There was a thrift store near where Cookie tended bar, and she liked to go in every day before her shift and treat herself to a gift. It was usually something useless, like a broken clock with cherubs on it, or a ceramic cat with giant blue eyes. Sometimes she bought records even though we didn't have a record player.

"Looks like garbage to me," Cookie snarled, then looked at me as if I'd snarl with her.

Jackie reached into the bag and pulled out a crystal goblet with etched flowers encircling it. "You think this is garbage?" Jackie asked. "I bought this at an antiques store; it's Depression-era glass."

"Well, that's nice," Cookie said. She leaned to the side as if she were trying to see the TV around Jackie.

"Cookie!" Jackie backed closer to the TV. "Your sweaters and shoes were in this bag, too."

I lowered the footrest on the La-Z-Boy and sat up straight.

"Well, why'd you put your stuff in the bag with my sweaters and shoes?" Cookie asked and took a slug of her Schlitz.

"I didn't. You did. You're stealing my stuff." Jackie turned around and punched off the TV.

"Wait, let me see that glass—" Cookie held out her hand. Her long pointed nails were painted orange. When she wiggled her fingers, it looked like flickering flames.

Jackie held up the glass but wouldn't hand it to Cookie. I counted the empty beer cans on the coffee table near Cookie's feet. Four. There was no way to count the cigarette butts in the overflowing glass ashtray.

"That's mine!" Cookie said. "That was my grandma's glass that I inherited from her."

"Who's your grandma?" I asked. Cookie rarely even mentioned her parents except to say they were a *coupla assholes.*

"Did you get these from your grandmother, too?" Jackie pulled out a Bee Gees album and a Frankie Valli album.

"No, I don't know what those are doing there." Cookie whipped her head toward me. "Rosanne! Did you put those albums in the bag with my grandmother's glass?!"

"No!" Cookie wasn't as scary as usual when we were at Jackie and Kenny's house because there was no way she'd beat me in front of them. Still, I got up from the chair and stood near Jackie.

"Did your grandmother wear Jontue?" Jackie asked, and she pulled out a spray bottle larger than the ones Cookie usually shoplifted from the drugstore.

"No, but I've worn Jontue for years, haven't I, Rosanne?" My mother looked at me, and I nodded.

"This is my Jontue," Jackie said. "But you know what, you like the smell so much, I'll give it to you. But this—" Jackie pulled out a macramé purse with beads worked through it. "I bought this at the town fair this past summer."

"You're lying—" Cookie's head rocked back as she stifled a burp. "I've had that for, like, ten years. Give it back to me." Cookie lifted her free hand again and twittered her fingers as if calling the purse.

"Mack drove off with everything you had. This is not your purse."

My stomach dropped. I was nervous for Jackie. Cookie was on her fifth beer. It was during beer five when my mother seemed to have no more sense than a headless chicken.

"He didn't have everything." Cookie lit a new cigarette from her old one while still hanging onto the beer. "I was carrying it the night he left. It had my grandmother's glass inside it." I knew my mother was lying. The purse she'd been carrying was clear in my head—a big, white, plastic thing with a zipper pocket that once held my sisters' phone number.

"And my wedding rings, Cookie." Jackie reached into the bottom of the bag and pulled out two gold rings with diamonds on them. "Did you have the same exact wedding rings, too? You haven't been married since Norm was a baby, and he's fourteen now."

Jackie always took off her wedding rings and put them in a coffee cup when she did the dishes. She'd been looking for them for the past couple of nights and even had Kenny go under the kitchen sink and take out a part of the pipe to see if they'd washed down.

"Are you calling me a liar?" Cookie took a slug of Schlitz; the lit cigarette glanced against her hair.

"Well—" Jackie stood up straighter and shook her head. "I suppose I am."

"How dare you call me a liar?" Cookie stood. She rocked a bit as she lost balance and then resettled herself on her feet. She took a hit off her cigarette, and a clump of ash fell onto her jutting breasts. "How dare you!" Smoke puffed out of my mother's mouth.

"You need to move out before Christmas," Jackie said. She put down the bag and then slowly and deliberately put on the wedding rings. Cookie smoked her cigarette while glaring at Jackie.

Now my stomach really dropped. Without a car to sleep in, we had no place to go. I wondered if Flavia's parents would allow me to move in with them. Their trailer had three tiny bedrooms—her parents in one, her brother in one, and Flavia in the third. I was so skinny, I could easily fit in Flavia's single bed with her.

"You have ten days to get out." Jackie picked up the bag and walked toward the kitchen.

"Are you kidding me?!" Cookie yelled. "I wouldn't steal your worthless shit if someone were payin' me for it!"

Jackie was already in the kitchen. No one made a sound.

"FUCK YOU!" Cookie yelled, and she threw her Schlitz toward the kitchen. It landed on the orange shag carpet. I ran to the kitchen, grabbed a dishcloth, and then went back to the living room and cleaned up the spilled beer. Cookie was already repositioned on the couch, smoking. *Three's Company* was back on and she didn't even look my way.

Before Jackie's ten-day deadline, a trailer became available at the Paradise Homes Trailer Park. I was thrilled because it was across the parking lot and a couple of trailers down from Flavia's trailer.

Norm was unhappy. He sat on the fold-out couch where we slept and watched me gather my things and put them in a garbage bag.

"Remember the last trailer?" Norm asked. I was six then and remembered the stories Gi had told me about it more than the experience itself. Cherie and Camille had each moved in with a friend while Cookie had abandoned me, Norm, and Gi in a trailer next to horse barns across from the sprawling Smith Haven Mall. Gi and Norm mucked out the stalls every morning in exchange for the food the Mexican workers brought us: warm rolls or Hostess cakes. Eventually my brother and sister were riding horses, both of them fearless as they trotted around the ring. The one clear memory I had was of Gi putting me on an enormous mare. I was enjoying myself until a rutting stallion tried to mount her. One of the Mexican workers had snatched me off the mare's back while trying to kick away the stallion.

"These aren't trailers like that," I said. "They're more like houses."

"It was so cold we had to wear socks on our hands

inside," Norm said, and an image came to me of Gi blowing on my numb hands and then covering them with her own hands, like a shell over a seed. When I could feel my fingers again, Gi wrapped my hands together in one of Norm's old shirts and then fed me a Twinkie.

"Flavia's mom will feed us for sure," I said. "And her trailer's heated."

"I don't want Flavia's mom. I want our mom," Norm said.

I wanted to whisk my brother away to Flavia's house and make him sit at the little table, eat tamales, and make Mrs. Feliciano laugh. Then he might understand how a good mother mothered.

"Well, I guess Mom's nice to you," I said.

"She loves us," Norm said.

"If she leaves, maybe you could just go with her." I put the last headband Tina had given me into the bag and then shook everything down. I pulled up the top corners of the bag and tied it.

Cookie came into the room. She was smoking a cigarette and singing a Kenny Rogers song about gambling and knowing when to hold your cards.

"One day," Cookie said when she finished singing. She leaned against the doorway to Tina's room, tilted up her head, and blew out a stream of smoke.

"One day what?" Norm asked.

"One day I'm gonna fuck Kenny Rogers." Cookie laughed. By then, I had grown to understand *fuck* as a verb and had to create thought-noise in my head so I could pretend I hadn't heard my mother.

"Think he'll be able to find you at the trailer park?" Norm squinted his eyes at our mother, waiting for an answer in earnest. These conversations never seemed to ruffle him.

"We won't be there long," Cookie said. "I finally got a hold of Vito's brothers and they're gettin' ready to turn over Rosie's birthright."

"What's a birthright?" I asked. I had a birthmark on my left leg; were Vito's brothers going to do something to *turn it over*? I liked my birthmark, it was the shape of Africa—a discovery I'd made while flipping through the atlas in the library one day.

"*What's a birthright?*" Cookie mocked me and then laughed. "You know Kenny—he calls himself *Kinny*—I bet he'd like settling down at Lake Havasu."

"So we're going to Lake Havasu after all?" Norm asked, and now he seemed happy.

"They're not going to touch my birthmark, are they?" The image of uncles I couldn't remember, wearing sunglasses, as they had at my baptism, and handling my leg was making me anxious.

"Birthright, not birthmark, you dunce cap!" Cookie said.

"When are we going to Lake Havasu?" Norm asked.

"In the spring," Cookie said. "They'll pay for the trip an' everything." Cookie rolled her back against the door like a bear rubbing against a tree. Then she sauntered upstairs. I had a feeling she was counting dollar signs in her head. And though I liked the idea of owning land, I hated the idea of leaving Flavia, school, the library, and Mrs. Connor.

10
Paradise

The trailer came with the things the last tenants had left behind: bedframes with sweat-stained mattresses that were as lumpy as oatmeal; greasy blankets and waxy sheets that were balled up in the corners of the rooms; food so overgrown with mold it was unidentifiable; trash that ran from balled-up toilet paper to a soiled diaper to liquor bottles and soup cans. In the closet-sized bathroom there was a hairbrush, toothbrushes, toothpaste, and shampoo. Cookie wanted Norm and me to use the toothbrushes since we'd forgotten to bring the ones we'd been using at Kenny and Jackie's. We both refused, and I threw them all away the moment my mother passed out on the bare mattress in her room.

There was a couch the color of wet dirt in the center

room, and an oval dining table with one wooden chair and two stools that were too high to use for eating at the table. Norm and I scooted the table toward the couch so we could sit there while we ate. We looked even smaller than we already were when we sat on the low, slumpy sofa and reached up toward our plates. When we weren't eating, Norm sat on the stool, maybe because it made him seem tall. Cookie liked the threadbare couch. And I sat on the wooden chair that reminded me of my teacher's chair at school.

The only luxury of the trailer was that we each had our own bedroom. My room, like Norm's, was about a foot wider than the single bed pushed against one wall. Cookie's room had less than a foot beyond the double bed. Between our bedrooms was a back door that led to a square of cement Cookie called "our yard." Unlike our neighbor's yards, ours wasn't fenced and had no plants or chairs.

About three days after we moved in, on the first day of Christmas vacation, Cookie slipped and fell on the slush of snow I'd tracked in after returning from Flavia's house. Norm had already made friends at Paradise Homes and was running around in the snow with them.

"The fuck?!" Cookie rolled over, grabbed the seat of the wooden chair and hoisted herself up. "Who put this shit here?" My mother pointed to the wet pool by the door.

Instead of answering, I ran to the bathroom, grabbed one of the two towels Jackie had given us and dropped onto my hands and knees to mop it up. My mother grabbed my hair at the nape my neck and yanked back my head. I felt like a dog on a very short leash.

Cookie said, "I asked you who put this here. I didn't fucking ask you to mop it up."

"I guess it's from my shoes," I said.

"Then take your fucking shoes off outside!" With those words my mother kicked me once—swiftly, powerfully—in the belly with her rubber-heeled moon boots. I contracted into a tight little spiral, my body like a conch shell. While still holding my hair, my mother kicked at me several more times. When she had kicked so much that she was panting for breath, Cookie released my hair and staggered to the couch. She dropped onto it, her feet up on the arm rest. I stayed on the floor, crying as quietly as I could so as not to bring my mother's boot to me again. My stomach churned on the edge of vomiting.

"Shut the fuck up," Cookie said. I took the deepest, quietest breaths I could and prayed that the tamales Flavia's mother had fed me didn't come pouring out.

When I heard the flick of a lighter, and then the TV going on, I figured it was safe to get up and go hide in my room.

Lying in bed, my belly and ribs as tender as an open wound, I tried to puzzle out how I could avoid future beatings. Things had been so peaceful at Jackie and Kenny's house. But now I knew my mother had been holding her breath while we were there, just waiting to exhale so her fists and feet could fly at me.

The only way to avoid beatings, I finally decided, was to not be home to receive them. So over the following days of Christmas vacation, I spent as much time as possible at Flavia's trailer. I was there so often that Mrs. Feliciano invited me, Norm, and Cookie to have Christmas dinner with them.

We had no tree or stockings, but Norm and I each got mittens and a hat for Christmas. Cookie gave herself a jug of vodka. By the time we were due at the Felicianos' for dinner, Cookie was passed out on the brown couch. Neither Norm nor I was interested in waking her.

Mr. Feliciano was home on Christmas Day. This was the first time I'd met him as he worked multiple odd jobs and was gone from dawn to dusk. That day, he helped Mrs. Feliciano make the meal; Flavia, Norm, and I set the table; Luis was in charge of filling the bumpy orange glasses with milk.

While Mr. Feliciano carved the turkey breast, I said a quick prayer in my head. I prayed that my sisters would soon find me, and I gave God each of their first, middle, and last names in case that would help him get them to me. I prayed for Brian, too. That he would stop shaking soon and that he was out of the Callahan house. I prayed that Cookie wouldn't ever beat me again. That Norm would be warm and have enough food to grow some more. And I prayed that I would do well in school so that I could go to college like Mrs. Connor hoped I would. Lastly, I thanked God for the Felicianos, and for Mrs. Feliciano's tamales in particular, which were sitting on a platter to my right.

When I finished my prayer, I noticed Norm staring at the turkey breast as if he were hypnotized by it. I decided I wouldn't eat any of it so there would be more for Norm. That would be my Christmas present to him.

Back in our trailer that night, when we were brushing our teeth with our fingers, Norm said, "How come you didn't eat any turkey?"

"I dunno." I was embarrassed about the present. I thought Norm might make fun of me for doing something nice for him.

"Was it so there would be more for me?" he asked. It was dark in the trailer. We could hear Cookie snoring on the couch; there was a pretty good chance she'd stay there all night.

"Yeah, I guess," I said.

"I didn't eat any tamales so there'd be more for you," Norm said. He knew I loved Mrs. Feliciano's tamales; I'd eaten three of them the day we moved into the trailer park.

"Thanks," I said. It was one of the nicest gifts my brother ever gave me.

The first Sunday after Christmas, Flavia and her family went to visit relatives, leaving me alone in our trailer with Cookie and Norm. Cookie was on her fourth beer; there was an electricity in the air that I felt in my bones. If I stayed in the house, I knew, a beating would come soon.

"I'm going to Flavia's," I said, and I ran out before my mother or Norm could ask any questions. I walked past Flavia's trailer, past the playground with the half-buried tires and over to Kenny and Jackie's house. They wouldn't be home; they went to The Domes church on Sundays.

I paused near the train tracks and waited for the train. When the train didn't come, I walked toward The Domes. Going to church with Kenny and Jackie had been one of the nicest parts of living with them.

Though I had been there many times before, my stomach rolled with nerves when I approached the church. I stood outside for several minutes trying to imagine what I'd do when I opened the door. I could hear the congregation singing on the other side. Would everyone stop, turn their heads, and wonder why the kid with the purple braided headband, jeans, pink top, and too-big handed-down coat was going to church alone? I unzipped my jacket, looked down at the dirt spot on my shirt and tried to clean it with my thumb and some spit.

One of the houses where my sisters and brother and I had lived alone had a church across the street. Gi had told me she liked to go there to relax and gather up a store of calmness. She felt like she was sneaking in, though, and never went back after the day when the priest asked her if she'd been baptized. Suddenly she felt like an outsider, and that warm feeling was gone.

The singing inside The Domes stopped, and my stomach gurgled. Still, I opened the door and stepped inside. Only a couple of people turned their heads to see who was entering and one of them was Jackie. She had a huge smile on her face, and she waved her arms toward me. I walked up to the pew where she, Kenny, Tina, and Sam stood, my head pointed down as I was scared to see if anyone else was watching me. When I reached them, Tina and Sam each scooted aside so I could stand in between them. I felt so happy just then. So warm and contained. It was like I was with my sisters again.

After that day, I rarely missed a Sunday at The Domes church. The pastor never asked if I was baptized, or where my family was, or if I believed in God, or even if I was Christian. He just took me as one of them. And even though I was one of the few kids who showed up at church alone, I never felt like the outlier—the foster kid, the new kid, the fatherless kid, the homeless kid, the kid with aching, bruised ribs—who was different than the rest. I was in the congregation.

Jim Nettles didn't live at Paradise Homes, but he liked to slowly drive his long, black, four-door car through the trailer park. Lines of kids followed the car as if he were the Pied Piper. Eventually he would park, and then he'd open the passenger-side door and sit in the car with the heat running and Top 40 radio on low. If you sat with him, he'd give you a donut or candy. If you were brave enough to drive away with him, he'd take you to Baskin-Robbins and buy you an ice cream. Flavia and I always got in his car together, and never in the front seat. Mr. Nettles would turn around and pat our heads or rub our knees while he listed all the candy he had in the front seat. He spoke slowly and with a spitty little lisp that made it seem like his mouth was too wet and full of saliva. His hair looked wet, too. Shiny dark brown, swooped over to one side.

Once Mr. Nettles had handed us the candy we'd chosen, we'd run out of the car and hurry to the park where we'd gobble our sweets in the nest of one of the giant tires.

On the weekends, when we weren't at the park, Flavia and I liked to skip circles around the cement-block storage bunker that was in the middle of the trailer park. It had half-size doors that only an Oompa Loompa could fit through and so we'd named it the Oompa Loompa house. We'd named our neighbors' trailers, too, according to how they'd differentiated themselves. The people with colored Christmas lights up all year were the Red Bulbs; the old woman with plastic flamingoes on sticks in the plants around her trailer was the Pink Lady; the family with the blue-slat fence and flower boxes was the Tulip Family.

Of all the places I'd lived, the people at the Paradise Homes Trailer Park were the most generous. If anyone noticed Norm and me hanging around outside near dinnertime, we were invited into their trailer and fed. Bags of fruit were frequently left on our doorstep, and a carton of milk showed up every now and then.

Once the snow melted, the Paradise Homes kids took up jumping rope, joyously shouting out rhymes during double Dutch. Flavia and I organized a jump-rope competition one weekend, and I came in first. I had never been a champion of anything until that day.

Eventually, after months of Mr. Nettles showing up, stories about him touching boys and girls on their private parts began to circulate among the kids. No one wanted to confess that it had happened to them, but everyone knew someone else he'd touched. It wasn't long before the stories drifted up to the parents. Cookie appeared to be the only adult who didn't believe the kids. Mr. Nettles was her friend, she said. He came to the bar where she worked and always left a generous tip.

"I swear," I told her, "he gives them candy and then he touches them while they eat, or he grabs their butt when they leave the car." It was likely that the only reason Flavia and I had escaped unscathed was because we'd only gone in his car together. And we never even considered sitting in the front seat.

"He's not interested in any snot-nosed kids!" Cookie said, and then she shouted at Norm, who was in his bedroom with the door closed, "NORM! Did Nettles ever grope your dick?!"

There was silence for a moment. Cookie shouted, "NORM!" And then my brother barked out, "No!"

Cookie said the Paradise Homes parents were a bunch of gossips that were trying to take down Mr. Nettles the way the bad guys had taken down my father. My mother claimed that her high moral standards prevented her from taking part in the Nettles "witch hunt."

The Nettles controversy happened around the same time that the mothers of Paradise Homes began to notice my lumps, scrapes, and bruises. No one asked if Cookie was beating me, but they stopped by the trailer from time to time to check on me and Norm. And more than one person told me I was welcome to come stay in their trailer if ever I needed to get away. It was clear they were suspicious of my mother.

One school night, my mother woke me up after midnight and dragged me by the hair into the living area.

"Nettles wants to talk to you and explain himself." Cookie's words were slurred, and there were several empty beer cans scattered across the table. She let go of my hair and lit a cigarette.

I backed away, out of her arm's reach. She'd overdone the Jontue, and the smell, combined with her ashtray and beer breath, made me slightly nauseous. "Why me?" I asked.

"'Cause you're one of the little bitches who's spreading rumors about him." Cookie collapsed onto the brown couch, her head rocking as if she were in a car that had just stopped short. She dropped her cigarette on the couch and then picked it up again, leaving a perfectly circular burn mark in the cushion. Hopefully she'd pass out before she got the idea to beat me.

"I don't want to talk to Nettles," I said.

"He's in my room waiting for you." Cookie tapped out her ash onto the floor.

"What?!" I looked toward my mother's closed bedroom door. Was Nettles going to pop out and start beating me along with Cookie?

"Just go in my room and talk to him," Cookie exhaled. "If you don't, I'm going to kick your ass from here to New York." Cookie started to stand but fell back onto the couch again. I could definitely outrun my mother if I took off for Flavia's; I was one of the fasted kids in my grade. But I was too embarrassed to wake the Felicianos at this time of night. It seemed wiser to do as Cookie had asked.

"He better not touch me," I said.

"He's not gonna touch you, you moron! He's here to explain himself." My mother waved her cigarette hand toward the door and shouted, "GO!"

I went into Cookie's room, leaving the door open behind me. Mr. Nettles was in boxer shorts and a white undershirt with yellow marks fanning out from the armpits. He sat on the edge of Cookie's unmade bed. The room was stuffy and overly warm. It smelled like a wet sneaker. On top of Cookie's dresser were three twenty-dollar bills fanned out beneath a round-eyed porcelain doll my mother had bought at the junk store. Cookie was never one to leave money around, and I wondered if Mr. Nettles had put it there for her. Was it a loan?

"Rosanne," Mr. Nettles said in his spitty-soft voice. "Sit down."

"I'm fine," I said.

"Sit." He patted the bed beside himself.

I went to the bed and sat as far from Mr. Nettles as I could.

"What do you want?" My stomach gunned like an engine revving to get me out of there.

"I just wanted to explain a few things. I heard that the community here was under the false impression that I was hurting kids." He lifted himself and scooted closer.

"Yeah." I squirmed so I was half off the end of Cookie's bed.

"I would never hurt a child." Mr. Nettles smiled, revealing teeth that were so short and widely spaced, they looked like baby teeth.

"Okay." The engine in my gut roared. I stood.

"Sit!" Mr. Nettles grabbed my arm and pulled me down again. I looked from him to the open door. Cookie and a beating were ready for me if I came out too soon, that was certain.

"I have to go to bed," I said. "I have school tomorrow."

"I know," Mr. Nettles said. "I just want to give you a little lesson about safety, because there are many bad men out there who will try to harm you." He smiled again, with his mouth open this time. A small bubble of spit sat on his tongue.

"Okay," I said. The gunning in my gut turned into a slow, long, howling pain.

"The first thing you should know is to never let a stranger touch you here." Mr. Nettles placed his doughy white palm on my crotch. I tried to brush his hand away, but he held it in place. I took my two hands and wedged him off. He giggled as if it were a game.

"I got it." My lungs stuttered as I took a deep breath.

I stared out the door again. How long, I wondered, would be long enough to avoid a beating?

"And don't ever let a stranger touch you here." Mr. Nettles turned and placed each of his fatty white hands on my breasts. With all my force, I pushed him off me and stood. Everything inside me was racing, yet I was as still and quiet as my mother's porcelain doll.

"I'm not going to hurt you, Rosanne," he said. "I'm trying to protect you."

"Thanks, Mr. Nettles," I said, loudly enough so Cookie could hear. Then I ran to my room, slamming the door behind me.

My heart beat so fast and furiously, there was no going back to sleep that night. The next day, when I slept in the beanbag chair after school at the library, Mrs. Connors woke me and asked if I was okay.

"I'm just tired," I said.

"Do you want to tell me anything?" she asked. It was time for school to close. Flavia had already gone home because it was her brother's birthday. No one else was in the library.

"Tell you something?" I asked, and I thought, *Yes, I want to tell you that my mother frequently beats me, there's no food in the house but the neighbors feed me, and last night my mother forced me to go into her bedroom with a pervert who touched me in my private places.*

"Is everything okay at home?" Mrs. Connors asked.

"Yeah, I'm just tired." If I told her even half of it, Social Services would be called. And if Social Services were called, I would likely have to leave school, Flavia, and the Paradise Homes community only to end up someplace like the Callahans' once again.

Spring brought the relief of warmer days and more hours of sunshine during which I could stay outside playing with Flavia and the other kids. Someone found an inner tube and one of the parents bought the gang of Paradise Homes kids an inflatable raft that we dragged over to the culvert just past the neighboring trailer home park. Norm named it Paradise Beach, even though there was no sand, just cement walls that held fuzzy, slate-colored run-off water. Sometimes, especially if there'd been rain, this sludge moved like a river. In our shorts and T-shirts, or even in our jeans, we kids floated along the current, ducking under low-hanging branches, dipping power lines, corroded pipes jutting from the cement wall, and overpasses that we thought of as bridges. Once, when the water was particularly high, Norm forgot to duck at the overpass and smacked his head straight into the concrete.

When Flavia and I weren't at Paradise Homes, we

jumped rope and skipped around the streets and the cemented common areas. One clear, bright afternoon, Flavia and I found ourselves alone near the Oompa Loompa house. We were skipping in circles while singing *Miss Lucy* songs. The other kids were at Paradise Beach, and the grown-ups were either at work or holed up in their trailers. Other than our high, fluty voices, it was eerily quiet. I stopped suddenly when I noticed a black car with black windows parked in front of our trailer.

"Do you think that's Mr. Nettles?" I asked Flavia, and suddenly I had to pee so badly I crossed my legs and bounced up and down.

Flavia made an awning with her hand over her eyes. "I don't think so," she said.

I hadn't told her about the night Mr. Nettles had been in my mother's room. It seemed that if I didn't say the words about what had happened, it would be easier to pretend it hadn't happened. Also, there was the horror of having seen Mr. Nettles on my mother's bed. Flavia knew most of Cookie's flaws, but she'd also seen fun Cookie, who would turn up the radio and dance while singing at the top of her lungs. If Flavia knew that my mother spent time alone with Mr. Nettles, it might be something that would make her never want to step into our trailer again. It certainly made me not want to step into our trailer.

"I have to pee," I said.

"Nettles's car had a different shaped roof," Flavia said. "And it didn't have that tiny window in the back." She looked away from the car to me, legs crossed, bouncing. "I have to pee, too!" And off she went.

I ran just behind Flavia as we raced toward our trailers. Flavia peeled off and ran into her home before I reached mine.

I slowed at the car parked in front of our trailer. The engine was running, and a man in black sunglasses sat in the driver's seat. My body tensed even though he definitely wasn't Mr. Nettles, and he made no indication that he was going to get out of the car.

I walked in the front door. Two men in black sunglasses stood with Cookie. My heart thumped once, a warning. I turned and started to leave when one of the men grabbed me from behind, picking me off my feet. Cookie screamed, and the other man lunged for her. As she struggled with him, my mother made the same grunting animal sounds and used the same curse words as when she beat me. I felt oddly calm as I fought against the man who tried to contain me—maybe because of the sounds Cookie was making, the experience felt familiar.

Only a few seconds had passed when I bucked so hard that the man who held me tripped backward and let me go flying away from him. "RUN!" my mother screamed, and I did. Past Cookie who was now rolling on the ground with the other man, straight out the back door onto the cement backyard, and then around the periphery of the Paradise Homes Trailer Park. My lungs scraped and burned and I could barely get air when I circled back into the trailer park straight to Flavia's house, where I banged on the door, screaming. Mrs. Feliciano yanked me inside and bolted the door behind me.

"A man grabbed me!" I yelled. Mrs. Feliciano hollered a stream of words in Spanish as she ran to the windows and pulled the flounce-trimmed curtains shut. Flavia came out of her bedroom and rushed to the front window with me, where we pushed the curtain aside and looked out. The black car was parked in front of Flavia's now. The passenger-side window came down, and the man who had grabbed me lifted his sunglasses and stared at me.

"Who is that?" Flavia asked.

"I don't know." I ducked below the window and yanked Flavia down by the hem of her shirt. It was only then that I started shaking, and my heart raced as if I were still running.

Mrs. Feliciano pulled the curtains shut further. "Do not tempt Mr. Nettles!" she said.

"That wasn't Mr. Nettles," Flavia said.

There was pounding at Flavia's door. My mother was yelling from the other side. Mrs. Feliciano opened the door, pulled my mother in by the hand, then shut and bolted the door behind her. Cookie had tears streaming down her face. I'd seen her cry before, but never when sober. I felt a pang of pain for her, hugged her, and then ran to the bathroom to finally pee.

When I came out of the bathroom, Cookie, Flavia, and Mrs. Feliciano were at the table with a plate of orange-colored wafer cookies between them. My mother was the only one eating.

"But why does Rosanne's father's family want to kidnap Rosanne?" Mrs. Feliciano asked. I had missed whatever my mother had already said. This was the first I'd heard that it was my family.

"Wait." I sat at the table. "Were those my uncles?"

"Well, sort of your uncles." My mother picked up another wafer and bit it in half.

"Rosanne has never met these uncles?" Mrs. Feliciano asked.

"Well, they're not uncles, or family, really, in the blood sense," Cookie said. "They're family in the . . . well, in the Mafia sense."

"Ei!" Mrs. Feliciano threw up her hands and started

speaking in rapid-fire Spanish. "Rosanne's family is the Mafia?!"

"Her dad was in the Mafia."

"What's the Mafia?" I asked.

Cookie lit a cigarette and turned her head to blow the smoke away from Mrs. Feliciano. "The Mothers and Fathers Italian Association."

Mrs. Feliciano shook her head and mumbled in Spanish. Then she picked up my hand, squeezed it, and said, "Rosanne, you do not need that family! Stay away from everyone who says they are your family!"

I trusted Mrs. Feliciano and knew I should believe her. But my sisters were family, and I definitely needed them.

"I wished they'd kidnapped me," Norm said later that night. We were lined up on the brown couch, my mother in the middle, watching *The Facts of Life*.

Cookie looked at Norm, then lifted the bottle of vodka she'd bought after we'd left the Felicianos' and took a slug. "You wan' some?" she held the bottle toward me. This was an act of tenderness from my mother. She felt bad about what had happened.

"No," I said.

"If they'd kidnapped me," Norm said, "I'd be hanging out on the shores of Lake Havasu right now, kicking back—"

"How did they know where we live?" I asked.

"I gave them the damn address," Cookie said. "They said on the phone that they'd take us all down there, but then when they showed up here, that mother-fucking smarmy asshole said he was only taking Rosanne."

"You shoulda let them take you!" Norm sat up and looked at me on the other side of Cookie. "I mean, you'd be living in Arizona, you'd have tons of money. How cool would that be?"

"I'm not so sure they were takin' her to Arizona," Cookie said.

Norm and I both looked at our mother.

"Well, where were they taking her?" Norm asked.

"I think they came to kill Rosanne." Cookie took another slug of vodka.

"Why would they kill me?" I didn't feel anything when I heard this news. It didn't seem any more real than Blair's problems on *The Facts of Life.*

"I guess 'cause I'd been ragging on them about that land. They know it's yours and instead of giving it to you, they were gonna, maybe, eliminate you." Cookie lit a cigarette.

"Wait," Norm said. "Does this mean we're never, ever gonna get Rosie's land in Lake Havasu?" Cookie and I, in a moment of synchronized delirium, broke out laughing.

"Fuck, no!" my mother finally said. She laughed straight through the commercial and when the show came back on, she shut her eyes, passed out, and started snoring.

11
Pathway to Perilous Peak

A week after the Mafia had showed up, Norm intercepted me on the way home from church. I'd never told him that's where I went every Sunday, but I had a feeling he had guessed.

"Come home now," he said. "We're moving."

I started running and Norm ran faster, beating me to the trailer. Cookie was on the couch, the TV on, nursing a beer. There were three empty cans on the coffee table.

"We're moving?" I was panting from the run. I bent over my knees to catch my breath.

"Yup. Pack up." My mother didn't turn away from the TV.

"When are we moving?" I asked.

"I dunno, maybe tonight, maybe tomorrow." Cookie burped and then took a sip of beer.

"Can't we just finish the school year?" As far as I could remember, I had never started and finished an academic year in the same school.

"Nope." She was still watching TV even though a Gillette commercial was on.

"Why not?"

My mother whipped her head to me. "There are people who want to kill you. And they know where you live. What kind of mother would I be if I didn't move you out of harm's way?"

My hand automatically went to the spot on the top of my spine where two nights earlier Cookie had dug her spike heel into me as if she were trying to extinguish a burning cigarette.

"Are the Mafia coming back for me?" I'd barely thought about that afternoon since it happened.

"Well, yeah, probably!" Cookie pulled a pack of Virginia Slims from her cleavage. She popped one out and lit it.

"Where are we going?" Norm asked. Cookie didn't answer. She smoked as if nothing had been said.

"Where are we going?" I asked.

"*Where are we going? Where are we going?*" Cookie

laughed. "You'll see when we get there. I put a garbage bag in each of your rooms. Go pack up. And then, Rosanne, you pack my stuff."

I went into my room, shut the door, and let the tears come down. My chest heaved as I tried to tamp it down, make it silent. The more we moved, the harder it would be for my sisters to find us. Gi had been friends with Tina and knew Jackie and Sam. Through them, there was a trail leading to us. If we left Caldwell, the trail might dry up.

"ROSANNE!" Cookie hollered from the couch.

It took me a second to find my voice, to find air enough in my lungs to respond. "Yeah?"

"IF YOU BREAK ONE THING FROM MY ROOM WHEN YOU'RE PACKING ME, I'll KICK YOUR FUCKING ASS FROM HERE TO NEW YORK!"

Flavia helped me pack Cookie's things. She and I both cried while we shoved my mother's stuff into numerous trash bags. Since Mack had driven off with all our belongings, Cookie had refilled her life with abundant junk. I hadn't thought much about these objects when they were stored in trash bags under the couch at Jackie and Kenny's. And I didn't really think about them when they sat on Cookie's dresser or along the walls of her bedroom in the trailer park. But when I had to pack it all, carefully so that nothing would break, I wondered what the point of this stuff was; why she had so many useless things when I was in need so many useful things. My breasts were now noticeably poking out of my T-shirts; I desperately needed a training bra. I also needed underwear to replace the three pairs I had as each one of them was ripped along the seams. And I wanted pants that didn't end above my ankle bones, inspiring the kids at school to say I was wearing *floods*.

On the other hand, my mother had a set of twelve copper bells in descending sizes, three plastic Hummel clocks painted with cherub-cheeked girls milking cows and boys with cowlicks and lederhosen, and a giant fan made of peacock feathers.

I told Flavia how my sisters used to argue about who was going to pack my mother's "lady things." They never wanted to go anywhere near her large, stained underwear, or her ripped grayish bras they called over-the-shoulder boulder holders. To protect ourselves from these items, Flavia and I put socks on our hands. The sock-gloves proved useful when we found a *High Society* magazine and a thick rubber wand that neither of us could identify as anything in particular but which we both sensed was something we shouldn't see. With my head pulled away from it, I dropped the wand into the bag. Then I looked up at Flavia, who also had her head pulled back. We burst out laughing and laughed until we started crying again.

Fortunately, we didn't move that night. The next morning Cookie, with a rolled wad of cash the size of a man's fist, headed into town to buy a car from a man who would also sell her a set of unregistered plates. Norm tagged along: he wanted Cookie to buy California plates. I went to school.

When I told my homeroom teacher, Mrs. Roahr, we were moving, she said, "Oh, Brooks, we're going to miss your big smile!" And then she clapped her hands together and changed the morning schedule. Instead of continuing our lesson on decimals and fractions, each student in the class was instructed to write what they liked about me on an index card. I sat at my desk and nervously read my book while they did this. Some kids wrote quickly and then took their index card up to Mrs. Roahr, who hole-punched the corner and then placed it on a silver ring. Some kids appeared to be laboring over what to say. I felt twinges of anxiety as I watched Charles Skillens chewing on his pencil, which he rotated like a piece of corn on the cob as he stared at the blank card.

When everyone had finished, Mrs. Roahr put the

ring of cards in a shoebox and handed it to me with the instructions that I should read the cards whenever I missed my friends in Caldwell. I missed them right then, even though they were in the room with me.

Through each part of that day, I narrated what was happening in my head: *That's the last time I'll say the Pledge of Allegiance in this room; that's the last time Flavia and I will play double Dutch on the playground; that's the last time I'll turn in my vocabulary words, alphabetized and with the two bonus words defined as well.*

When the other kids had gone home, I went to the office to get photocopies of my records to give to the next school. Then I went to the library and found the book David Collins had been reading the last time we'd worked together. On a piece of scrap paper I wrote, *Good-bye from Brooks.* I crossed it out, turned the paper over and tried again: *Good-bye forever. From Brooks* I stared at that a minute. It sounded like something terrible was about to happen to me. I balled up the piece of paper, found a new piece of paper and started once more: *Bye David. From your friend forever, Rosie.* I secretly kissed the paper and tucked it into the book.

Mrs. Connors's eyes looked watery when I said that

I was leaving. She couldn't understand why my mother wouldn't tell us where we were going. I told her I didn't understand either. Cookie claimed the secrecy was so that the Mafia would be unable to find us. And maybe that was true, but I also sensed that our secret destination had something to do with not letting the parents of Paradise Homes find us either. It was like Cookie had been under unofficial surveillance that had forced her to temper herself, if only just a little. Whenever I ran out of the trailer, my mother never followed. She knew I was fully protected outside those flimsy walls.

"Well, Brooks," Mrs. Connors said, "You might not know where you're going, but wherever you go, *you'll* be there and that will make it a wonderful place."

My throat felt weighty and stiff. I took a couple of steps closer to Mrs. Connors and then dove in for a hug. It felt so good when she wrapped her arms around me and rocked me a little from side to side. Without my sisters holding me, grooming me, reading to me, and tucking me into bed, I was desperate for affection. Desperate for kindness. "I'll miss working here," I squeaked.

"I'll miss you," Mrs. Connors said. She held each of my shoulders and smiled at me. "Wait, I'm going to give you a present." Mrs. Connors went behind her desk and opened a box of books. She pulled out a brand-new copy of *The Secret Garden*, placed it on her desk, and wrote something on the inside cover page with a pen. I'd never seen anyone write on a book before, and I laughed. Mrs. Connors held out the book over her desk.

"Is this for me?" I asked.

"It sure is," she said. "I was going to give it to you at summer break so you'd have something to read when school was closed."

I took the book and smiled in a quivering closed-mouth way. Mrs. Connors hugged me again, and I couldn't help but cry a little. Before she could say anything else, I ran out.

On the way home, I stopped at Jackie and Kenny's house. No one was there, so I went into the backyard, said hello to the chickens, then slipped out behind the fence and waited for the train.

First I opened the shoebox with the ringed index cards and read them all. Skittles had written in pencil marks that looked like scattered pick-up sticks: *You are the prettiest girl in the world.* The rest were equally kind. I was called out for my jump-roping skills, my smile, my big laugh, how fast I could run, and my ability to spell long words. The notes meant more to me than was, perhaps, intended by the writers. After reading through the cards three times, I had almost memorized them. They were words I wanted to hold deep inside me, far beyond my mother's reach.

Next, I opened *The Secret Garden* to see what Mrs. Connors had written. It was a long note, with big words and big hopes for my future. And then she quoted what she said was her favorite line from the book: *She made herself stronger by fighting with the wind.*

I was thinking about this line and what it meant when the whistle sounded as the train approached. I closed the book and stood so I could feel the wind on my face. This wasn't a wind I was fighting, but for those few minutes when the train powered by and I thought of everything my class and Mrs. Connors had written, I did feel strong.

When I got home Cookie and Norm were loading the Hefty bags into the new car. It was low and wide, four doors, the color of an old faded lemon. There was an AM/FM radio and a built-in cassette player that was only a year old, Cookie told us.

"It's a Chrysler," Norm said, and he rubbed a spot of dirt off the door. It was clean now, but that would last about as long as Cookie's sobriety.

"Get some fucking bags," Cookie said.

I ran into the house and grabbed the Hefty bag from

my room. I didn't want to think about our departure. I didn't want to feel anything, and so I moved fast, robotically, as I put my belongings in the trunk and then went into the house for more bags.

"I need to say good-bye to Flavia," I said. The car was loaded and the trailer home door was left wide open, as directed by Cookie, so that *any motherfucker who wanted could go in there and mess up the place back to the way it was when we found it.* Norm and Cookie were already in the car. Norm was hanging out his open window, looking up and down the street as if to find someone to say good-bye to.

"I'm gonna miss Paradise Beach," Norm said. The pack mentality of the trailer park kids created constant playmates for me and my brother. It was the most social place we'd ever lived.

"Get in the fucking car!" Cookie said, and she honked the horn once as a warning.

I got into the backseat and rolled down my window. "Honk again at Flavia's, okay?" I asked.

Cookie slowed in front the Feliciano trailer. I felt like we were the Mafia now. My mother laid her left palm on the center steering-wheel horn and honked three times. Flavia came to the front window, the ruffle-edged curtains framing her. She waved both her arms and yelled good-bye over and over again.

I stuck half my body out the open window and screamed, "BYE, FLAVIA, I'LL MISS YOU!" I wanted to shout it again, but my voice was gone—closed up from sadness.

Cookie zoomed off so quickly I jerked back and hit my head against the top of the window frame.

"FUCK YOU, PUSSY PARADISE HOMES!" my mother shouted, her middle finger waving out the open window. "We were here, but not to stay, we didn't like it anyway!"

Neither Norm nor I joined in with her chant. My brother continued to hang out the window. I slid down low into the backseat and watched the trees blur by my window like a smeary watercolor painting. I knew Norm was thinking the same thing as I was. Here we go again. A new place where we'd have to make new friends. We had to figure out how they dress and try to dress like them as best we could with our overused clothes. We had to figure out how they talk and try to talk like them so we wouldn't stand out as the outsider weirdos. We had to figure out who we could bring home when our mother was drunk, swearwords buzzing out of her mouth like flies, and who should never come near our house or meet our mother on the street even. There was going to be a new school bus. New teachers. A new librarian. A new bedroom, assuming we got one. And a new bed, assuming we weren't on a couch or a floor.

A few minutes later we pulled into a trucker motel along the highway.

"This where we're gonna live?" I asked.

"*This where we're gonna live?*" Cookie imitated me. "Fuck no. We've got more class that that."

Starting when, I wondered.

Cookie cut the engine, leaned back in her seat, and said, "You know this car is a '72, just like you, Rosanne." She pulled a Virginia Slims pack from her cleavage, tapped out a cigarette, and then threw the pack onto Norm's lap.

"Is it October sixth, 1972?" I asked. For all I knew, cars had birthdays, too.

"It's just a fucking '72," my mother said. "But that will bring us good luck. It's good luck to have a car from one of your kids' birth years."

"Why didn't we get a car from my birth year?" Norm asked.

"'Cause all the ones from your birth year were too old and broken. And this thing is big enough that the three of us can comfortably sleep here if that's what it comes down to."

Norm turned in his seat, looked over at me, and whispered, *But we're too classy to stay in the motel?* Cookie ignored him.

My brother turned back and the two of us sat quietly, patiently waiting for something to happen while Cookie smoked her cigarette. It wasn't long before Hal Pinkerton approached Cookie at her window. He had a six-pack of Miller dangling from one hand. Norm and I had barely seen Hal even though he'd been Cookie's boyfriend since we'd lived at Jackie and Kenny's. He was a trucker who liked to stop in Caldwell to drink for the night because, as he told me the first time I met him, "It has a pulse." Whenever he was in town, Cookie drank with him and then stayed in his motel room. This was always a huge relief to me, a periodic night off from dealing with my mother.

Cookie put her hand out and Hal popped off a beer and gave it to her.

"Hey, kids!" Hal had a nice smile and shiny silver hair that swooped up into a pompadour. His belly was big and hung out over his low-hanging jeans.

"Hi." I scooted up and leaned over the front seat. I liked Hal. His friendly way of talking reminded me of Ricky, the tow-truck driver.

"Let's blow this shithole," Cookie said.

"We're gonna convoy," Hal said.

"Where are we going?" Norm asked.

"We're going wherever we go." Cookie pulled the tab off the beer and sipped from the frothing foam.

"We're going to my house." Hal took a sip of beer. "Didn't your mother tell you you're moving in with me?"

"These two are on a need-to-know basis." Cookie took a slug of beer, her cigarette clamped between her first two fingers.

"We're gonna live with you?" I asked. I hoped that Cookie wouldn't accuse me of trying to steal him, like she had with Ricky. And I hoped that I'd have a bedroom with thick walls so I couldn't hear my mother and Hal in their room. The kinda things she did in a bedroom, my mother had once told me, kept men interested in her enough that they'd put up with me and Norm.

"He's my boyfriend, you idiots! Yes, we're gonna live with him!"

Hal laughed and pulled another beer off the plastic holder. He handed it to Cookie, and she stuck it between her legs. Then he slowly walked away, his stride so wide I could have run between his legs.

"Put on the Convoy tape!" Cookie said. We had a C. W. McCall cassette with the song "Convoy" on it. Norm and I loved saying the spoken lyrics—CB radio lingo with phrases like *Smokey Bear, Rubber Ducky,* and *Taco Town.*

Norm dug through the shoebox of cassette tapes Cookie had "borrowed" from the bar where she worked. He popped in "Convoy."

Hal pulled up beside us in a blue pickup. Cookie dropped her empty beer can out the window, onto the pavement. She opened the beer between her legs.

"Why's he in that?" Norm asked. "We need a big truck to really convoy." The song was playing. Norm turned it up.

"We just need to drive behind him for it to be a convoy, you idiot." Cookie took a slug of beer and then rolled out of the lot behind Hal.

It wasn't hard to follow Hal; unlike in New York, there were few cars on the road. We drove up Highway 84, listening to cassettes, Cookie singing along the whole way. I sat in the backseat and thought about everyone I missed: Cherie, Gi, Camille, Flavia, Mrs. Connors, David Collins, and Kenny, Jackie, Tina, and Sam.

After we passed the populated towns of Farmingville and Sheeps Meadow, the landscape turned to desolate mountains. There were shrubs and grasses, and lots of cattle grazing. The fields were dotted with red barns, silos, and white farmhouses with green shingled roofs.

I started to feel more and more lonely. And the lonelier I got, the more panicky I became.

"There are no people." My chest felt as if it were being clamped shut.

"Hell no!" Cookie said. "Just the way I like it. No nosy parkers trying to tell me what I can and cannot do with my kids."

"But is there a school?"

"Yeah, there's a fucking school. There just isn't a bunch of dumbass do-gooders passing judgment on me. No one's in your business here."

Norm looked over the seat at me. He must have sensed my anxiety, for he reached his arm back and I grabbed his hand. I held on as if my brother were keeping me from sinking into quicksand.

"But I like having people around." I was almost whispering. *People around* was the thing that kept me safe. The Paradise Homes mothers, and Kenny and Jackie before them, were the buffer between me and Cookie. And until I was taken away from my sisters, Cherie, Camille, and Gi encircled me in so many layers it was rare that Cookie could get her hands on me. Who would watch out for me in Nowhere, Idaho, with no *nosy parkers* looking into my mother's business? Surely not the trees. Not the massive mountains looming ahead. Not the fields that spread out like shimmering green blankets thrown across the ground. Nature was indifferent to suffering, that was certain.

I squeezed my brother's hand. I wanted to sew the two of us together so we'd be a bigger beast, a wilder animal to fight against our mother.

"You know, Hal said there are so few people out here, I could pop a squat in the front yard and no one would see!" Cookie laughed.

"Gross," I whispered so she wouldn't hear.

"Norm. Cigarette!" Cookie barked, and Norm released his hand from mine so he could find Cookie's cigarettes and light one for her.

I slid into the corner of the seat and searched for my sisters in my head. Cherie would tell me to hang tough. Camille would say that I was brave and strong and I could make it through anything. And Gi would say, *Mia bambina, je t'aime, je t'aime.*

Soon we were driving through one nearly empty town after another. Hal slowed his truck each time the buildings popped up on the sides of the road, and I'd wonder if this was where we were stopping, if this was our new home. One of the towns looked like it was from a cowboy movie: flat-fronted buildings, wooden porches, low pitched roofs. I expected there to be nothing behind them, like a Hollywood set, everything held up by wooden scaffolding.

"Looks like *Blazing Saddles*," Norm said. *Blazing Saddles* was my brother's favorite movie. He could talk for hours about the bean-eating and fart scene.

"I think it looks more like *Little House on the Prairie*." I loved the Laura Ingalls Wilder books. Laura's life seemed hard at times—living in the mud house or surviving the dust storms—but there was so much love in her family that all of it seemed tolerable. Fun even. When I had lived with my sisters, without my mother around, we were a riff-raff, parentless, Dumpster-diving version of the Ingalls family. We had the love.

"Looks like fucking hickville to me," Cookie said. We'd been in the car for an hour and a half and her two beers were long gone.

At the next town, Hal slowed, honked his horn and then pointed out the window to the green sign on the side of the road. It said: OAKVIEW, POPULATION 360.

Cookie honked her horn and shouted, "Lookout Oakview, 'cause Hurricane Cookie is here!"

"Is this our new town?"

"*Is this our new town?!*" Cookie imitated me. "What? You don't like country towns?"

"I liked Paradise Homes." With only 360 people,

how many girls my age could there be in Oakview? Would it be possible to find a friend like Flavia? Would the librarian be as nice as Mrs. Connors? Would there even be a librarian?

A block later we passed a wooden billboard stuck in the roadside grass. It said: WELCOME TO OAKVIEW, PATHWAY TO PERILOUS PEAK. Below the giant words was a painting of snow-capped mountains. And below that, on a white plastic billboard, with black letters placed in slats, it said RODEO BIBLE CAMP STARTING JUNE 21. FARMERS MARKET SAT.

"Perilous Peak?" Norm said. "This better not be a sign of how things are around here."

"It's just a fucking name," Cookie said.

"Can I go to Rodeo Bible Camp?" I asked. Would kids actually ride on bucking bulls while learning about Jesus? I wanted to go if only to answer that question.

"You think I have money for camp?" Cookie asked. When I didn't answer, she said, "Well? Do you?!"

"No," I said.

"Damn right, no," my mother said. "You're going to Camp Hal Pinkteron."

"Does Hal live on a farm?" Norm asked.

"Hal lives where Hal lives," Cookie said.

I stared out the window as we cruised through town. We passed the Prairie Motel and RV Park that had a pack of fat, low motorcycles parked in front. There was a gas station, a Senior Center that looked clean and tidy and had a bench by the front door, a small market, and, just past it, a grocery store. There was a lumber store, a feed store, and a brick hotel with peeling white paint. Hal pulled his truck up in front of a flat, formstone building with a sign that said RODEO EXPRESS. Cookie brought the Chrysler up beside him and rolled down her window so they could talk. I tried to look in the glass front door to see if there were any kids my age, but it was too dark inside to see anyone.

"Let's settle in quick and then come back here for a drink," Hal said. I could tell by the urgency in his voice that he was someone who liked to drink as much as Cookie did. As in many of her relationships, the common love of alcohol was a binding force.

"I'm drinkin', as long as you're payin'," Cookie said and laughed.

We turned down a rutted road, occasionally lined with low-hanging trees that dappled the light into bouncing white spots. As far as I could see in any direction were rolling fields framed by mountains. There wasn't a human in sight but plenty of cows, horses, pigs, and sheep. I counted five tractors left standing in fields as if the rider had simply disappeared. And there was more than one rusted-out horse trailer sitting near the road. Every now and then a driveway would show up with a leaning mailbox marking the turn. The houses looked lonely, patchworked; one had a front door hanging by a hinge at an angle, like a loose tooth. It was the opposite of New York, where buildings fill up all the space you can see, and dirt and grass are only freckled in among them.

Soon enough, we arrived at Hal's property. He had a red barn, a silo, and a few other outbuildings. I wondered if Hal had chickens, and if so, if he'd named them. The house was a one-story ranch, white clapboard with a red roof. In front of the house, near the post-and-wire fence, was a beautiful willow tree with boughs that hung like a thick head of hair all the way to the road.

"Look at that willow tree." I was turned in my seat staring at it. My sisters had told me about a house they had lived in before Norm and I were born. None of them could remember whose house it was or why they were there, but they called it the Happy House because they all remembered feeling loved and being fed there. There was a willow tree at the Happy House; the three of them picnicked under it, napped beside it, and swung on a swing hanging from one of its low-hanging boughs. I'd liked hearing stories about the Happy House—it was nice to imagine my sisters smiling, warm, swinging under a tree. I hoped that one day we'd all be together in another Happy House with another willow tree.

"Oh, little Miss Smarty Pants thinks she's an arborist."

"What's an arborist?" Norm asked.

"You know, I'd like to pop a squat right under little Miss Arborist's willow tree!" Cookie laughed.

I thought then that Hal must really be desperate for a drinking and bedroom partner if he'd put up with a woman who wanted to poop on his lawn.

Cookie looked out the window as Hal approached. He leaned his forearms on the window ledge.

"Welcome home," Hal said.

"Can I go to school here? Can I start tomorrow?"

"Little Miss Arborist doesn't want to miss school," Cookie said.

"We'll get you in school." Hal opened the door for Cookie, and then put out his hand and helped her out of the car. I looked at my mother through the frame of my rolled-down window and realized for the first time that she had thinned out since we'd left New York. Her belly—normally part of a barrel that started at her neck—had disappeared. She was all hips and breasts now, an hourglass on legs.

I got out of the car and stood next to Norm, who was staring at the house.

"Can I walk to the library from here?" I asked.

"Ignore the bookworm." Cookie did a shimmy against Hal. "I really could use a burger and a cold one."

"Can we go with you to get a hamburger?" Norm asked.

"You two unpack the car." Cookie pointed toward the house, then got in Hal's truck and slammed the door shut.

Norm approached Cookie's open window. "Can we get a hamburger after we unpack the car?"

"Just unpack the fucking car!" Cookie said. "You'll get what you get when we're back."

"Rosie," Hal said, "your bedroom is the first one you walk into straight from the front door. Norm, your room is right next to your sister's."

"So we just go in?" I asked. "Like, it's really our house, too?"

"No. I get the house, you get your fucking willow tree," Cookie laughed, Hal waved, and then they drove off.

Norm opened the trunk. Together we stared at the bulging green plastic bags. For people who had nothing in life, we sure had a lot to unpack. All but two of the trash bags belonged to Cookie.

"You pick it, you put it away," Norm said. He was

quoting my sisters, who had shouted those words every time we moved. The purpose of the game was to eliminate the fight over who had to unpack Cookie's things. With my sisters, once *you pick it, you put it away* had been shouted, we each grabbed random bags and put away, without complaint, whichever bag we first laid hands on.

"I packed Mom up." I wanted to weep. "We both have to unpack her." I grabbed the Hefty bag that I knew to be mine as I had tied a thick, short knot in the top, hoisted it out of the car and walked into the house.

It was a fine house. Not too messy, not too clean. There was the living room and an eat-in kitchen area. I liked that other than the bedrooms and the bathroom, there were no corners around which someone could hide. I'd always know where my mother was.

My bedroom didn't look out at the willow tree, but it did have a view of a field and the mountain beyond it. I opened my trash bag and pulled out the ring with the index cards. There were no nails on the wall for me to hang it, so I laid the cards on the water-stained wooden dresser. It looked too plain. I fanned the cards out as if they were something to be displayed. Next to the index cards, I lined up my notes from David Collins—he hadn't been in my homeroom and so hadn't written on a card. One by one, I picked up David's notes and reread them. Even when he just wrote *It's so hot in here today, I need a fan!* I smiled and swooned. With my school-sharpened pencil, I poked a neat hole in the corner of each note and then added them to the silver ring that held the index cards.

Next, I removed my clothes from the garbage bag and laid them out on the bed. I needed to envision the possible outfits I'd wear to my new school. I had three pairs of sweatpants, one pair of purple jeans (too short), one pair of blue jeans (too short), one pair of corduroys (holes in the knees and too short), five shirts (most stained), and the ratty underwear.

The Secret Garden was the last thing I pulled from the trash bag. I laid it on the dresser, facedown and open to the page I was on, right next to the index cards. I stared at the dresser, at what amounted to all my things, and wished I had a photo of my sisters. Or even one of the board games we'd played when we lived together. Like ghosts or saints, my sisters often seemed invisible. Believing in them felt like an act of faith.

The next day Cookie drove me to the elementary school so I could register for the fifth grade class. The curly-haired principal, Mr. Jackson, was a smiley, friendly man with the gentle voice of people on children's television shows. He said there were only three weeks left in the school year but he was glad to have me at Oakview Elementary. The fifth grade was made up of twenty-four kids—twenty-five now that I was there. The school was populated by kids from many different townships, Mr. Jackson explained. And we'd all be together through twelfth grade when we graduated. He seemed so enthusiastic about the idea of this pack making it to the end together that I didn't dare admit I'd never made it nine months with the same group of kids before moving on to another town.

When my mother left Mr. Jackson's office, I realized I didn't know where she was going to pick me up at the end of the day. I ran down the hall, caught her, and said, "Where do I wait for you after school?"

Cookie snorted. Then she leaned into my ear and whispered, "I'm not your fucking chauffeur."

"So how do I get home?"

"The bus, you idiot!"

"I didn't know they had busses out here." I'd barely seen any cars on the drive to school.

"There's a bus." Cookie pinched me hard, right where my rib cage turned into my back. It silenced me. She let go and walked away.

"Wait!" I shouted, and then I caught up to my mother again. "How will I know where to get off the bus?" I took a couple of steps back so she couldn't reach me for another pinch.

"Did you memorize the address?"

"No, what is it?"

My mother shrugged her shoulders. "I hope you don't end up at some cow pasture where you'll have to walk knee-deep in manure." Cookie laughed as she left the building.

My heart clanged in my chest. I imagined myself wandering endless dirt roads, every barn looking like the last one, no distinct landmark to point out Hal's house. What if I didn't make it home by nightfall and had to sleep in a field of cow manure? What if a stallion tried to trample me? I'd been terrified of horses and hadn't touched one since Long Island when the enormous stallion tried to mate with the mare whose back I was on. But there were even worse animals than rutting stallions out here. What if a bull that had broken free from the Rodeo Bible Camp attacked me?

Mr. Jackson met me in the hall and walked me to my classroom. Twenty-four heads turned and stared at me.

"Friends," Mr. Jackson said, "this is the first New Yorker to ever sit in a chair at Oakview Elementary." One boy said, "Whoa," as if I'd just arrived from Mars.

My teacher, Mrs. Muse, had a pretty round face and curly brown hair. As I lined up to go to lunch, she put her hands on my shoulders and asked me to stay behind. I wondered if I was in trouble for something I hadn't realized I'd done. My mother frequently got angry at me for things I hadn't realized I'd done, as well as for things she'd only imagined I'd done.

"Rosanne, are you okay?" she asked.

I shrugged my shoulders. I didn't want to answer until I knew what the right answer would be. Would I be in trouble if I weren't okay?

"You look worried," she said.

I'd been worried all morning long about getting on the bus and getting off the bus. As the new kid, I'd be stared at like someone on a stage as I did the first terrifying walk down the aisle. Then, once I'd made it on the bus, I had to magically figure out where to get off. I'd barely been able to hear anything except the anxious thoughts swirling in my head.

"I guess I'm kinda worried," I said, and I hesitated to see if this would make her angry. But it didn't seem to make her angry; her face was still soft, and her eyes were gentle.

"What are you worried about?" Mrs. Muse leaned her head down so that it was even with mine.

There was no point in sharing the new-kid-on-the-bus anxiety as there was nothing she could do about that. I simply said, "I don't know where I live and I don't know how to take the bus home." When the words left my mouth, I wanted to cry. But I didn't. I just pulled in my lips and stared at my white tennis shoes that had originally belonged to Tina.

"Oh, Rosanne." Mrs. Muse rubbed a quick little circle on my back. "I can understand why that would worry you. Just put it out of your mind for now and I'll figure it out before you have to get on the bus. Okay?"

"Okay," I said, but still felt too scared to look at her.

In the cafeteria, I sat alone in the corner where I could watch all the kids. They were noisy and restless like kids at every school I'd ever been at. The boys sat together, or barely sat, many of them standing. And the girls clustered in tight half circles at the ends of the long tables. Hal had given me an apple and a piece of fried chicken leftover from his dinner last night at Rodeo Express. I ate them slowly so I would have something to do the entire lunch break.

In spite of Mrs. Muse's offer to help, I continued to worry throughout the day. What if Mrs. Muse didn't know we were living with Hal? What if she didn't know where Hal lived? What if the bus didn't even stop near Hal's house? What if she sent me to the wrong house?

And what if the bus came and left while she was explaining it all to me?

At the end of the day, Mrs. Muse gave me a hand-drawn map that showed landmarks and named each road or farm where the bus stopped. At my stop, Mrs. Muse had put a big red X on the map.

"Rosanne," she said, "you're wound tighter than a wet bale of hay." She laughed and I looked at her, slightly panicked. Was there something wrong with me? I didn't understand what she was saying.

"Sorry," I said.

"You're fine!" She smiled, her eyes turning into tiny arcs.

Mrs. Muse stood near the door of the bus and watched as I got on. A barbed-wire terror ripped through my gut. I remembered Gi's instructions for the first walk on a new bus: *Hold your head high, don't appear needy or nervous, don't look anyone in the eye, and sit in the back so you don't have people staring at you from behind.*

I fully accomplished the head hold and the avoidance of eye contact. But the back of the bus was full, so I slipped into a window seat at an empty middle row. Mrs. Muse was still near the door. I waved at her and then opened the map and studied it. I wanted to memorize every stop leading up to mine so that I was sure to get off at the right place.

A short, freckle-faced girl slid into the empty seat beside me. She had fine, curly hair that looked like it would slip through your fingers like water. My mother, who loved to yank my hair, would have a hard time with this girl's orangey wisps.

"Hey," she said.

"Hey." I recognized her from my class. She had sat two desks away from me.

"Do you wanna do homework together?" she asked.

"Okay." I glanced at my map one last time, then took out my homework folder from my backpack.

"That's neat that you're from New York," she said.

"I guess," I said. "What's your name?"

"Paige Paisley," she said, and I started to laugh.

"Sorry," I said. "But my best friend at my last school was Flavia Feliciano and now the first person I meet here is Paige Paisley."

"The boys call me pee pee," she said.

"They're gross," I said, and Paige Paisley agreed.

We did our homework, and Paige Paisley talked. She told me that she lived on a farm with two hundred cattle. Her mother and older sister moved two hours away to Boise last year, so Paige lived with just her dad and her brother. She had lots of chores before and after school, so she always did her homework on the bus.

I was so happy to make a friend that I forgot about the anxiety I'd been having all day.

"You get off in three more stops," Paige said as she gathered her things. "There's a red barn and a silo you'll see right there." She stood, and the bus jolted to a stop. "I'll see you tomorrow!"

The yellow door squeaked open and Paige hurried off. Maybe Oakview wouldn't be as bad I'd thought.

12

Bookie or Cookie

As long as she was getting free housing, food, ciga-rettes, and alcohol, my mother could tolerate any-thing in a man. From what I'd seen so far, she preferred ruddy-faced, barrel-bellied alcoholics—guys who paid for her needs in return for the pleasure of her company. In this way, Hal and Cookie were a perfect match. Hal appeared to adore my mother. Whenever I sat with them at Daisy's Café or Rodeo Express, Hal seemed proud of Cookie in her spandex clothes with her thin hair fluffed into a black cloud around her head. He usu-ally had a hand on her somewhere: her back, her waist, her hip. And Cookie acted like she loved him equally. If he was sitting in a chair at home, she'd drop into his lap, stroke his chest, and touch him over the fly of his blue jeans so that I felt compelled to retreat to my room, or turn my head at least.

But when Hal asked my mother to pitch in for rent and food because he had lost most of his paycheck gambling, Cookie shut off the charm and turned as bitter and stormy as I'd ever seen her. From that day on, nothing Hal did was right. The two of them engaged in a one-sided, violent war where my mother let everything out. Once she even threw knives at Hal, who hollered plenty but never—no matter how explosive my mother got—physically fought back.

If it was daylight when their fights started, and I could make a clean escape, I did. Through my bedroom window, out the bathroom window, out any hole my body could slip through. I'd run the twenty minutes to Paige Paisley's house. I knew the way so well, I could easily have done it in the tented black of an unlit sky. But like most people in town, Paige's family went to bed early and woke early. The only souls that stirred after eight or nine were the drinkers, smokers, and gamblers, like my mother and Hal.

If Norm and I were together, we fled the blowouts by hiding in the red barn at the back of the property. I never went there alone, however. The lingering smell of horses and the abandoned rust-edged farm tools, which looked like dinosaur bones in the dark, made it far too scary. Instead, I risked being found by my angry mother—who would beat anything in her path—and took refuge in the front yard, under the willow tree. While I was there, I liked to think of my sisters in the Happy House. In my fantasy, we were all there together, our current ages, picnicking on a giant, fuzzy blanket spread under the willow tree. We'd have books scattered around us and so much food that only half of it could be eaten. Together, we'd laugh and laugh until we fell asleep with the long, leafy branches rustling like tambourines above our heads.

In the high heat of summer one night early in Cookie and Hal's season of fighting, the two of them and I sat down for dinner. Norm was out playing video games with his friend Colton. We were eating chicken from the farm down the road, fried potatoes from another farm, and applesauce from a jar. The meal had just started and my mother, who had been singing Johnny Mathis songs while she cooked, was now angry at Hal, who had just told her he couldn't go to Rodeo Express with her tonight because he had to be at a poker game. My mother quickly tapped her foot under the table. I took several quick bites of chicken breast and then stared at my plate and hoped that Cookie's anger wouldn't be turned toward me.

"Can I be excused?" I wanted to run to Paige's before the battle erupted, before it got dark.

"Yes," Hal said. He stabbed his fork into my half-eaten piece of chicken and put it on his own plate.

"No, you *cannot* be excused." Cookie stood, picked up the chicken on Hal's plate and dropped it back onto my plate. "Eat." She licked the chicken juice off her fingers before sitting down again.

I cut into the breast and ate several more bites. Hal refocused on his own plate.

"You really outdid yourself with this." Hal pointed at the chicken. He was trying to soften Cookie, but he should have known by then there was no softening her. She was as tough as gristle.

"Glad you like it because it's the last good meal you'll get until you quit gambling." If Hal had been a thief, a cheat, a liar, a pervert, a tax evader, a welfare defrauder, or even a fake churchgoer stealing money from the collection plate, Cookie would have been content with him. But a gambler? His money was her money and she wanted him to have nothing to do with any enterprise that took that money away.

"Ah, c'mon, Cookie. We got enough here. We got each other—" Hal reached an arm across the table to stroke Cookie's cheek. She scooted the chair back quickly as if he'd electrocuted her.

I stood and picked up my plate to clear it.

"You are NOT excused!" Cookie leapt from her seat, took my plate, and flung it against the kitchen wall where it fell, along with the food, to the floor. Oily streaks painted the wall like an amber waterfall. Above and below these streaks were other spotted marks where Cookie had thrown food on previous nights.

I sat again and tried to shrink inside myself. If my mother didn't notice I was there, she might not hurt me.

"Honey, that was a good piece of chicken." Hal sounded more sad then angry.

"You don't fucking deserve it!" Cookie picked up Hal's plate and threw it against the same wall.

Hal took a deep breath, then scooted his chair out. Slowly, as if he were exhausted, he went to the cupboard, took out the puffed rice cereal, and emptied half the box into a mixing bowl. Just as he was pouring in the milk, Cookie leapt on top of him, knocking the milk carton and the bowl to the ground.

Hal dropped to the floor in a puddle of milk. He curled into an armadillo shape, his arms over his head, as Cookie punched and kicked and hollered about how he'd failed her, he was a disappointment, he had ruined a great thing by gambling away the rent money.

Often these fights ended when Cookie grew bored

of being the only one doing battle. That night, Cookie stopped punching and kicking, went to the table, and Frisbee-tossed toward Hal the remaining plate and the platter with the chicken. He scrambled away and stood in time to duck again as Cookie overhand dart–threw each piece of silverware toward him.

I had slipped off my chair and was trying to leave the room unnoticed when Cookie said, "Rosanne! Clean this shit up!"

"Ah, come on, she doesn't have to clean our mess," Hal said.

Cookie's response was to pick up the overflowing glass ashtray from the table and hurl that at Hal. "THE FUCK SHE DOESN'T!"

I hurried to the kitchen area and started cleaning the floor. Hal moved in on Cookie and tried to wrap his big body around hers as she punched and screamed. Eventually she broke free and a start-and-stop chase ensued with Hal periodically trying to contain my mother, who was, it appeared, uncontainable. They rolled around on the carpet, knocking over the coffee table and two chairs. When I was done with the kitchen floor, I plugged the sink, poured in the green dish soap, and started what I thought of as a bubble bath for the dishes. My hope was that I could clean everything while Cookie was still engaged in the battle. Then maybe, just maybe, I could escape the scene without having to interact with my mother again.

Cookie and Hal's yelling and commotion soon turned into a background noise that I was able to filter away as I narrated in my head what I was doing: *Now wipe up the wall. No, wipe it better. Mom will be mad when she sees that brown spot. Turn the water off. Scrub the plates first. They take up less room on the drying rack.*

And then there was silence. I whipped around in time to see Hal rushing out the front door. My mother stared at me, tapping her foot

"I'm cleaning up." I plunged my hands into the hot sudsy water and continued scrubbing the plates. My back tensed and I could feel my mother walking toward me. She paused at the table and lit a cigarette.

"You know I was young once." Cookie's voice came out like a sparking silver cable. "And pretty, too."

"You're still pretty, Mom." I washed faster, barely rinsing the suds from each plate.

"And you fucking kids took all that away from me." She came closer. I heard the pop of her lips as she took a hit off the cigarette.

"Sorry," I whispered.

"You took my body, you take all my money—Hal and I wouldn't even have these problems if I didn't have to support your waste of skin—" Cookie grabbed my hair at the nape of my neck and yanked me back so I was leaned in against her body, which smelled steamy and rank. I had a sponge in one hand and a glass in the other. I reached the hand with the glass out as far as I could toward the sink so I could let it drop safely into the water. Cookie flicked her lit cigarette into the sink and then thrust me, by my hair, straight to the floor. My face banged into the linoleum. The grit and grease from the food that had landed there earlier rubbed into my cheek. My mother knelt beside me, my head pinned down by her grip. She pulled back her fist and punched me over and over in the gut, the chest, the ribs.

I had come to think of my mother's anger as having a distinct length and width—a physical entity that had to be fully dispensed. If she didn't get rid of it all with Hal, the leftovers came to me. When I was able to escape, her anger was either burned out by the time I returned, or she and Hal were engaged in a truce, which inevitably ended in the bedroom. But without anyone else nearby to sop up what was left of Cookie's emotion, I was the sole receptacle and the single source of all her miseries. And that night, her miseries seemed to be greater, larger, more sweeping than ever.

As Cookie carried on, I felt my mind swoop out of my body so that I was in two places at once: on the ground, my flesh swelling and throbbing in places I'd never felt before; and in the air, quietly floating above it all. The pain was so enormous that I couldn't allow myself to be present for it. I didn't land back inside myself until Norm came home and yanked my mother off me, wrestling her to the ground.

The trip from the kitchen to my room felt nearly impossible. I lay in bed in a delirious half-consciousness. My body pulsated as one giant, painful heartbeat.

I was moving slowly the next morning and winced when I sat at the kitchen table. Norm and Hal were there, each eating a bowl of puffed rice.

"Where's Mom?" I asked.

"Thrift stores," Hal said. Cookie had opened a checking account at the local bank and, as I'd heard in her arguments with Hal, was writing bad checks from it everywhere she went.

"She said she was getting groceries, too," Norm said.

"You okay?" Hal asked me.

"Yeah." It felt like there was a single open wound from my collarbone to my belly button. It hurt each time I took a breath.

Norm made a grunting noise to indicate I was lying.

Hal looked at Norm; Norm picked up his bowl and drank the grainy gray milk.

Hal said, "Why are you sitting so stiff like that? Are you hurt?"

Norm got up and cleared his bowl. Hal stared at me until I looked up at him. "Mom got mad at me after you left."

"Did she hit you?"

"If you're not around to take it," Norm said, "she goes after Rosie."

Hal's eyes were like giant, wet marbles. He looked back and forth from Norm at the fridge, now drinking milk straight from the carton, to me stiff in my seat at the table.

"Jesus Christ," Hal said. "You two pulled a bad straw in the mother draw."

"She's not so bad when you manage her right," Norm said.

"She's great when she's happy," Hal said. "But I don't know if I can keep her happy and I sure as shit don't like that she's takin' out our problems on Rosie."

"I'm okay," I said, shrugging. If Cookie thought I was complaining about her to Hal, yesterday's beating would only be a warm-up. Though her moods and responses were as irregular as a bouncing crazy ball, there was one way in which my mother was entirely consistent: we were never to utter a bad word about her to anyone. It was the ultimate betrayal. It was what my sister Gi did after she went to her new foster home and told her social worker and the courts everything she could about our mother. Since then, Cookie said to anyone who would listen that Gi was a terrible person who should have been aborted.

"Well, if that's what happens after our fights, I'm just not leaving, you hear?" Hal said.

I reached for the box of cereal on the table and bashfully said, "Thanks."

"Norm, bring your sister some milk," Hal said. "We got to give this girl a little rest today."

My head dropped and I smiled into my lap. I was in pain, but it hurt much less simply knowing that Hal was looking out for me.

As promised, Hal never left the house again when he and Cookie fought. I didn't know how or when or where to thank Hal for this. But every now and then, if I were standing real close to him, I would tilt my head so that it landed lightly on his arm. It felt so good to feel him there, holding me up in a sense, someone who would never hurt me. Invariably, Hal would gently stroke my hair. And once he kissed the top of my head. Just the way my sisters used to.

Like the Feliciano trailer in Caldwell, the Paisley house in Oakview was my retreat. There were no tamales, and we couldn't spend the day jumping rope because Paige had farm chores. But even farm chores could be fun when Paige and I did them together with her goat, Shadow, and her furry black and brown dog, Pup. Shadow and Pup were best friends who wandered the farm together and followed Paige wherever she went. I'd never lived among pets before, and I immediately loved these two—they were a couple of clowns, two four-legged goofballs who were happy just hanging around us. They'd run after Paige's bike with me sitting on the seat and holding onto her waist while she stood and pumped the pedals. And they'd stand outside the barn when we mucked the stalls. Paige talked to them as if they were human, as if they could understand every word we said. She even whispered to me so they couldn't hear when she said something that we wanted kept secret, like who we thought was the cutest boy at school.

The first time I tried to bring Pup into the house with us, Paige looked at me like I was luring a bull inside.

"He can't go in," she said.

"But he's one of us," I said.

"He's gotta keep the wolves away from the sheep." Paige showed her sheep at 4-H.

"But what if it gets cold out? What about when it snows?" I had dropped to my knees and was nuzzling Pup face-to-face.

"His coat gets thick in the winter, and at night he curls up with the sheep."

I buried my face in Pup's neck. "I love you," I said to Pup. Shadow butted his head into my belly.

"You have to treat them equally." Paige scratched Shadow behind the ears while I continued to dote on Pup.

I looked back once before we went into the house. The goat and the dog were side by side watching us. They were an alternate version of Paige and me.

In order to cover his gambling debts, Hal took more trucking jobs and was away for days at a time. While he was gone, Cookie spent more time out of the house, entire days sometimes on a barstool at Rodeo Express. Norm was frequently gone, too. He and Colton freely roamed Oakview from end to end.

One afternoon when I was home alone, there was knocking at the door. The front window was so dusty that the sun beating down on it made it impossible to see out. Still, I could see that there was a man out there: tall, broad shoulders, standing with acutely bowed legs.

"Hello?" I shouted through the closed door.

"Sweetheart," he said. "Is your mother home?"

"No," I said.

"Do you know where she is?"

"Probably Rodeo Express." It was Cookie's favorite bar.

"Is she eating or drinking?" he asked.

I didn't answer. I knew Cookie was drinking. She was always drinking, but I wasn't sure if I should tell that to the shadowy stranger.

"Sweetheart?" the man said. "Tell your mother that Clyde stopped by. And I'm leaving a present for you right here on the porch."

"Okay," I said.

I waited until I heard the rumble of a truck engine, and then I opened the front door. There on the ground was a glass jar, almost the size of a coffee can, filled with milk. I took the jar into the kitchen and stuck it in the refrigerator. I wasn't going to drink it. My sister Gi had frequently warned me that most gifts come with a price. She always said to be wary of anyone who offered me anything for free.

When Cookie got home that night, I showed her the milk.

"Well, how'd'ya like that?" Cookie smiled. She opened the jar and took a few slugs. "Did you ever think that anyone would give you milk for a gift?"

"No." Though I wasn't surprised. Everything in Oakview seemed different than it had in New York. Things were even different than they'd been in Caldwell. I had the uneasy feeling that the rules weren't the same here and that every person in town, all 360 of them, knew those rules but me.

Sometimes when Hal was home, he and Cookie took Norm and me to Rodeo Express with them. Hal would let us order burgers and fries while they ordered burgers, fries, and beer or vodka tonics. After we finished our meal, Cookie and Hal continued drinking. Rather than sit in a booth and wait for them, Norm and I liked to sit on the curb in front of Rodeo Express and watch the people in town come and go. There was a market next door that had Pac-Man, Tetris, and a pinball machine so a lot of the kids in town—always older than me, but sometimes Norm's age—hung out there. Unless Colton showed up, Norm stayed with me.

One night when we were standing outside Rodeo Express, a woman with softly curled hair, high-waisted jeans, and a black T-shirt came out of the market.

"You kids okay?" Her voice was soft-edged, kind. She reminded me of Mrs. Connors, the librarian in Caldwell.

"Yeah," Norm said.

"I'm Sheryl. You new in town?"

"Yeah." Norm stared out toward the street.

"What are your names?" Sheryl turned her head to try and catch Norm's eye.

"I'm Norm." My brother finally looked at her. "This is Rosie."

"Rosie talk?" Sheryl smiled at me.

"Yeah," I said.

"Where'd you move from?"

Norm explained that we'd gone from New York to Caldwell to be near Mom's friends, Jackie and Kenny. Then we'd moved here so our mother could live with Hal.

"So your mom moved you all the way from New York to be with her friend and then left her to move in with Hal?" This question made us both a little nervous. Norm kicked at a crack in the sidewalk with his sneaker.

"They're still friends," I lied.

There was silence for a moment and then Sheryl said, "You know the market is named after me"—the three of us looked up a the sign that said SHERYL'S

SHOP—"but everyone calls it The Bird Cage after the high school mascot, the Oakview Owls."

"That's cool," Norm said.

"Listen," she said, "I care about all the kids in this town—I want everyone to be safe and happy. So you tell your mama she can spend her food stamps here. And if you kids ever want food on credit, that's fine by me. I know you'll be good for it." Sheryl winked at me.

"Thanks," Norm said.

"Thanks," I said.

"Here's five bucks"—Sheryl handed Norm a half roll of quarters—"go inside and play some video games. It's a lot more fun than standing here watching the cars go by."

"Thanks." Norm shoved the roll into his pocket and waited for Sheryl to enter the store before we went in behind her. I couldn't help but think of Gi's words again, to be wary of anyone who gave us things for free.

The next time Clyde showed up, Cookie was home and Hal was on the road. I opened the door this time. Clyde was wearing a green John Deere baseball cap and fresh blue overalls, and he was holding a shiny clean pitchfork upright beside himself. I didn't understand the pitchfork; it seemed fantastical, like a warrior with a spear. Norm came to the door and stood next to me. His mouth hung open, and I could tell he was trying not to laugh.

"Your mother home?" Clyde smiled, revealing the whitest, most perfectly aligned teeth I had ever seen. His eyes were blue and caught the light as if they were made of crystals. He stared at me a couple of seconds too long, and my stomach revved the way it had that day in my mother's bedroom with Mr. Nettles.

"Just a second," Norm said. I followed my brother to the bedroom where Cookie was on her back, smoking a cigarette, watching television.

"Mom, it's the guy who brought that milk," I said. "He's at the door and he's holding a pitchfork!"

Cookie rolled off the bed. "Keep him busy, and tell him I'll be out in a second."

"You mean Mr. Haney from *Green Acres*?" Norm said, and we both laughed.

"Yes," Cookie pushed Norm on his shoulder. "Get the fuck outta here and keep him there while I freshen up."

I sat on my mother's bed and watched Cookie pull her breasts up in her bra so they met in the middle like two bald heads. She sprayed Jontue in her cleavage and on the back of her neck.

"Did you steal my new lipstick?" Cookie turned to me, suddenly furious. I jumped off the bed and sorted through the impossibly dense cluster of things on her dresser. There were many different lipsticks, compacts with powders and blush, dusty color-smeared trays of eye shadow, false eyelashes that looked like dead spiders half-glued to the dresser top. With Cookie, there was always excess—even when it came to something as small as lipstick. Finally, within the jumble of objects, I found the newest-looking lipstick.

"Here." I handed the lipstick to my mother and watched her smear her lips into a bloody red.

She pinched her cheeks. "How do I look?" she asked.

My mother had never asked this question before. My sisters had asked it of each other frequently—on school photo day or when one or the other of them was going out with friends. But Cookie always seemed pleased with herself, unavailable to the opinions of others. "Well?!" Cookie said.

"You look pretty," I said. If you took away the rage, the dangling cigarettes, the smell of booze and tobacco mixed with Jontue, the waxy makeup, and the in-your-face breasts, she was, indeed, a pretty woman.

I followed my mother to the living room where Clyde and Norm stood. Cookie's face softened and sweetened at the sight of this cleanly overalled man holding a pitchfork. She spoke in a voice I almost didn't recognize when she said, "It's so nice to see you again." I wondered when she'd seen him before, and where she'd seen him before.

Cookie whisked Clyde into the kitchen and they sat at the rickety wooden table. Norm and I hung out in the living room where we could easily hear them. Clyde told Cookie about his dairy farm, his eighty acres, his steer, horses, chickens, and his farmhand, Boone. Cookie oohed and aahed like he was talking about cute babies or kittens. At one point my mother said, *Well, there is nothing sexier than a bow-legged farmer*, and then she and Clyde both laughed.

"Say hello to our new dad," Norm groaned. Where I preferred Cookie to have a boyfriend, someone to suck up her attention so we'd be mostly left alone, Norm preferred to be the man of the house.

"This guy's really gross," I said.

"They're all gross," Norm said.

I didn't bother to disagree, though I did. Hal was a great guy who made sure Cookie didn't beat me. And Ricky, the tow-truck driver, had been kind, too. Of course I couldn't remember my dad, but from all the stories I'd heard about him, I'd decided that Vito had been best of all.

A couple of weeks later, Norm, Colton, and I were in Sheryl's Shop playing Pac-Man when I noticed Sheryl with a blonde woman whose body was swollen and soft, like a marshmallow in slacks and a blouse. They stood on the customer side of the counter and appeared to be talking about me because they looked in my direction every couple of seconds. I wondered if the woman was a social worker from New York who had caught up with us—something that would be either terrifying if it led to another foster home like the Callahans' or a relief if it led me back to my sisters. Her thick blonde hair appeared more done-up—frozen in a swooping wave—than that of most social workers I'd seen, so this made me wonder if she was from the Mafia, searching for me so she could "extinguish" me, as my mother had said. I realized that couldn't be the case as she seemed to know Sheryl well and, other than her swooping hair, she had that pretty, wholesome, milk-fed look of many of the locals.

Sheryl caught me watching them and waved me over.

"This is my friend Betsy," she said. "She wants to talk to you for a second." Sheryl winked at me and then went behind the counter where the cash register was. I stood next to the candy and packs of gum with Betsy.

"What's your last name?" Betsy smiled, but it looked painful, an unhappy smile.

"Brooks." I glanced back at Norm and Colton. They

were so engrossed in Pac-Man that Betsy could have been holding a machine gun to my head and neither one would have noticed.

"Is your mother Camille Brooks?" she asked.

"Yeah," I said. "Everyone calls her Cookie."

"Cookie?" That smile again. I felt my mouth mirror hers and was swept with a flush of sadness.

"Like the food."

"Do you know where your mom is now?" Betsy asked.

I looked at Sheryl behind the counter. I wasn't sure if I was supposed to answer this or not. Sheryl nodded her head at me, as if to tell me to trust Betsy. "Next door at the Rodeo Express," I said.

Betsy gave that pained smile again and put a handful of quarters in my hand. "Thanks, honey. You go play some games now, okay?"

"Okay." I looked toward Norm, who still hadn't turned away from his game, and then shoved the quarters in my pocket. I had a feeling Cookie shouldn't know I took money from this woman.

Betsy left, and I looked back to Sheryl.

"Don't worry," she said. "She's a nice lady. But listen—" Sheryl paused for me to answer.

"Yeah?"

"You and your brother can spend as much time as

you want here, okay? If you ever need a meal or anything like that, just come on over and Sheryl's got you
covered." She leaned over the counter, picked up a
Snickers bar, and handed it to me. "Share that with
your brother now."

I had a pocket full of quarters and a Snickers bar. If
Gi was right, and nothing was ever really free, how was
I going to end up paying for this?

Later, when the quarters were gone, the Snickers
was long ago eaten, and Colton and Norm were still on
Pac-Man, I went to the Rodeo Express to see if I could
convince Hal to take me home. Norm was sleeping at
Colton's that night.

Hal wasn't there. Neither was Cookie. I asked the
bartender about them.

"Went home at least an hour ago," he said and turned
back to the paper he was reading, *The Oakview News*.

I returned to Sheryl's Shop and tugged on Norm's
sleeve. "Mom and Hal went home without me," I said.

Norm continued to play. He used his foot to tap
Colton's calf. Colton was on the game machine beside
him. "Your mom give Rosie a ride home?"

Colton nodded and kept playing.

Norm and Colton talked Pac-Man the whole way
home. Colton's mom chatted with me, telling me about
who had been in her beauty salon that day. Everyone

wanted to look like Heather Locklear, she told me, but no one really had the hair for it.

"You can call me for a ride anytime," Colton's mom said as I got out of the car. Her eyes flickered, she looked anxious, and I wondered if she thought Norm and I were better off getting rides from her than from our drunk mother any night or day.

I waved to my brother as they drove away and then watched the car wind down the long dirt drive.

That night, the sky was like a black velvet cape hanging above my head. All the lights were out in the house, making it look shadowy and eerie. The red dot of a burning cigarette bobbed on the front porch.

"Mom?" I walked closer. Cookie took a drag off her cigarette and I could see her face now. Her foot was tapping and a leather belt dangled in her free hand.

"Where's Hal?" I prayed he was home to save me.

"So you like talking to Clyde's wife, huh? You like telling her my business?" Cookie took a deep sucking drag off her cigarette.

"I don't know who Clyde's wife is." I scrunched my eyes shut for a second and hoped with everything inside me that Betsy wasn't Clyde's wife.

"Betsy, you dumb twat! You told her all my business!"

"I didn't tell her any of your business." What was

Cookie's business anyway? Hanging out in a bar and drinking? Everyone already knew that.

"That bitch is a liar."

"Yeah. Okay." I couldn't think of anything she had said to me that would have been a lie. All she'd done was ask a couple of questions.

"Clyde's a Mormon. LDS don't molest little girls." Most of the kids in school were Mormon. They called it LDS for short, from Latter-Day Saints.

"Right." Were there people who thought LDS *did* molest little girls?

"Did Betsy tell you Clyde molested that little girl? The daughter of the widow in Eagle Rock Township?" I thought of Mr. Nettles. His shiny hair, his whispery voice, his teeth like bits of corn lined up in his gums. When I didn't answer, Cookie said, "Well?!"

"No, she didn't tell me that."

"Explain this to me, Little Miss Smarty Pants—" Cookie took a couple of steps toward me. She flicked her cigarette out into the dewy grass. The belt was still dangling from her hand. "If Betsy really believes Clyde touched that girl, why does she want to stay with him? Why is she spreading rumors about me in town?"

"I don't know what you're talking about," I said.

"*I don't know what you're talking about,*" Cookie mocked me. She moved closer and I stumbled back a step.

"Hal home?" I looked around in the blackness as if Hal might jump out and save me.

"And even if Clyde did molest that girl when she was twelve"—my mother ignored my question. She was stuck in her head now, in an anger whirlpool that wouldn't release her until she'd released it—"she probably deserved it. She's probably a dumb little slut, trying to seduce every grown man she meets . . . just like your sisters and just like you." My mother smiled, and I could see the shine of her wet teeth.

"She didn't tell me about any of that." I took a few more steps back.

"Well, Hurricane Cookie's in town now, so guess who's getting kicked out of Clyde's bed?" Cookie whipped the belt against the ground a couple of times as if she were in a rodeo.

"Betsy?" It always seemed safest to answer one of my mother's questions when I could.

"Exactly. And I won't be havin' a jealous, nosy little idiot like you stepping into my business and trying to stop this from happening. Understand?" She lifted the belt again.

I dropped to my knees and went into the armadillo pose I'd seen Hal do so many times. The belt felt like a giant, heavy rubber band snapping on my back. I tried to leave my body and float with my thoughts. I imagined the Happy House, which was growing in my mind into a lush Garden of Eden dominated by weeping willow trees. My sisters were always with me in my Happy House fantasy—napping in hammocks, reading, playing Talent Show. There was no belting in my Happy House. No kicking, pinching, or punching. No Cookie.

Eventually the belt slaps grew weaker. My mother, wasted, was losing power quickly. She dropped the belt at my feet, kicked at me, but missed.

"Stupid waste of skin . . . dumb slut . . . ungrateful little shit . . . ," Cookie mumbled and cursed as she staggered back into the house. I waited in the darkness until it felt safe to get up. My back sparked and burned, as if there were live electrical wires plugged into my skin. When I tiptoed into the house, Cookie was asleep, facedown on the couch. Her snoring rang out like the harmony to Hal's snoring booming out from the bedroom.

13
Collateral Damage

Norm and I were banned from Sheryl's after that night. We didn't stop going as it was the only kids' hangout in town; we just stopped telling our mother that we'd been there. When we were sent to the store to buy cigarettes for Cookie or macaroni to make for ourselves at home, we walked past Sheryl's to the next market, just in case Cookie wanted to examine the receipt.

In the height of the summer heat, it was a brutal trek along the open road from our house to the store. The blacktop reflected the heat straight back to our faces with only glimpses of shade when the trees grew closer to the road. But walking to the store was better than sitting home with Cookie, especially when Hal was out of town and Clyde was sniffing around the house.

It wasn't long before Clyde's wife, Betsy, told all her friends about Cookie trying to poach her husband. With only 360 people in town, the fact that Betsy would do just about anything to keep her marriage intact was something even Norm and I knew. And then there was Cookie's story. Anyone who was near our mother long enough—in a bar, at Colton's mother's hair salon, at the thrift store a few towns over where she regularly shopped—got the tale of how Cookie had lost her virginity, just this summer, in Clyde's red pickup truck. I didn't understand if it was a joke, or if it was something my mother, who had five kids from five different men, really wanted people to believe. Either way, that was her story and she stuck to it as fiercely as she stuck to the story about being a go-go dancer or singing backup on tour when she was in her twenties.

One day when the heat was pushing toward a hundred, Norm and I walked to the grocery store. Norm had a handful of food stamps in his back pocket. I had two dollars in my pocket so I could buy two packs of cigarettes for Cookie.

The store felt wonderfully chilly. I held my hair up off my neck as we walked the aisles and Norm put food in the cart. There wasn't a long line, and we only had to wait a minute before being rung up. The cashier was a big woman with bright orange-red hair and cakey orange-red lipstick. The collar from her jewel-green blouse stuck out over the edges of her blue apron. She looked back and forth between our groceries and our faces.

"Aren't you the Brooks kids?" she asked.

"I'm Rosanne Brooks." I wondered if she was the mother of someone in my grade.

"I'm Norman."

"And your mama's that New York lady that calls herself Cookie, right?" The cashier paused with a box of pasta in her hand. There was a woman with a full cart behind us in line. I wondered if she was anxious for us to pay and move on.

"Yeah," Norm said.

The woman shook her head and clucked her tongue. "It's not nice of her to be spending so much time with Betsy Hapner's husband."

Norm dropped his head and stared at the food on the belt. I reached into my pocket, pulled out the bills and said, "Can we also have two packs of Virginia Slims menthol?" Diversion and distraction was a skill I'd learned from my sisters. When drunken Cookie tore around the house after one or the other of my sisters, Cherie would hold me on her lap and play clapping games; Camille would style my hair; Gi would read library books to me.

"Owner doesn't like us to sell cigarettes to minors."

In a town made up of mostly LDS, cigarettes could be a little harder to procure than they'd been in Caldwell or New York.

"Sorry." I picked up the two dollars and put them in my pocket.

"How old are you?" The cashier held up a can of Ragu as if she were about to read the label.

"Ten. I'll be eleven in October."

She rang up the Ragu and said, "Someone told me that widow's girl was eleven when Clyde started messin' with her." I assumed this was the rumor Cookie had been talking about when she told me that LDS don't molest little girls. If Cookie, who wasn't very well connected in town, knew this story, then there wasn't a soul who didn't. I felt a flush of embarrassment for my mother, who was now dating a married child molester. And I felt embarrassed for Norm and me as the children of this woman.

The cashier reached to the cigarette display behind herself and pulled out two packs of Virginia Slims. They weren't menthol.

"Can we have menthol?" Norm asked.

She returned the packs, took out the menthols, and said, "I heard he molested her for years until her mommy found out and then they left the state lickety-split."

"Why would Clyde's wife wanna stay married to a man who had molested a little girl?" Norm asked. It was exactly what I had been thinking though I wasn't bold enough to ask a stranger a question like that.

"Even a bad husband's a husband." The cashier slowly bagged our groceries. "Better than nothing, don't you think?"

"Can you put it in three different bags?" Norm asked. He would carry two and I'd carry one all the way home.

She opened another brown bag and continued to load. "You watch out, Miss Rosanne Brooks." The cashier handed me a bag. "It's not the big Cookie Clyde wants." She winked, and I could see the smears of green eye shadow on her eyelid.

Right then, I wasn't afraid of Clyde. All I felt was the humiliation of a stranger pointing out the sloppy ways of my mother while pretending to look out for me. Moving was always hard, starting a new school was even harder. But there was one thing I liked about each move: we were starting fresh, where no one knew anything about any of us. Now, though, we'd barely been in Oakview for two months and

already there was an embarrassment I was ready to
flee.

Norm picked up the other two bags and pushed
ahead of me. I didn't catch up to him until we were on
the hot road walking home again.

"Please don't tell Mom," I said. Fear was an emotion that burned so brightly, it dimmed everything
around it.

"Mom needs to know people are talking about her."
Norm walked faster. Sweat spots painted a dark spine
down the back of his green T-shirt.

"But if you tell Mom, she'll find a way to blame me
for everything that woman said." I took extra fast steps
and caught up to Norm so we were side by side. "She'll
beat me so bad."

"Okay. I won't tell." Norm slowed so I could continue to walk beside him. If he hadn't been holding a
bag in each arm, I would have tried to hold his hand.

The next couple of weeks Norm and I spent waiting
for Hal to find out about Cookie losing her virginity
in the back of Clyde's milk truck. Each time I left the
house with my mother, heads turned as if a movie star
were walking down the street. Cookie liked to pretend
they were looking at her because of her form-fitting
clothes, her black hair fluffed out, her flapping fake

eyelashes. But I knew what they were thinking, and I hated being associated with her.

When Paige asked me to sleep over one night, I pitched the idea that I sleep over more than one night. Paige had no idea about the beatings at home, but she did know I liked being at her house more than mine. Together, we hatched a plan that I'd tell Cookie that Paige, her brother, and her dad needed me to help with the farm over the weekend as there were a few new sheep.

I brought it up after we'd made it through an entire meal without my mother yelling or throwing food. Cookie was smoking a cigarette, and Hal and Norm were each eating a soup bowl full of butter pecan ice cream Hal had brought home that evening. I was doing the dishes, trying to stack things in the drainer according to sets. There were no more than two of anything because so much had been broken against the kitchen wall.

"Mom," I said.

"That's my name, don't use it up," Cookie said.

"Paige Paisley wants me to stay at her farm for a few nights to help her and her brother with the chores."

Cookie laughed. "You're gonna go do chores at her house?"

"Yeah, I'll help them out."

"Why would you wanna do their dishes instead of ours?"

"No, not house chores. Farm chores. I'll help with the new sheep. She's gonna show them at 4-H."

Cookie took a drag on her cigarette, her eyes closed for just a minute. "Get me a beer."

I took a can of Schlitz from the refrigerator, opened it, and stuck it on the table in front of her.

"I think that sounds nice," Hal said.

"No one asked what you think," Cookie said.

"She'll learn about farming. That's a good thing in these parts."

"I don't need your fucking opinion." Cookie chugged the beer.

"They really need me." I picked up Norm's and Hal's empty bowls and took them to the sink.

"You know," Cookie said. "Since we might be living on a farm soon . . ."

Norm and I both looked at our mother. Was she going to tell Hal about Clyde? Hal seemed not to notice. He lit a cigarette and leaned back in his chair. His silver pompadour shone under the hanging lamp.

"Can I go?" I asked.

"I think it'll be good for you to learn farming. It'll come in real handy before you know it." My mother winked at me, as if I would be thrilled to be secretly talking about her not-so-secret affair right there in front of Hal.

"Thanks!" I threw down the dishrag and hurried to the bathroom to get my toothbrush. Before my mother could change her mind, I was running down the road to Paige's.

When we weren't feeding the animals or cleaning pens with Pup and Shadow following, Paige and I sewed. Already that summer, we'd set out to make new school clothes for the next year. I was awed by Paige's skills and clumsily worked alongside her— adding uneven inches of fabric to my too-short pants, putting buckling trim on the sleeves of my shirts and decorative buttons on the shoulders.

Paige's dad was so happy with our hard work, he drove us all the way to Ontario, Oregon, where we visited the fabric store, which Paige thought of as *heaven*. We spent two hours picking out fabrics, buttons, zippers, and patterns. It was shocking to witness her father paying for all that stuff without a single bad word about spending money on his daughter. It wasn't until right then that I realized there were people who just bought their kids things because they needed them. And they did it perfectly sober.

Our big sewing project that week was something

Paige had spent several days thinking through and designing on paper. She called it the Topsy-Turvey. The basic pieces were two pairs of thrift store jeans and some fabric. First Paige cut the jeans open and, using a floral fabric we'd picked out at *heaven*, she turned them into short skirts. Next, Paige sewed the skirts together, bottom to bottom, so there was a button and zipper on each end. You could wear the skirt with either end at the top and the flowers either hanging down or pointing up. I thought it was the cleverest, coolest piece of clothing I'd ever seen. I worked as Paige's assistant and within a few days we had two of them that we decided we'd share during the school year—swapping with each other from month to month.

On Saturday, Paige asked me to cut her hair. She liked it short so it didn't fall in her eyes during farm chores. We were on our way to the bathroom with a pair of sewing scissors when Norm showed up.

"Mom says your time's up," Norm said.

"But I'm cutting Paige's hair," I said.

"You think Mom cares?" Norm asked, and then Cookie laid in on the horn and stuck her head out the open window.

"GET IN THE DAMN CAR!" my mother shouted.

"I'll do it myself." Paige took the scissors from me and lopped off a hunk of her bangs right there in the doorway. We both laughed and then I hurried off to the car before my mother honked again and scared Pup and Shadow, who liked to hang out near the front door.

"Where are we going?" I was in the backseat. Norm was in front, fiddling with the radio.

"None of your fucking business." Cookie slapped Norm's hand away when he'd landed on a Kenny Rogers and Dolly Parton duet. My mother and Norm both sang along.

"Do you think they slept together?" Cookie asked us.

"Huh?" I leaned up from the backseat and looked out the front window. The car had been swerving so much I was feeling a little nauseous.

"Dolly and Kenny, when they recorded that song. You think she got him in the sack?"

"Probably," Norm said. "She's got big boobs."

"Gross," I said.

"She's no Cookie!" my mother said. "If I was doin' backup for Kenny, I guarantee he'd want some of the Cookie."

"You'd call him Kinny," Norm said. My brother made dealing with our mother seem easy.

"That's right, I'd call him Kinny." Cookie laughed at the fantasy, and Norm laughed, too.

A few minutes later we were at the local hardware

and feed store. There was room enough for two cars between the two farm-dirty pickup trucks where Cookie was trying to park. She pulled in, almost hit one truck, pulled out. Pulled in again and almost hit the other truck, pulled out again. After the fourth time, she killed the engine and stomped down the parking brake. We were at an angle, the front bumper almost touching the truck on our left, the rear bumper just an inch from the truck on our right. The three of us got out of the car and stood on the sidewalk for a moment staring at the Chrysler.

"I'm gonna wait for you out here," I said.

"Fuck you are." Cookie grabbed my hair at the nape of my neck and tugged me with her toward the hardware store. Before we walked in, one of the employees, a bone-thin man in a green apron, came out pushing a cart with giant bags of feed stacked on it. He gave Cookie the celebrity stare she'd been getting lately and then nervously looked behind himself.

"Ma'am," he said, quietly. "I believe it would better if you came back later. This is feed Mrs. Hapner is picking up for her husband's farm." He looked behind himself again.

"You think I give a shit?" Cookie took a couple of wobbly steps forward. The man moved in front of her again.

"Ma'am"—his voice was slightly higher now, louder and faster—"*Clyde Hapner's wife is in there*. This is her feed."

Rather than backing down, my mother saw the clerk's pleading as a challenge, a way to draw more attention to Hurricane Cookie, so she began to speak even louder, dropping her *R*s in her dramatic New York accent, as she said, "I don't give a fuck who's in your store, I'm here to buy flower seeds. So step outta the way."

"Ma'am, I'd really advise—"

"Outta the way," my mother repeated, "'cause Hurricane Cookie is here!" Cookie shoved past the clerk just as Betsy Hapner came out. We all paused. There was silence. Betsy looked at Cookie, the whites of her eyes flashing, and then she scurried a few yards down the sidewalk, the clerk following with the cart of animal feed. At her backed-in truck, Betsy Hapner watched as the clerk lowered the gate and started unloading bags. Her body was rigid as a flagpole.

I prayed my mother would walk into the store and leave Mrs. Hapner alone. "Let's go get seeds," I said.

Cookie snapped her head toward me as if I'd awoken her from a dream. She staggered down the sidewalk toward Mrs. Hapner. Norm and I followed.

"You're just the person I was looking for," Cookie announced.

Betsy held up her left hand and flashed her ring finger. She waved it in front of my mother's face. "We're married, Cookie! Married! So back off!" The clerk was moving so quickly, he was almost throwing the bags into the truck.

"He doesn't want you anymore! The man brings me milk every day 'cause he likes his milk and Cookie!" My mother put her hands on her hips and shook in one of her go-go dancer moves.

"You're a fool if you think he wants you! He wants your kids to work on the farm. He doesn't want you!"

The clerk turned to look at me now. With one side step, I stood behind Norm in an attempt at invisibility. I hoped the clerk was too young to have kids in my school—then, maybe, this story wouldn't follow me into the sixth grade.

"Oh fuck off!" Cookie laughed. "You've turned into a fat heifer since you married and now you've lost him. Face the facts!"

"Have you looked in the mirror?" Betsy said. "I mean, seriously, have you looked in the mirror because you're no slim—"

Before Betsy could say more, Cookie slid her purse from her shoulder and swung it toward Betsy, who screamed and covered her head just as the purse hit.

The clerk and Norm both ran to my mother, each of them grabbing one of her fleshy arms, and walked her back to our car. Cookie was laughing, staggering as if she were being dragged out of a New Year's party.

"Ma'am," the clerk said, "I don't want you in the store again. None of our customers deserve this kind of behavior."

"Blah blah blah, fuck you." Cookie jerked herself free from the clerk and Norm, and then got into the car. Norm quickly got in the front seat and I went to the backseat, where I slunk down so my eyes were just at the bottom of the window.

The clerk stood on the sidewalk and watched Cookie back the car into the truck on our right. She turned the wheel, drove forward and nicked the truck on our left. She backed up once more and hit the truck on our right again.

Cookie pulled forward slowly and then backed out once more, this time clearing the trucks.

We tore down the street, past Betsy, who sat in her truck, probably waiting for us to leave. Cookie honked the horn and shouted out the window, "FUCK YOU, BETSY HAPNER! CLYDE IS MINE!"

And he was. Or she was his.

Not long after that day at the hardware store, Hal

came home, sat at the dinner table, and pushed his food around with his fork. We were having mashed potatoes and meatloaf.

"What's your problem?" Cookie asked. She dipped her fork into Hal's mashed potatoes and took a big bite.

"Betsy Hapner left town. Seems she and Clyde are divorcing." Hal put down his fork and ran his hands over his pompadour. He took a deep breath and then blew it out like he was blowing out smoke from a cigarette.

Norm and I both stopped eating. It was hard to guess how Cookie might react to any piece of news. My mother could warp, mutate, and butcher the most innocent thing into a perverse and ugly crime. And things that I thought of as disturbing frequently glided past my mother, who showed no more interest than she had for the weather.

"Yeah, I heard the same." Cookie took a big bite of meatloaf and chewed it over and over, as if she were gnawing down a strip of leather.

"Also, according to Ray over at Rodeo Express, you and the kids are moving in with Clyde." Hal blinked, and a tiny drop of wetness caught in his eyelashes. I hoped he wouldn't cry. My mother wasn't worth crying over.

"First I heard of that," Norm said. It was the first

I'd heard of it, too, but I wasn't going to speak as I still wasn't sure how Cookie was digesting this.

"Is it true?" Hal stared at Cookie, who was working on another bite of meatloaf. If he hadn't been out on the road so much—trying to earn enough money to support Cookie—he would have found out about the affair much sooner.

"Nothing's set in stone." Cookie shrugged.

"Damn right it's not." Hal stood, pushed his plate forward to indicate he was done, and then walked to the front door.

Cookie got up and ran after him. She was smiling. "Where're you going?"

"Clyde Hapner's place. We're going to settle this man to man." Hal opened the door and left. Cookie stood at the threshold and watched until his truck drove away.

My mother returned to the table. She was giddy. Hungry. Happy. She chattered about the days when she was a go-go dancer. Men were always fighting over her back then.

"That was before you kids ruined this body. Ruined my tits." My mother put one hand on either side of her breasts and pushed them up.

"Doesn't seem like Hal or Clyde care," Norm said.

"That's 'cause in a town like this, I'm the best thing they can get!" Cookie hooted and then lit a cigarette.

She smoked and talked while I cleared the table and did the dishes. I'd rarely seen her happier.

The following day, everywhere I went, people were whispering. And though I sensed what they were murmuring about, I never really *knew* until years later. What was being said was that Clyde and Hal played a poker game that night. LDS aren't allowed to gamble, and Clyde considered himself among the faithful, so no money was involved. The only thing on the table was Cookie. So by extension, Norm and I were on the table, too.

Our lives were irrevocably changed by the outcome of that card game.

14

Pitchfork and Dagger

The night before we moved into Clyde's place, Cookie put Frankie Valli on the stereo and played "I've Got You Under My Skin" over and over again. From my bedroom, with the door closed, I could hear my mother's voice better than Frankie's.

There was a quick rapping at my door. It wasn't my mother, she didn't knock. And it wasn't Hal—he'd gone on the road a couple of nights earlier. It could only be Norm.

"Come in!" I shouted, and my brother opened the door and dove across the room and onto my bed in one swift motion.

"Think she's played that song enough?" Norm turned sideways and propped himself up on one elbow.

"I've got it memorized now." I started singing, and Norm sang with me. We both imitated Cookie's voice, which was sounding slightly operatic in her enthusiasm, though still New Yorkish.

"You know she stole that record from Jackie," Norm said. I did know this. Just before we took off for the trailer park, Cookie ran through Jackie and Kenny's house and restole most of what had been returned.

"Yeah." I rolled to my side and did the head prop, too.

"I really, really hope we move again before school starts," Norm said. My brother rarely cried and he swallowed his emotions down like horse pills. The rare times Cookie hit him, she could never get the satisfaction of even a whimper. *Take it like a man* was something I'd heard frequently, and Norm usually took everything just that way. (Though my experience so far was one where girls were the ones who, more often than not, were called on to *take it like a man*.) But that night, on the eve of our relocation to Clyde's house, Norm was struggling.

"I hope we move, too," I said. We were both acutely feeling the humiliation of Cookie's poach-and-switch act. If there had been more people in town to dilute the story, if there had been other women seducing married farmers, it might not have been so bad. But we were the only headline in the Oakview gossip that summer. The embarrassment felt like Pig Pen's dirt cloud, always visibly encircling my brother and me.

All went silent as the song ended. Norm and I each lifted our heads an inch in anticipation of that opening note. The song started again, Cookie let loose with the vocals, and Norm started talking. Really talking. It was like a drainpipe had been unplugged that night, and every gunky, wadded hairball was flushing out of my normally unruffled brother.

Norm and I swapped Cookie stories late into the night. First we each reported who in town had said what about our mother. Next, we pulled out and examined past humiliations in Caldwell and in various towns, bars, motels, and parking lots scattered across Long Island.

Late that night, or early the next morning, Norm and I speculated on where we should move in order to escape further humiliation.

"We should head west," Norm said. "Hollywood or Las Vegas, where people like Mom don't stick out."

"I've gotta be in New York," I said. "With Mom in a different state. Or maybe on a different planet."

I wanted family, my sisters, the comfort of people who knew my story and didn't think there was anything wrong with me. Norm wanted total anonymity, the gift of being only and exactly the person he chose to be on any given day. Someone who reflected nothing of his past or even of the people who knew that past.

Our fantasies were different, but the places in our minds that drove those fantasies were identical. We both wanted to simply feel normal. And safe.

I never told my brother I loved him. But I felt it strongly that night as our tethers of pain connected like two grasping octopuses. For now, I couldn't get to New York, and he couldn't get to Las Vegas. Instead, we would bob through this murky mess together.

Clyde's house wasn't far—the farthest end of his property met the farthest end of the land Hal's rented place was on. When we drove down Clyde's long dirt drive, dust kicked up and created clouds that were impossible to see through. Cookie barreled ahead as if she knew the road by heart. She never slowed for the potholes, and every few feet I flew up in the backseat as the car bucked and lurched.

"Why doesn't he spray down the road?" At Paige's farm, they sprayed the road when they watered the fields in order to keep the dust down.

"Oh, Little Miss Smarty Pants spends a couple of days at the Paisleys' and thinks she knows more about farming than Clyde, huh?" Cookie slammed the brakes when we reached the house. It was white, one story, with a green roof. A white split-rail fence surrounded the house. Inside and outside the fence was the greenest grass you'd ever see—it looked like it had been colored with a Crayola crayon.

On one side of the drive, lined up like tombstones, were three old cars: a station wagon and two trucks. They were rusted, and the tires were flat or missing. Most of the farmhouses I'd seen had old dead cars on the property. Vehicles weren't traded in or sold to make room for the new—they were driven until they couldn't drive. Sometimes the old cars were put to good use, like at Paige's house where her father had removed the engine from a car, planted trees in it, and called it Farm Art. Cats lived in the Farm Art car, changing the landscape of it so it was a work in continuous progress.

A furry gray-and-white dog the size of a lamb ran to us as we got out of the car. He barked a little but was wagging his tail and clearly had a dog smile on his face. I leaned down and petted him. He reminded me of Paige's Pup; I figured he was a working animal, too.

"Stand up straight," Cookie said under her breath, and she pinched me in her favorite spot on my back where my rib cage wrapped around.

We approached the house, the dog sticking by my side. The windows were small and had ripped yellow shades pulled down so you couldn't see inside. I wondered why a man surrounded by so much land would have to cover his windows.

Clyde met us at the door. He was in his bright, clean overalls again. No pitchfork this time. He flashed his Crest ad teeth at me, then he kissed my mother on the cheek. Unlike the other times I'd seen him, Clyde wasn't in his John Deere baseball cap. His bare, balding head was the shape of a bullet, pointed on the top near the back.

"Let me give you a tour of your new home." Clyde had a tinge of a southern accent.

"Can the dog come in?" I asked.

"Of course Blue can come in." Clyde winked at me. "Whatever makes you happy."

Whatever makes me happy? Why didn't I believe this? Nonetheless, I was glad to have Blue by my side. He was warm and fuzzy, and I loved the way his bottom swung from side to side when he wagged his tail.

We started in the mudroom that had a large white freezer big enough for the four of us to sleep in. Clyde popped up the lid and showed us the giant slabs of meat. "All my cattle," Clyde said. Cookie oohed and aahed as if he was displaying a show horse. All I could see were dead animal parts, frosty and pink like the marzipan candy I'd seen at Paige's house. "And we got chicken, eggs, and milk, too. Only thing you need to use your food stamps for is fruit, vegetables, and cereal."

Also in the mudroom were boots, gloves, hats, and coats. Clyde explained that everything you wear out on the farm gets taken off in the mudroom so you don't drag manure through the house. *Manure* was a word I hadn't heard until I'd moved to Idaho. But here, *manure* was everywhere. You pitchforked manure out of stalls; you dumped wheelbarrows full of manure into *manure pits;* you watched for manure when you ran across a field; and you wiped the manure off your shoes before you entered a house. I'd thought the poop hole at the Callahans' was bad. But that was nothing compared to the amount of manure I'd already encountered just helping out Paige on her farm. Seemed there was as much manure as dirt in the ground.

Clyde opened a door off the mudroom that went to a small, spare bedroom. "This is your room, Norm." He smiled down at my brother, who just stared at the empty space. "You like it?"

"He loves it!" Cookie said, and she reached up and pinched Norm on the top of his ear.

"I love it," Norm said.

We left the mudroom and entered the main living area

where the kitchen, living room, and dining room were combined. As in many farmhouses, masses of flies circled and buzzed. The rugs, furniture, and cabinets were a dull brown. It felt like I was inside a wooden blanket box.

Clyde moved in his bow-legged hobble to the wood-burning stove in the kitchen. Cookie followed him and then looped her arm in his.

"This here is our only source of heat. You'll need to learn how much of these here wood chips, wood shavings, and newspaper to put in." He pointed to the wooden crates nearby. "It's not hard, but you gotta do it right to keep the house warm."

"Norm can be in charge of the fire. Can't you, Norm?" Cookie smiled real big like she was the friend-liest mother around.

"I guess," Norm shrugged.

"All right then, that's your job." Clyde's eyes lit on me, and he said, "And you and Rosie can feed the calves each morning before school and then again after school, in the early evening."

"That'll get you outta bed, won't it?" Cookie laughed.

We followed Clyde to the remaining two bedrooms. One was Cookie and Clyde's and it was as big as the whole dining area and kitchen combined. There was a built-in closet with multiple doors that covered an entire wall. Cookie opened all the doors. Over two-thirds of the closet was empty.

"I'm gonna be like Lady Di with all the clothes I'll have in here." Cookie leaned into Clyde and gave him a wet smooch.

"You're gonna be my princess," he said. Then he looked over at me and added, "I'll have two princesses in my house."

"That's okay," I mumbled. "I don't wanna be a princess."

"Of course you do!" Clyde said. "Let's go look at your princess room."

"I don't like princesses," I said.

There was a tiny bedroom just beyond the master. It had a fresh coat of pink paint on the walls, and the bed and dresser were both white with pink hearts painted on them. At each of the two windows, there were pink lacy curtains.

"Look how he set this up for you!" Cookie said.

"What do you think?" Clyde smiled at me as if he was going eat me up.

"I'll just stay at the other end of the house with Norm." I tried to speak with a light casualness, but I could barely breathe and was forcing out the words.

"Of course you won't!" Clyde said. "You're a princess and this is a princess room."

I stared at the bed with the pink ruffle-edged quilt. Did he go out and buy these things for me? Why would a man with no kids have a pink quilt? "I like sharing a room with my brother."

Norm said, "It's okay if Rosie wants to stay in my room."

"Rosie's staying in this nice room Clyde set up for her! Now can you two say *thank you?*" Cookie said.

"No thanks necessary," Clyde said. "Now why don't you kids put your things away, and then I'll show you how to do the farm chores."

Norm and I stood on the bottom rail of the calf pen peering in. Clyde stood beside me, his hand on my lower back as if I might fall, which I knew I wouldn't. I hopped down, went to the other side of Norm, and climbed onto the rail again. Clyde stayed where he was as he explained about the calves and how they were separated into their own pen when they were weaned. They stared up at us as Clyde talked, and I tried to make eye contact with each one of them.

"You two are going to be their mommies now," Clyde said. "You're going to feed them and take care of all their needs."

Norm and I looked at each other. To us, a *mommy* wasn't someone who took care of all her kids' needs. I decided then that I'd treat the twenty or so calves as if they were our younger siblings. Like Cherie, Camille, and Gi did for me and Norm, I'd do all I could to make sure these babies were safe, fed, and warm.

Norm hated getting up early, and I didn't like it much either. But once we were in the calf pen, it all seemed okay. The calves had fur as soft and shimmery as velvet. Their giant eyes were like disks of melted chocolate. When they had suckled their mothers, they butted their heads into her udders to release the flow of milk. This practice didn't let up when Norm and I fed them from what looked like giant baby bottles. As soon as my brother and I approached the pen, they ran for us, butting their bony rectangular heads into our legs and hips, often toppling me over. I found the best way to approach them was to leap into the pen and immediately straddle a calf as if I was going to ride it. With the animal gently pinched between my thighs, I'd lean over its head and feed it. If the bottles ran out before they were full, they'd buck and kick. I'd stick my fingers in their mouths to pacify them as I dismounted. Bruises tattooed my legs, but they didn't bother me. They were proof of my devotion.

When Norm and I tried to leave the pen, the calves chased us, charged, and kicked as their way of begging us to stay. We'd hop onto the fence, climb over, and look back down at them as they mooed in grief, their voices sounding like tiny creaky engines. I usually told them I loved them and that I'd be back at the next feeding. I swear they smiled at me.

One morning, when Norm had slept at Colton's house and I was alone feeding the calves, Clyde showed up. He leaned with his arms folded on the top of the fence, talking to me. We'd been living in his house for over a month, but I still felt like he was a stranger, and my body surged with a hyperawareness whenever he got near.

"You're doin' a great job," Clyde said.

"Thanks." There was a nuzzling calf between my legs that was just getting to the end of her bottle. I stuck my first three fingers in her mouth, swung my leg off over her back, and stepped backward to the fence before she charged me. I hopped on the rail, and several calves ran toward me, their big long mouths ajar as they moo-begged me to stay.

"You're a heck of a worker." Clyde helped me down off the fence, though I didn't need help. "You're strong and you gotta good work ethic. A darn good farm girl."

"Really?" I looked up at Clyde. It was so nice to get some praise. To be appreciated. My mother only claimed to see the bad in me.

"Honestly, Rosanne. I don't know what I'd do without you around here."

"What about Boone?" I asked. Boone Westley was the farmhand that showed up Monday through Friday. He had thick black hair and a furry black mustache that crawled up over and down the sides of his mouth like a giant caterpillar. Boone was friendly and chatty, and I didn't feel the strangeness with him that I did with Clyde.

"Boone's a great worker. But, I'm tellin' ya, Rosie, you are one of kind." He cuffed my cheek lightly and I blushed. I was glad he could see how hard I was trying. It made it feel worth it. And the fact that he complimented me made Clyde seem not so bad. Maybe people were jealous of him because he had so much land; maybe that's why there were the terrible rumors about him molesting the widow's daughter.

"I love the calves," I told Clyde.

"You'll love the cows, too. And starting tomorrow morning, you're gonna be milking them." Clyde smiled as if this were a gift. More chores. More work. More to do before school when it started in a couple of weeks.

"What about Norm?" Everything was easier and more fun when I did it with my brother.

"He's got other assignments," Clyde said.

At five thirty the next morning, Clyde took me out to the chilly pasture where the cows huddled in small groups, half of them sleeping. The sun was a few minutes from coming up, and the world was slowly changing from black and white into full color. Blue, the dog, who had already started staying in my room at night, was by my side. Clyde looked down at Blue, whistled and then said, "Gets 'em Blue, go gets 'em!" At his words, Blue bolted into the wide field and ran circles around the cows, who got up as if an alarm had gone off. The dog circled them back and forth, drawing them closer and closer together. A couple strayed far from the herd and Clyde said, "You missed one boy, go get 'em!" I'd seen Paige's dog herd the sheep, but that wasn't as dramatic as this. The cows were enormous—they could kill Blue just by sitting on him—and yet they obeyed as he ran in a zigzag and then bounded toward them to keep them moving toward the milking parlor. Eventually, Blue had corralled them into one massive clump. He darted back and forth to encourage them forward, sometimes nipping at an ankle or two to move them along. When the cows kicked their feet back, they never hit Blue; he was too fast, too loose, while they seemed earthbound, trudging ahead.

"Why do they do what he says?" I asked. Clyde had already told me that the dog weighed forty pounds and each cow weighed at least a thousand pounds. It seemed miraculous to me that they followed Blue's orders. Clyde explained that cows are prey and dogs are predators. Their innate nature made them respond to each other the way they did. One group was always scrambling to stay alive, while the other charged forward to get exactly what he wanted. I thought then that people could be divided into predators and prey, too. My mother and Mrs. Callahan were predators. Me, Norm, and my sisters were prey. I wasn't sure what Clyde was yet. He was friendly, kind, and full of praise for everything I did. When he taught me about farming, however, I always listened carefully with two parts of my brain. One part took in everything he said, so I could learn as much as possible. The other part examined him, the way he moved, how he used his hands, the whiteness of his teeth—as if all that could tell me what I needed to know about him and whether or not I should beware.

The milking parlor was a building made up of two wall-to-wall, floor-to-ceiling cement rooms. The cows entered one room, where they walked up two separate ramps in a line, penned in by metal gates on the side. Four cows were milked at once while crated in by metal bars, still up on the ramp. Clyde and I stood in the area below the ramp. The cows' teats and the suctions were at arm level for Clyde. We wore plastic bib-top aprons to keep from getting wet as we cleaned each cow before it was milked. We used what looked like a garden hose, but the spray was powerful, like water from a fire hose. The cows didn't seem to mind as we washed off the manure, grass, and dirt that stamped their bodies in what looked like a camouflage pattern.

"Focus on their teats, where the milk comes out. It's gotta be pink and fresh looking." Clyde mussed the top of my head as I looked up at him. "Don't want any dirt in our milk now."

I redirected the spray and cleaned each cow until she was glossy clean.

After hosing the cows, Clyde showed me how to attach the suctions, which, with their four tentacled silver caps, looked like something from a movie about Mars or aliens. The "top" of each cap was connected to a hose that drained the milk into the containers below the ramp. Each cow milked for around four minutes. With almost eighty cows being milked, four at a time, the whole process took just under two hours.

At five thirty that evening, Clyde and I went out and milked them again. This time I knew what I was doing, and we were finished in an hour and a half.

"You're a heck of a fast learner!" Clyde said when we were done. He whistled and then added, "Heck of a smart girl!" I couldn't stop myself from beaming with pride.

"So when do we do it again?" I asked.

"Tomorrow."

"Already? The cows don't get a day off?" At Paige's farm the chores were done every single day. But her cattle were for beef, so none of them were milked.

Clyde laughed. "Nope. There's no day off on a farm. Not for the cows and not for the farmer. And you're a farmer now."

Clyde mussed my hair again, and we walked back to the house. I was starting to feel more comfortable with him. And as for having to work morning and night—I didn't dread it the way I should have. Mostly I saw it as time out of the house, away from my mother. Beyond her predator's bite.

Fortunately, that bite was less frequent after we first moved in with Clyde.

Cookie only hit me when Clyde was way out in a field or at the store picking up feed. By the time he walked in the door, my tears were dry and everything appeared normal again. Cookie would rush to Clyde with an enormous smile and a girlish squeal. She'd wrap her arms around him and plunge her lips against his.

When they weren't kissing, my mother stroked Clyde's cheeks; if he sat down, she rubbed his shoulders; if he sat for long, she took off his shoes and massaged his feet; or, she sat on his lap and nuzzled her breasts in his face. At least once a day, she laid her hand over his crotch and told him how handsome and big he was.

When Clyde was in the room, Norm and I were invisible. And that was fine by me.

Just as the summer was ending, Clyde taught me my last chore: mucking the cow barn. After showing me the pitchfork, the wheelbarrow, and the hay, Clyde walked me over to the end of the corrals to the edge of the manure pit that spread out in front of us. I thought of the La Brea Tar Pits, which I'd read about in school last year. Animals died in those pits, along with anything else that fell, crawled, landed, or was dumped in them. There were dead animals in Clyde's pit, too: lame calves, cows, sick chickens that wouldn't lay and couldn't be eaten.

I read that the tar pits gave off a smell sort of like gasoline. But whatever that smell was, it had to have been better than Clyde's manure pit, which smelled worse than any bucket I ever carried out of the Callahans'. Inhaling the manure pit stink made my skin feel itchy, like there was something that needed to be washed off me.

"Once a month, someone gets on a tractor and pushes all the manure into this pit." Clyde stared out at it as if we were looking at something beautiful or majestic. Mrs. Callahan would probably have loved Clyde's manure pit as much as Clyde seemed to.

"There's no people poop in there, right?" Who knew where waste went when you flushed a toilet.

"No," Clyde smiled. "But you know what?"

"What?" I was still staring out at the giant pit.

"I think I'm gonna teach you to drive the tractor so you can do this job, too. You're smart enough and tall enough."

"You know I'm only ten, right?" Maybe Clyde just didn't understand that I was a little girl. I'd grown so much over the last year that people often mistook me for a thirteen-year-old.

"Ten's my favorite age." Clyde winked, and my stomach gunned like it had with Mr. Nettles.

Sometime before school started, my mother called Cherie. She didn't seem to hate my oldest sister with the same passion and depth as she hated Gi and Camille. Thankfully, Cherie was able to get our phone number and address out of Cookie, so soon enough all three of my sisters were calling for me and Norm.

There was only one phone in the house; it was beige and hung on the wall in the kitchen. The phone had an extra-long cord so you could pull the receiver far from the base. When my sisters called, I stretched that cord as far as I could to get away from Cookie. But that rarely worked. As soon as she heard me answering questions with a simple yes or no, my mother pushed her head against mine and tilted the earpiece so she could hear what we were talking about. I always said something that would let my sisters know Cookie was there. Soon enough, Gi came up with a plan that Norm and I were to answer *yes* questions by talking about life on the farm and *no* questions by talking about the weather. This seemed to work in keeping Cookie away while we talked.

"Is Mom beating you?" Gi always asked.

"Yeah, I love feeding the calves the most."

"Is Clyde beating you?"

"No, it hasn't rained since we moved in."

"Oh, *mia bambina! Je t'aime!*"

"*Je t'aime,*" I'd whisper.

Then one day, my sister said, "Tell me the name of your school, but say it casually so Mom doesn't wonder why I'm asking."

"Okay." I couldn't think of a sentence.

"I'm going to call the school counselor and see if we can get you and Norm out of there," Gi said.

"All the kids are nice at Oakview Elementary," I said.

Gi was one of the most strong-willed and determined people I'd ever met. And knowing she was going to try to take care of me all the way from New York made me feel a little safer, a little calmer. It created an end point.

From then on, each time Cookie pinched me on the back, or yanked my hair, or slapped me across the face, or whipped my back with a belt, or kicked me in the stomach, or stomped her wooden-heeled shoe into my spine, I saw Gi in my head. She was only sixteen years old, but my sister was as busy and bossy as the president, and she called grown-ups all the way in Idaho, at a school she'd never even visited, and demanded that they do something about my mother. *This might be the last time,* I thought, after each beating, *'cause Gi's gonna take care of this.*

The Friday after my eleventh birthday, Cookie handed me a note to give to the principal. I was to be released at two thirty so she could take me to the doctor for my annual checkup. Of course I'd never had an annual checkup. Other than the hospitalization after the car crash with Ricky, I'd never seen a doctor. My mother had forged doctors' signatures, turned in forms that she herself had filled out, or told the school she'd get them to them eventually. Eventually never came before we'd moved on. But in a town with one family doctor, there was no faking medical records. The school had been after my mother since last May; it was more than a month past Labor Day, and they were insisting on a checkup, proof of immunization, actual doctor-signed medical records.

After lunch, Mrs. Muse was giving a math lesson. She seemed so enthusiastic talking about long division, that I worried she wouldn't tell me when it was time to meet my mother. Every few seconds I looked to the door to see if Mr. Jackson would show up to tell me it was time to meet my mother. Mrs. Muse never stopped her lesson, and Mr. Jackson never showed up. But my mother did. She filled the frame of the doorway with her big black hair and her tight red sweater.

"Mrs. Muse," my mother said, her voice as falsely sweet as I'd ever heard it. "I need to take Rosanne for her annual checkup."

I gathered up my things and shoved them into my backpack. The sweeter my mother's voice, the angrier she probably was. Once I was out of the classroom, she grabbed a fistful of hair at the base of my neck and dragged me out of the building and then toward the car, cursing in a quiet mumble.

Cookie let go of me with a little push, and then we each got in the car. The keys dangled in the ignition, and the engine was already running.

My mother looked at me, her face a flat circle with craggy angry lines at her mouth and eyes. "Making me wait like that . . ." Cookie grabbed my hair at the nape of my neck again and slammed my head forward into the dashboard. I swallowed the yelp that tried to come out of me—I wanted to be a little more stoic, like Norm.

Cookie lurched out onto the road while simultaneously lighting a cigarette.

"TWO THIRTY!" she shouted. "I TOLD YOU TO HAVE YOUR LITTLE ASS OUT HERE AT TWO THIRTY!"

The head bang along with the cigarette smoke made me queasy. I rolled down my window for fresh air. "I thought Mr. Jackson or Mrs. Muse would tell me when it was time to go."

"Why didn't you just read the fucking clock?!" Cookie stuck her cigarette in her mouth and used two hands to make a sharp right turn. The car screeched.

"I don't know how." My hand went to the spot on my forehead where a cartoon-quick lump was growing.

It was hot and throbbed like a loose tooth being pushed out with a tongue.

"The fuck you don't know how! Who the fuck doesn't know how to tell time? You're eleven fucking years old!"

"No one ever taught me." When I had lived with my sisters, I hadn't needed to tell time. They woke me, got me to school, and picked me up from school. Whenever we had a TV (and, strangely, even when we didn't have heat, we often had a TV), I always knew what time it was according to which show was on. On Saturdays, if *Scooby-Doo and Scrappy-Doo* was on, that meant it was nine. If *Fat Albert* was on, it was eleven. When I lived at the Callahans', I knew it was eight at night when the bunkroom door was locked. I knew it was six in the morning when that same door was unlocked. I knew it was eight twenty and not eight fifteen if we missed the school bus. When we lived in the hotel, once the social worker had shown up and the heat knew were my mother was, Norm woke me, got me to school, and walked me home. I didn't go anywhere without him then. When we lived in the car with Cookie, the radio announced the time every hour. But time didn't matter so much then. We weren't in school, so we didn't have anywhere to be. Instead, time was organized in blocks around my mother: the time she was in the bar, the time she was sleeping in the car, the time we were waiting outside the car while she was doing things in it with a man. At Kenny and Jackie's, Jackie woke me and made sure I got to school on time. If Jackie's family was getting ready to leave for church, it was quarter to ten. At the Paradise Homes Trailer Park, Norm woke me for school. And I knew it was time for church when I saw the Flynn family in the trailer beside ours leave for their church. Since we'd moved to the farm, Clyde woke me up for chores. When chores were done, it was time to go to school. When school was done, it was time to go home and do chores again.

"What a dumb fuck!" Cookie laughed. I didn't know how to tie my shoes either, but now didn't seem like the time to reveal that. This had been less of a problem as the one pair of shoes I owned had laces so old and knotted there was no tying or untying them.

We pulled into the parking lot behind the doctor's office. Cookie cut the engine, got out of the car, and flicked her cigarette across the parking lot. I watched it roll under a car and imagined it igniting the gas tank and the whole thing blowing up.

The nurse at the reception asked my mother for my

immunization records and medical history. Cookie put on the sweet voice and said, "Sweetheart, we fled an abusive man in New York and there was no way to get the medical records."

"Oh." The nurse seemed stunned. Her cheeks looked like milk with rose petals floating in it. "Can you call and have them sent?"

"Absolutely not," Cookie said. "If my ex finds out where we are, he'll come after us and he'll probably kill me. He might kill the kids, too!"

"Okay, yes, I wouldn't want that to happen." The nurse blinked her eyes rapidly and then nervously looked down at her papers.

Doctor Phillips had warm hands and an even warmer smile. He was nice and spoke slowly and calmly.

"How was school today?" he asked.

"Fun," I said. "We played dodge ball."

"Ah, that's a dangerous game," he said. "I think they should separate the boys and girls when you play."

"Then there wouldn't be enough kids." I was now taller than half the boys and stronger than many of them. Playing against them was fine by me; I preferred it even.

"Did you get that bang on your head in dodge ball?" the doctor asked.

"Yeah." I put my hand on the lump. It felt like a warm, curled-up baby mouse was living under my skin.

"Good for you. Playing hard." Before I knew it, he had given me a shot.

"Yeah," I smiled. I did play hard. It was fun to push myself, to feel my strength.

"What's your favorite subject in school?"

"Reading and—" Another shot went into my arm. "I like everything at school."

"I bet you're an excellent student." Doctor Phillips landed his third shot, and I barely flinched. He had no idea how minuscule the pain was compared to the shots Cookie landed on me.

Clyde liked to talk about farming, milk, and his teeth, in that order. Farming we covered during chores morning and night. Milk we discussed when milking the cows and during dinner when Clyde drank at least two glasses of milk and urged Norm and me to do the same. His teeth were part of the milk conversation. He'd never had a cavity. Never had even a shadow dim the whiteness of his fangs. Never had any dental work whatsoever. And that, Clyde claimed, was all due to his daily consumption of milk. Ice cream was worked into the milk diet. According to Clyde, if you really wanted nice teeth like his, you had to eat only vanilla ice cream, preferably with peanut butter on it.

The four of us were doing just that after dinner the day I'd had my checkup.

"Doctor said Rosie has pretty good teeth, too," Cookie said.

I looked up from my bowl. Was my mother saying something nice about me?

"You finish that ice cream, your teeth might look as good as mine." Clyde winked at me.

"It's because I gave her milk her whole life." Cookie banged her spoon against the bowl, scraping up the last bits of ice cream. "No matter what our circumstances, I always made sure my babies had milk."

Norm and I shot each other looks across the table. We never had milk except with our free lunch at school. Or at Paradise Homes when someone left it outside our door. The only beverage that was continuously on hand when Cookie was around was Schlitz.

"You're a good mother," Clyde said. I wondered if he believed this, or if he knew he had to say things like that to keep Cookie fawning over him, which she did whenever her hands were free.

"You know we almost didn't make it to the doctor today because that one"—Cookie pointed at me with the end of her spoon—"can't tell time and didn't know she had to leave the classroom."

Norm laughed. "Seriously?"

"This true?" Clyde asked.

"Yeah," I mumbled into my spoon.

"I'll teach you," Clyde said, and he reached across the table and put his hand on mine. I pulled my hand away, got up, and started doing the dishes.

"I'll teach her," Cookie said. "The girl's an idiot. She doesn't need someone to be nice with her; she needs someone who will beat it into her thick head." More and more Cookie was slipping up in her good-mother act. I knew it wouldn't be long before she started throwing dinner against the wall and felt free to beat me in Clyde's presence.

"Sweetheart," Clyde said. "I got this one. You take the night off from mothering."

"Aren't you the best," Cookie cooed. She got up from her seat and sat on Clyde's lap, whispering in his ear while Norm and I cleaned the kitchen. When we were done, Norm and Cookie went to the couch and turned on the TV.

Clyde took me out to the dairy barn, where there was a rectangular clock radio on one of the shelves. It looked like a miniature TV console from the 1970s—a brown plastic speaker on one side, a clock face beside the speaker. There were little white knobs below the clock to move the hands and set the alarm. We stood side by side as Clyde spun the dials and explained the big and little hands: quarter after, quarter of, half past, and the hour. After forty minutes I could read time in an instant.

"It's easy now," I said.

"That's 'cause you're a smart girl." Clyde mussed my hair. "Not only can you farm as well as big ol' Boone Westley, you just learned to tell time in under an hour."

Whenever he complimented me like this, whenever he noticed how hard I worked or what a good job I did, I felt a surge of warmth in me—a form of happiness. And that happiness made me like Clyde a little more. It edged me toward actually trusting him.

Back at the house, Clyde removed his boots in the mudroom. I looked down at my sneakers, the black laces knotted like a clump of inky seaweed.

"Can you show me how to tie my shoes?" I asked.

"You don't know?" Clyde lowered his voice.

"What are you two whispering about?!" Cookie yelled from the couch.

"We're still working on time here." Clyde winked at me.

"Gi always tied my shoes," I said to Clyde.

"Well, what have you done since then?"

I slipped off my shoe and handed it to Clyde. He flashed his ghost-white teeth into a smile. Then he leaned over and picked up Norm's sneakers. We walked past Cookie and Norm on the couch. My mother lifted her eyes, as if she were suspicious, and then jerked her head back to the TV. Clyde and I sat at the table. He untied each of Norm's shoes and then handed one to me. I followed his movements as he retied the shoe in his hand. We did it over and over again. It was a little more difficult than reading a clock, but by the time Cookie's show was over, and she was splaying herself across Clyde's lap, I had it down pat.

The following Saturday, after we'd milked the cows, Clyde said, "Now that you got time and shoe-tyin' under your belt, it's high time I taught you to drive the truck."

"Really?" My mouth was open. I didn't want to make a move until I was sure he wasn't kidding.

"Really," Clyde smiled and handed me his keys. I ran, the keys jingling, straight to Clyde's red truck. I sat in the driver's seat and watched Clyde walk toward me. His knees sat wider than his hips. I wondered if he'd be taller if his legs were straight.

"Scoot over," Clyde said.

"I thought I was driving," I said.

"Gotta get you out in the middle of a field," Clyde said. "Where you can't run over anything and no one can hear if one of us starts screamin' and hollerin'."

I slid to the passenger seat and Clyde got in. We drove down the road to the one of the more remote fields where Clyde leased land to grow hay. He shut off the engine in the middle of nowhere. The field was flat, mostly brown, and brownish green hills rose up in the distance. Clyde scooted across the seat. I hopped out before his body got too close to mine, ran around the truck, and got into the driver's seat.

"Steering wheel," Clyde said, and he put one hand next to mine on the wheel. Then he pointed down past my leg and said, "Gas." I remembered Becky at the Callahans' pointing out the kitchen, dining room, and living room. I wanted to say *obviously* the way Becky had, but I didn't.

Once he'd shown me all the parts, Clyde quizzed me on them. When he said *clutch, brake,* or *gas,* I had to put my right foot on it as quickly as I could. He explained the gas/clutch relationship—illustrating what my feet would be doing—by pushing his hands back and forth in the air. It looked simple.

"Now put your foot on the clutch and push down as far as it goes," Clyde said. I did and he whistled as if my long legs were something I'd chosen, worked for, rather than something I'd just been born with. "Your mama probably couldn't drive until she was twenty-one, with her little itty bitty legs."

Cookie's legs were far from itty bitty. But she was short and surely wouldn't have been able to reach a clutch as I did then at age eleven.

"Can I turn the key?" I was ready to go. Fearless.

"I'm ready if you're ready." Clyde rolled down his window and casually let his arm hang out over the side of the truck.

I started the engine and then jolted off across the field. The truck lurched and screeched as I changed gears. We were thrown toward the ceiling as I barreled over ruts in the dirt. The few times I stalled out, Clyde patiently talked me through starting it up again, and off we'd go.

"Heck of a fast learner!" Clyde smiled, thrilled, and I felt the softness of trust coming over me. How bad could he be if, within one week, he taught me to tell time, tie my shoes, and drive a truck?

Around the end of October I came home from school and found Cookie staggering slowly around the living room, like an enormous bug that had been stepped on but hadn't yet died. She looked at me and smiled. And then she started laughing.

"What?" I looked down at myself to see if there was something funny on me, or about me.

"Your sister." Cookie dropped onto the couch and patted the seat beside her.

"Which one?"

"The crazy, juvey, slut, trouble-makin' bitch." Cookie's words were slow and thick, as if she were just learning how to speak English. She patted the couch again and said, "SIT."

I sat. "Gi?"

"See, even you know wha' a crazy fuckin' lunatic she is." Cookie tried to light a cigarette, but she was too drunk to hold the match to the tip. She dropped the lit match on the couch. I leaned over my mother's lap to make sure it went out.

"What about Gi?" I took the pack of matches from the coffee table, struck one, and lit my mother's cigarette.

"She called your school. I hadda go down there and sit in the principal's office like I was the bad kid and—" Cookie's head rocked back against the couch. She appeared to have forgotten she was in the middle of a sentence.

"What did they say?" My body felt electric. Was I about to be sent to New York to be with my sisters? Gi promised me that she'd make sure I didn't go to another foster home.

"That stupid, crazy twat called the school, and I tol' them, I tol' them all right."

"What'd you tell them?"

"That she's crazy! And a delinquent! And tha's why she doesn't live with us!" Cookie started laughing again.

"And they believed you?" The electric feeling was shutting down, powering off.

"O' course! I am an upstanding member of this community! I am LDS!"

"You're not a Mormon." Everything inside me went quiet. Numb. If they believed her, there was no getting away from Cookie. "You went to Catholic school."

"It was a Mormon-Catholic school. I jus' never told you."

"Yeah. Right." My body felt heavier and heavier. It seemed like I might plummet straight through the couch.

"They love me a' your school. The love me 'cause—" Cookie shut her eyes and fell asleep. Or passed out.

I took the cigarette from my mother's hand and tip-toed away. Norm walked in the door from his school bus. I lifted my finger to shush him, and the cigarette banged against my lip. The intimacy of my mother's lipstick-blotted, spit-wet cigarette tip against my mouth was almost as unbearable to me as the beating I'd just escaped.

By the time Christmas had passed, Cookie had brought four cats into the house. I'm not sure who named them or how, but they were called Socrates, Aristotle, Plato, and Snowy. There was a litter box in the mudroom, but with so many cats it filled quickly, and they seemed to prefer doing their business in the corner behind the kitchen table, or in the hall outside the bathroom. Since Cookie did very few farm chores, cleaning the inside of the house was her responsibility. Either she didn't do it, or she did it so poorly and infrequently that the mess couldn't be wrested under control. The grime spread from one surface to another. The kitchen walls near the table were stained with grease spots and various splatters as Cookie started throwing food again. Every now and then, a dead mouse would show up under the table—they dried out quickly and traveled from room to room as the cats batted them around. In short, the inside of the house wasn't much cleaner than the outside. And though I still took off my boots, gloves, and jacket in the mudroom so as to avoid tracking manure into the house, it wouldn't have made much difference if I hadn't.

After a day of chores, school, and more chores, I was so tired at night there was no drifting off to sleep. It was more like falling off a cliff into an abyss.

On the weekends, I spent as much time with Paige and the third person to join our best-friend bond, Jasmine Bailey. Jasmine had deep brown eyes, brown hair, and the energy of fireworks. Like Paige, she was game for anything. Because Paige and I were penned in by chores, we often did them together. Paige's chores were easier, so we three started there, ripping through pen-mucking and feedings as quickly as we could. Once we were done, we'd tear down the road to Clyde's farm, where we'd milk the cows, muck the barns, and feed the calves. There was more to do on my end and it was harder work, so I tried to make it fun for Paige and Jasmine. We created games where we climbed on the bigger calves' backs and rode them around the pen. We'd sit back on their hips and lean over their bodies, our arms wrapped around their luxuriously soft middles as we raced until someone tumbled off. If the calf wasn't big enough, my feet dragged on the ground—I was growing so fast I was already taller than my mother and not that much shorter than Clyde.

Once a week, Sister Price and Sister Elson from the Mormon church stopped by the house. It was their job to check in on everyone in the ward as often as they could. Since Clyde was Mormon, Cookie had decided to pass herself off as Mormon, too. Jack Mormon, it was called, the term for LDS who weren't practicing the church laws of not smoking, drinking, or consuming caffeine.

After supper, the family sat in the living room with the women. They were pretty with big, toothy smiles and voices that sounded like cream and honey. My mother was exceedingly nice when they visited. She'd bring us cookies on a plate, and plastic cups of Hi-C punch. If Clyde was there, she brought milk. Sometimes Cookie snuck outside and smoked while the sisters were there. Or, if it was really cold out, she stood as far away as she could in the kitchen waving her smoke away with one hand.

Norm didn't say much on these visits. He and I both ate as many cookies as we could while they were being offered. I asked questions every now and then about Joseph Smith and what kind of man he was. Did he really talk to Jesus, I wanted to know. Or was it like when I talked to my sisters in my head? Clyde seemed pleased when I asked questions as he always sat up straight and smiled at me or mussed my hair.

I figured it would be pretty easy for me to become a Mormon. I didn't drink. I didn't smoke. I could easily give up Coca-Cola and other caffeinated beverages, and I had no problem believing in Joseph Smith as well as Jesus Christ. Also, since everyone who visited from the church was a woman, I thought then that women were running the Mormon church. After watching my mother move her life here and there according to the men she was after, a place with women in charge seemed good to me.

The more I learned about the Book of Mormon and the more I learned about Joseph Smith and Jesus, the more normal I felt when we started going to the Mormon church every Sunday. With our cleanest clothes on and the dirt picked out from under our nails with tooth-picks, you couldn't tell the difference between Cookie, Clyde, Norm, and me, and the Mann family who lived a few farms over. And though everyone knew my mother was the person who had bewitched Clyde Hapner, people were nice to Cookie at church functions. She, in turn, was the best version of herself. Her New York accent clanged among the voices, but at least the words that came out were gentler and kinder than the words she used at home.

Clyde and Cookie allowed me to go anywhere and do anything that was church related. So there wasn't a rafting trip, a picnic, a hike, a visit to a factory that I didn't go on. The church was like a lifeboat floating just a few feet away from the terrors of my mother. Cookie now freely dispensed her beatings in front of Clyde, who usually left the room as if it was none of his business. Just the idea of a church outing, knowing that something was coming up in the next week or month, made things at home slightly more tolerable.

15

Up to Her Boots

One afternoon in early spring, when we'd been living with Clyde for almost ten months, I came home from school, walked in the house, and halted at the sight before me. My mother was naked, except for a pair of red cowboy boots, galloping in front of naked Clyde. She had one hand back and appeared to be pulling Clyde across the living room by what I thought of at the time as *his thing*. The image was so strange, I didn't know where to put it in my brain, how to see it. It was a puzzle that felt upside down and backward. As soon as I realized this horsey game had something to do with sex, I rushed out of the house to the fields. There I met up with Boone, who was moving the irrigation pipes to water the alfalfa and grain.

Boone was always kind and good to me. He sent me

off early whenever he could so I wouldn't have to work in the dark of night. And he was endlessly patient when he taught me new tasks. I thought that with his enormous mustache and burly body, he should be rough and mean, like my mother. But he wasn't. Ever. And there was never a moment when I was alone with Boone that the engine in my stomach started up. I trusted him completely.

Still, when Boone asked why I seemed so rattled, I didn't tell him what I'd seen. I just picked up a pipe and helped him the best I could. By then I was too old to innocently blurt out things and too young to think I had a right to report the bad behavior of the adults in my life.

On Clyde's property was a trailer that was used for storage. Much of what was in there must have belonged to his ex-wife. My mother went there frequently and rummaged for things that she'd bring into the house. I never knew she could sew until she brought in a sewing machine and immediately began making clothes for herself. Drunk or sober, Cookie moved her hands quickly and fluidly across the fabric, a line of straight pins pinched between her lips with a scowl. She seemed to know what to do without really thinking about it.

Most of the girls in school were sewing miniskirts that year. Mr. Jackson, our principal, had told us that miniskirts weren't proper for good girls and we should not wear them to school. This didn't stop Paige and Jasmine from each making a skirt, and it didn't stop me from asking my mother if she'd sew one for me. That she agreed seemed miraculous. And that the skirt she made actually fit and was beautiful (sharp-lined black corduroy with a side zipper) was even more miraculous. I took Cookie's creation to Paige's house one afternoon and she helped me embellish it with white buttons down the front and white rickrack around the hem and waist. Paige's skirt was striped and looked like it was from a fashion magazine.

Paige, Jasmine, and I, along with five of our friends at school, decided we'd wear the miniskirts on the very same day in spite of Mr. Jackson's request.

Since I was one of the tallest people in my grade, my skirt seemed shorter than the others. My legs were as taut as a horse's, and I felt just as powerful as a horse when I walked down the hall that day. Mr. Jackson followed me into the classroom, stopping near the front door. His angry face had turned the color of an eggplant, and his mouth hung open. I imagined sparklers fizzing out of his eyes. In a firm voice, Mr. Jackson called each of our names and asked us to step into the hall. I shimmied my skirt lower on my hips as I followed Paige, Jasmine, and the others out of the classroom. We stood in a circle, shoulder to shoulder, our bare knees knocking and twitching.

"I am so disappointed in you girls," Mr. Jackson said. "You have made a very poor decision. Very poor indeed." He looked at us, one by one. A flush of shame rushed up to my head and I pushed my knees closer together.

"I have a mind to call each of your parents and tell them about your little shenanigans."

A couple of girls started crying. My lips shook. I turned to Paige and saw her face had turned a splotchy pink. She was probably worried for me, as she knew I got in trouble for the simplest things, like not feeding the chickens in time (I was beat for that, but as far as Paige knew, I was just grounded for it). Paige's dad appreciated her sewing skills and would probably side with his daughter on this.

Jasmine reached for me and squeezed my hand. Now I knew she was worried for me, too, and like Paige, she was aware that I often got in trouble but also had no idea the beatings occurred. Jasmine's mother was in and out of her life, in and out of their house, depending on the month. Her father rarely got angry over anything she did.

"Rosie will get in huge trouble," Paige blurted, and the two of us locked eyes for a second before I dropped my head, suddenly heavy as a bowling ball.

Mr. Jackson didn't speak for a minute. And then he said: "You all have detention every recess this week. And I want a letter of apology by the end of today."

When Mr. Jackson turned and walked away, I almost cried with relief. Once he was out of sight, we eight girls hugged each other over what we saw as a victory. Then we cautiously returned to the classroom.

That first recess detention, I pulled out a thick piece of blue-lined paper and held my pencil over it while I thought through my apology. What I wanted to say was that I was sorry I had disappointed him, but I wasn't sorry I did it. After the possibility of being beaten for my skirt had been eliminated, I felt triumphant. Wearing the skirt, going against the rules, brought to life the me-ness that had been dormant since I was a little girl and my sisters had tried to tend to my every wish. I wasn't just the farm girl who did her chores; I wasn't just the punching bag and repository of all ill thoughts from my mother; and I wasn't just the quiet one who tried to be so still no one would know she was in the room. Inside my obedient shell was the noisy, wanting, loving, happy me. And happy me liked wearing her black corduroy miniskirt with the white buttons and rickrack. Happy me liked having her strong, bare legs exposed. Even when it was forbidden.

My first big crush since David Collins at Caldwell's elementary school library was Davey Stewart. He was about six inches shorter than I was, with brown hair, freckles, and a big, winsome smile. Paige and Jasmine knew I was crushing on him and when we walked down the hall together, they would shift so that I'd suddenly find myself beside him. I'd laugh and hurry to catch up to them.

Mrs. Muse regularly had us correct each other's homework. We always wrote notes to each other on the papers, something fun or funny, to crack each other up. The best note I got was when Davey Stewart had to correct my homework. He put an arrow on the front so that I would turn the paper over. On the back it said, "Rosanne, will you go with me?" *Go with me* was what you asked someone when you wanted them to be your girlfriend or boyfriend. I suppose it was short for *go steady*, but no one ever used those words. Below Davey's question were two boxes. One said *yes* and one said *no*. I put an X in the *yes* box. I took the paper with me when I got up to sharpen my pencil, and I casually let it fall on Davey's desk. He read it quickly, and then he smiled so big I could even see the teeth in the back of his mouth. I picked my homework back up and returned to my desk. I couldn't wait to tell Paige and Jasmine. I was thrilled that I now had a date to my very first Spring Fling.

Spring Fling was the only thing the kids were talking about. When I stopped in at Sheryl's Shop to buy a small jug of bleach, she asked if I had a date to the dance. I blushed and mumbled something about going with my boyfriend; of course she wanted to know who that was. I told her Davey Stewart. She said, "Isn't that sweet! That boy's every bit as cute as you are, Rosie!" Though Sheryl knew the Cookie/Hal/Betsy/Clyde story from every angle, and I assumed Betsy was still her friend, she never blamed me or Norm for any of that. My brother and I always felt as welcome in her store as we were in the church.

I paid Sheryl for the bleach, and she dropped a package of Reese's Peanut Butter Cups in the bag, too, telling me to split it with Norm.

That afternoon, Norm said I could share his toothbrush so I could use my own to dip in bleach and clean my tennis shoes. I scrubbed and scrubbed until those shoes were as white as Clyde's teeth. While my tennis shoes dried, I ironed the only jeans I had that weren't too short and a long-sleeved white shirt I borrowed from Norm. Over the shirt I wore a blue chambray shirt Cookie got me at the thrift store, open and unbuttoned. I thought it was a nice outfit—casual, tidy, and clean.

Davey looked gorgeous that night in his jeans with a red belt and a long-sleeved white shirt with USA in bold red letters on the front. Below that it said CALIFORNIA. I knew where California was on the map: one state over and one down if you went through Oregon. But because I'd never been there, and only knew it from television, it felt even farther than New York—a magical place with beautiful, cool people; beaches; short skirts at school; and summer weather in January. Davey, with that shirt on, seemed like he was actually from California. And I felt like we'd run away there together as we danced through the night.

When Lionel Ritchie's "My Love" played, Davey held my hand while we danced. I'd never held a boy's hand before, and I didn't expect it to feel so good, like warm, electric water streaking across my skin. As soon as the song ended, I wished that we could go back in time and do the dance all over again.

That night I was so excited, I could barely sleep. I lay in bed, Blue on the floor next to my bed (where he'd been sleeping since we moved in), and tried to remember every song that had played. "My Love" had been the highlight, of course. It seemed like I had just fallen asleep when I heard Blue rustling on the ground.

"Go to sleep," I whispered to the dog.

At five a.m., Blue was restless again. I rolled over and looked at the dog. He was sitting up, panting on me.

"What is it?" I looked from the dog to the door, which was ajar even though I always slept with it shut. I got up, pushed the door closed all the way, and then went back to sleep.

A half hour later, my alarm clock, a gift from Clyde when I learned to tell time, went off. The dog was gone and the door was open. I figured Clyde had started the round-up early. I pulled on sweatpants and a sweatshirt, tied my hair back with a scrunchie, and then went to the kitchen, where I brushed my teeth with Norm's toothbrush at the sink.

I was half-dazed, tired, but happy when I stumbled into the milking parlor. The cows had already been herded in, and the first four were waiting on the ramps.

"You have fun last night?" Clyde unhooked one rubber apron, dropped the head tie over my neck and then tied it in the back. I was too off in my head to notice or care that he was tending to me like this.

"Yeah, it was great." Clyde had tied the apron so

loosely it hung like a flapping flag. I untied and retied the sashes in the back.

"Did you behave?"

"Of course I behaved," I said. "I'm eleven."

"Those boys weren't trying to touch you, were they?" Clyde wasn't asking this in the same way as when Cookie accused me of being a slut, so I knew he wasn't angry. He was even smiling. But I didn't understand his tone—I didn't know what he wanted from me. Did he really think I would tell him the private details of my life with my friends at school?

"Of course not," I said. "I have a boyfriend."

"A boyfriend?" Clyde took his apron off the hook and looped it over his head. "Well, you can drive a truck, so I guess you're old enough for a boyfriend."

I started toward the hose when Clyde came up behind me and flipped his apron over me so that I was trapped under it with my back pressed against him and my head coming out the top below his. I struggled but Clyde held me tight in place, both back ties to his apron pulled to one side with his left hand while his right hand roamed beneath my sweatshirt.

"Did your boyfriend touch you like this?" Clyde panted into my ear.

"No!" I jerked from side to side and Clyde jerked with me, pushing harder into my backside. I had a feeling he liked the movement, so I stopped suddenly. And then he let me go.

I ducked out from under his apron, picked up the hose, turned it on, and aimed the spray at the cow. My arms were shaking, and the water hit the cow everywhere from her tail to her nose.

"Steady, steady," Clyde said. He stood behind me and reached for the hose, but I stepped to the side.

"I've got it."

"Direct it on her teats," he said. "Make them pink and shiny."

I wanted to vomit. I wanted to run. I wanted to direct the spray at Clyde. But I didn't. I stood there and finished the job.

An hour and a half later when we were leaving the parlor, Clyde mussed my hair and smiled at me. "You did good today," he said "You're a great worker."

"Whatever." I kept walking.

"Rosie!" Clyde pulled my arm and turned me so I was facing him. "No one needs to know how I teach you your chores. We work well together on the farm. Let's keep it that way. Got it?"

"Yeah." I yanked my arm from him and ran into the house, into the bathroom so I could shower.

As I washed myself, I looked around for any marks. When Cookie hurt me, there was always evidence of it—bumps, bruises, dots of blood where she had held a pinch. I didn't like being hurt, and I didn't like my body taking on new shapes and colors from my mother's hands. But I liked that there was proof as to what had gone down. It was like a statement acknowledging how bad whatever happened had been. But with this, with Clyde, there was nothing to show for it. It was as if the act had vaporized as soon as it was done. I felt unwitnessed. Unreal. Invisible.

That summer, my sister Gi used saved money from her job plus money she got from for high school graduation to buy a round-trip ticket to Idaho. Between sidestepping Clyde, who pinned me from behind in the milking parlor any time Boone wasn't around, and Cookie, who was happy to slam my head into the dashboard or worse, I was desperate for my sister to show up. Every night I prayed that nothing—illness, hurricanes, broken airplanes—would prevent Gi from arriving.

Before Cookie would drive the two hours to Boise to pick up Gi from the airport, I had to clean out and organize the goods that filled her station wagon. The Chrysler, now dead, was lined up with other abandoned, rusted-out cars on the lawn beside the driveway. Recently, my mother had decided she was tired of farm life and was going to open a junk shop. With her New York sophistication and charm, my mother told us, she would lure in customers from all over the state of Idaho. The name of her shop would be Prismatic Fantasies. Just about every day Cookie drove out to other small towns, where she wrote fraudulent checks to pay for anything she thought would be fitting for Prismatic Fantasies: costume jewelry, antique jewelry, clothes both new and vintage, stained glass and other crafty items, display shelves, display tables, rolling racks, and even a working cash register. And she brought home cats, so many cats I didn't know all their names. You couldn't sit anywhere in the house without picking up a layer of the cat hair that clung to every surface as if it were covered in glue.

Paige and Jasmine helped me clean out the car. We examined each trinket we picked up and moved into the trailer where my mother was storing the goods for her store's grand opening.

"Where do you usually sit?" Paige asked. The car was filled so that the only available space was in the driver's seat.

"Sometimes I just sit on the stuff." I remembered when Cookie, Norm, and I lived in The Veg. We might as well have lived in a rolling garbage bin. I wanted to tell my friends about this, just as I wanted to tell them about what Clyde had been doing to me. Instead, I said nothing. Each time a family secret floated up toward my mouth, an imagined metal gate crashed down across my lips, locking it inside me.

Cookie dropped Paige and Jasmine off at the Paisleys' farm before she, Norm, and I headed to Boise to fetch my sister. My mother didn't seem happy or excited. She chain-smoked and talked about what a terrible person Gi was and how lucky Norm and I were that we had gotten away from her.

"A slut from the day she was born," Cookie said. I imagined my sister, probably swaddled in a blanket, definitely unable to hold up her head or talk, on the first day of her life with Cookie already angry at her for being a slut.

In the terminal I noticed Gi before my brother or mother seemed to. She was fit, tan, and had huge hair that looked thick enough to be used as a helmet. I watched her for a second, dazzled by the sight. And then Gi's eyes caught mine.

"*MIA BAMBINA!*" My sister shouted and ran to me. We hugged and I almost couldn't speak because I was so choked up, so happy. We pulled back from the hug, looked at each other, and laughed. Since she saw me last, I'd shot up and was now at least six inches taller than my sister. "You're gorgeous!" Gi said, and she leaned up to kiss me on each of my cheeks.

Next she hugged Norm. "Look how handsome you are!" she said, and Norm's face reddened. "You're like a grown man."

Then, without pause, she hugged Cookie, who grunted and frowned. I sensed that Gi was hugging her for Norm and me. To keep the peace during the visit.

Norm picked up Gi's suitcase, but then I took it from him. I wanted my sister to see how strong I was. She looped her arm into my free arm, and we walked like that to the station wagon with Gi asking my brother and me questions about the farm, our friends, our lives in Idaho. Cookie smoked a cigarette and didn't say a word.

I put the suitcase in the way back and then the three of us got in the backseat, Gi in the middle so that Norm and I both could sit next to her.

"I guess I'm the fucking chauffeur," Cookie said as she got in the driver's seat.

"Thanks for picking me up, Mom," Gi said.

"You owe me twenty bucks for gas." Cookie flicked her cigarette out the window and pulled onto the road.

"What?" my sister asked.

"It's four hours round trip. You owe me twenty bucks for gas." My mother lit a new cigarette.

"I'll help pay." I scooted up between the two seats.

"You don't have any fucking money," Cookie said, and she was right.

"I'll pay, I have money." Gi opened her purse, pulled out a twenty-dollar bill and handed it over the seat to Cookie, who shoved it into her bra. Then my sister put one arm around me and one around Norm and the three of us talked on and on in an excited twitter.

Cookie interjected several times to bring up the extra chores that had to be done that week. The lawn was in need of cutting; the bull pen needed mucking; and we had to pick up groceries for dinner, but we were to let Gi pay since she was about to be a "fancy know-it-all." In the fall, my sister would be going to college. Norm and I were excited for her and proud of her. Cookie's reaction to this news had been exclusively focused on how Gi would think she was too good for us once she had a degree.

"I didn't go to college and I turned out fine!" Cookie had said more than once. Each time she made this claim, I wondered why she considered herself fine. She drank continually, lived with a pervert, beat her daughter, hoarded garbage for her Prismatic Fantasies junk store, collected cats because she liked them better than humans, and of her five children only two spoke to her. And that was because they lived with her and had no choice.

The week with Gi was like a vacation. I still did my chores, but Gi did them with me. The high-wire tension and jangling fear I normally felt in the milking parlor was completely gone when my sister was with me. It was impossible for Clyde to touch me while she was around.

Gi loved learning about the animals, and I was excited to show her everything I knew. We talked nonstop, and nothing could break our happy mood. When Cookie demanded that Gi pay for her food, my sister handed our mother money. When Cookie threw two pairs of scissors at us and told us to cut the lawn with them, we laughed hysterically and then we got out the lawn mower and cut the lawn. And when Cookie refused to let us take two of the three vehicles Cookie and Clyde owned—he had two trucks, she had the station wagon—to the river so we could float down on inner tubes, we ignored her and let Norm take up that fight. My brother, when he put his mind to it, was the only one of us who could ever persuade Cookie to do something she didn't want to do.

Once Norm was able to wrangle the vehicles, we threw three inflated inner tubes into the back of one truck and drove both trucks to the end of the two-hour river ride. That truck would be our ride back to the original starting point, where we left the second truck. Gi loved floating down the river so much that Norm got us the trucks again two days later, and we did it once more. During the calm parts of the ride, my brother, sister, and I clasped hands and floated together like one giant, bobbing structure. Norm and I told stories about floating down Paradise Beach, the sewage-smelling runoff drain in Caldwell: how murky that water was and how much trash was in it. Here, the water smelled as fresh as ice and was foamy white as it crashed across car-sized rocks. In the calm pools, the water was as clear as glass.

Cookie didn't try to beat me while Gi was there. She knew as well as I did that as long as my sister had my bruised body for proof, Gi would call the police. Or the state senator. Or the president, if she could. And she'd keep calling until someone looked at me and listened.

When we drove Gi back to Boise for her flight home, Cookie asked for gas money again.

"I gave you twenty bucks when you picked me up," Gi said.

"She did," Norm said. "I remember." The three of us were huddled in the backseat again.

"No one fucking asked you to come out here and visit," Cookie said. "Pay up."

"Mom, the twenty I already gave you covered both trips," Gi said.

"Pay the fuck up!" Cookie held her open palm out toward the backseat.

Gi pushed her back against the seat so she could be as far from my mother as possible. She reached into her wallet, pulled out a ten, and handed it to Norm, who handed it to Cookie.

"You can send me a check for the rest." Cookie shoved the bill down her cleavage.

Norm sat in the front seat and fiddled with the radio the whole way home. Every now and then he glanced back at me and then turned up the volume. He didn't want Cookie to hear my crying since he knew that was a punishable offense.

I was mopey and sad after Gi left—stuck in a daze. Cookie seemed to thrive on this as the more depressed I was, the more chipper she was. Clyde pretended to care about me, however, and he decided that learning how to drive the tractor would snap me out of my stupor. He brought it up over breakfast.

"Whaddya say?" Clyde nudged me on the shoulder.

"Okay." I was starving and concentrating on my bowl of puffed rice.

Cookie whacked her hand across the back of my head. "A thank-you would be nice. You've been asking him to teach you ever since you started driving that truck!"

I looked up at Clyde and said, "Thanks."

"I wanna see this," Norm said

"Yeah, I wanna see it, too." Cookie got up from the table, shimmied her breasts in front of Clyde's face, and then went to take a shower.

After the morning chores were done, I got on the tractor and Clyde talked me through it. It was easier than the truck, which I'd been driving around the farm regularly. The only new thing I had to learn was that there were two foot brakes on the tractor—one to stop the right-side wheels and one to stop the left. Once I got that down, Clyde thought I should practice by driving in figure eights.

Cookie and Norm came outside to watch. My mother was drinking a Schlitz, and my brother was drinking a Mountain Dew. For a summer day in Oakview, this was high entertainment.

"Where's the popcorn?" I asked, and my brother smiled.

I was feeling a little proud of myself as I maneuvered the tractor in circles around my brother and mother. Clyde thought this was funny and clapped his hands. Norm laughed. Cookie tapped her foot and chugged her beer as if nothing out of the ordinary was going on.

"You're really good at it," Norm said.

"She's a smart girl and a fast learner." After what was now happening in the milking parlor, I could barely listen to Clyde's continuous flattery.

"Let's see you do what you were sent out here to do," my mother said.

I idled beside her. "I was sent out to learn how to drive the tractor."

"No, you were sent out here to shovel that shit into the pit." My mother pointed at the manure piles that had been shoveled and wheel-barrowed around the corral, waiting to be plowed into the pit.

"You can do it, Rosie," Clyde said. "Just lower that plow like I showed you, get under the manure, and scoop."

My mother, Clyde, and Norm followed me to the side of the pit as I plowed the first load. Clyde talked me through it, helping me get the tractor just close enough that the plow pushed the manure in without the tractor going over the edge.

I thought about the poop hole at the Callahans' and how the kids there would have had a great laugh over the size of Clyde's poop hole. Clyde's manure pit could have filled the Callahans' entire backyard—it was like the giant poop-hole yard Norm had predicted.

Everyone was in good spirits as I approached with

the next pile of manure. Cookie lit two cigarettes and handed one to Norm, who had recently started smoking. They looked relaxed and happy as they watched the manure-pit show.

Cookie said, "I hope you enjoy this, 'cause you're gonna be shoveling shit like this the rest of your life!" She hooted a laugh.

My head wasn't with my body thirty minutes later when I plowed the last pile of manure. I was thinking about who I was, who my mother was, and how odd it was that just because you were born from someone, you were then bound to them for life. Even if you didn't like them. Even if you thought the things they did were ridiculous and a waste of time. Even if they were people who were so unlike you, they seemed like aliens from another planet.

And just as I was trying to explain all this to myself in my head, I missed the clutch and the tractor started to roll into the pit. I slammed my foot on the clutch and the brake to stop the slow tumble. The tractor leaned forward, the plow dipping in, the seat riding high in the air. I imagined the pit was like quicksand and everything, including me, would slowly sink down and down and down. Suffocation. Silence. Nothingness. At least I'd get out of having to do any more chores. And

I'd get away from mother's flying fists and feet and Clyde's grabby hands.

Cookie, Clyde, and Norm fell over their knees laughing. I couldn't laugh. I was too scared. I leaned back as far as I could, trying to counterbalance the weight. They continued to laugh; Cookie was coughing for air.

"Help!" I said, and they roared even louder.

Norm ran to me first. And then Clyde. They pushed on the big back wheels while I shifted into reverse.

I had thought that was as close as I'd ever have to get to the manure pit, but unfortunately it wasn't. Norm and I were then given the new chore of walking through the manure wearing knee-high boots and wielding pitchforks to break up any lumps.

My mother, who loved a good scene of suffering when she could catch one, sauntered over to watch my first stomping in the piles. With a cigarette clamped in her teeth, she began taking photos of me in the middle of the pit—isolated and alone—manure up to the tops of my boots.

16
Baling Out

I n October, after my twelfth birthday, I decided I
needed a new hairdo. All the girls had been cutting
bangs, or wings—long bangs that they parted in the
middle and pushed to either side of their faces. Paige
and Jasmine agreed.

After school, we three rushed through Paige's
farm chores so there would be time for Paige—whose
sewing skills made her the presumed master stylist—to
cut my bangs before my chores. Unlike the few times
I hacked Paige's bangs into a zigzag, she cut mine
perfectly straight, with the same precision she used
when sewing. Afterward, we ran to my house where
my friends helped me feed the calves. It was my favorite job and the one I now always did first. Boone
was milking the cows with Clyde so we didn't have to

go into the milking parlor that day. But we still had to feed the bull, the pigs, and the chickens.

Following chores, Paige and Jasmine went home, and I went inside to clean up for dinner. A few of Cookie's cats—there were around thirty of them by then—rushed me in the mudroom as I took off my boots and jacket. I tried not to step on them and steadied myself against the wall as they tripped me up.

I could hear my mother in the kitchen, talking to the cats as she got dinner ready. She used a sticky-sweet voice, treating each cat as if it were a dimwitted child she loved more than anything in world: *Hello Socrates, my little man, my little gray man, my sweet little boy.*

"Set the table," Cookie barked at me.

I got the plates from the drainer and took them to the table. Before I set each plate in its place, I wiped off the floating cat hairs with the sleeve of my shirt pulled over my hand.

I went back to the kitchen and took out the mismatched silverware from the drawer. There was cat hair there, too—it was like dust, floating and entering every surface. I'd even found cat hair in the refrigerator. I wiped all the silverware with my sleeve and then grabbed a handful of paper towels and went to the table where I laid it all out, the paper towels folded into napkins.

I was getting out the milk glasses when Cookie

banged the spoon she was stirring spaghetti sauce with against the side of the pot and then stepped in front of me.

"What the hell happened here?"

"What?" I looked down at my shirt to see if there was something sticking to me.

"Here!" Cookie smacked my forehead with the wooden sauce spoon. I reached up and wiped the sauce away with my wrist. There were two glasses clasped in each of my hands.

"Everyone has bangs now so Paige cut mine." I hurried to the table and put down the glasses.

"Did I give you permission to cut your bangs?!"

"No." I straightened the place settings on the table. My stomach clenched.

"So why did you cut them?"

"I didn't think you'd care."

"You didn't think I'd care? You didn't think I'd care?!" Cookie stepped closer and closer.

I shrugged and stared at my bare feet. "Jasmine's dad didn't care when Paige cut her bangs. Paige's dad doesn't care when I cut her bangs, and I cut them all the time."

"I am not Jasmine's or Paige's dad," she said as she began to tap her foot.

"I know."

"Do you know?"

"Yes." I was still staring at my feet.

"You don't shit, piss, eat, walk, sit, sleep, bleed, or fuck without my permission! Get it?!"

"Yeah." I was mumbling.

"GET IT?"

"Yes." I looked up, made eye contact with my mother, and watched as a cloud of darkness came over her face. The switch was flipped; I knew this wouldn't end until she'd emptied herself.

Cookie grabbed my hair and yanked me straight to the ground. She wasn't wearing shoes, so the kicks she landed in my gut didn't split open my skin the way her spiked or wooden heels could. As I wailed in pain, I tried to send thought-messages to my brother to get home quick. My mother wasn't drunk enough to just peter out—she appeared to have the energy to go on for a very long time.

Thankfully, my brother was going through a growth spurt and was rarely late for a meal. He ran into the kitchen and pulled Cookie off me. She cried onto his shoulder as if she were the one who had been beaten. I stumbled to the bathroom and hung my face over the toilet, my stomach clenching in spasms. I'd barely eaten that day, so there was nothing to throw up. I didn't spend too much time in the bathroom. Dinner was ready. Cookie might go at me again if I was late.

My sentence was given that night with Norm and Clyde at the table: I had to do Cookie's and Norm's chores until my bangs grew out. My brother stared down at his plate. He reached his leg under the table and tapped me on the shin. Even though he was about to get out of chores, Norm felt bad for me. We both knew that there was nothing my brother could do about this. Anytime he argued on my behalf, Cookie made it twice as bad for me. She'd bullied us both into submission.

"Never a day off for a farmer," I said quietly, echoing Clyde's words.

"That's the spirit," Clyde said, and he mussed my hair.

I had no idea what Cookie's farm chores were, as I rarely saw her outside. But as far as I was concerned, there were only three farmers sitting at the table. And as of that night, just two of them never got the day off.

The following April, our second spring with Clyde, brought harder days and nights than I'd ever known. Now that I could drive a tractor, I was expected to participate in the extra work required during hay season, which happened every spring and summer. The morning routine was the same; I did my chores and then hurried off to school. After school, on top of my evening chores, I had to cut hay and then, later in the night, bale it. The fields were spread across Clyde's eighty acres, and there were more fields on the isolated forty-acre plot he leased from a farm a few minutes' drive down the road—the place where I'd learned to drive the truck. I liked working on the leased land, away from my mother, who couldn't wander out, stand in a field, and watch me with her craggy scowl and her burning cigarettes. I was far from Clyde, too—relieved of the continuous current of fear I felt when we were alone together. This was solitary work, as only one person at a time was needed to operate the tractor that pushed the machines used during hay season.

Cutting hay was done in the day with a swather. The swather was a wide, rotating, bladed bar in front of the tractor. Sitting on the tractor with the sun beating down on me, I felt a calm connection to the landscape. I drove in hypnotic rows of tight circles slicing down the hay. Each circle of cut hay stayed where it was to dry in the sun for a day or more, depending on the weather.

After swathing for a couple of hours, I went home, ate as much as I could of whatever supper was on the counter, and then went to bed. The sun was usually still up, but I was so exhausted, all I had to do was close my eyes and I was asleep. Around nine or nine thirty that same evening, I'd wake up—summoned either by Clyde or my alarm. When the alarm went off, I might lay still for a few more minutes, listening to the beep-beep-beep until I couldn't take it anymore. When it came to Clyde, however, my body was on full alert. He only had to crack my door to make me sit up, wide awake. I'd pull on my boots, grab a Mountain Dew and a bag of sunflower seeds from the kitchen, and then drive a truck to whichever field had dry, cut hay. This was Clyde's time to sleep. Cookie's time to sleep. And Norm's time to sleep, too, because my mother decided that as a growing sixteen-year-old boy he needed more sleep than I did as a twelve-year-old girl.

With no streetlights, the sky was like black velvet, and the stars were vibrating flicks of diamond. I looked up with amazement, never tiring of the sight. The baler—a boxy metal machine on the front of a tractor— sat like a sleeping creature alone in the wide field. It roared awake when I started it, a grumbling metal monster, but my metal monster. I brought a Walkman with me when I baled and always put in a tape I could sing along to: Madonna, or Cyndi Lauper, or even the Eurythmics. I sang loudly, shouting out the lyrics like a rock star. There was only me and the audience of stars above my head as I drove the baler over each circle of dry hay. The machine sucked up the hay like a vacuum. Moments later it turned what it had inhaled into a bound, compact, perfectly shaped rectangle that it spit out. My monster: sucking and spitting, sucking and spitting, while I sang, drank Mountain Dew, and used my front teeth to crack open sunflower seeds.

Around midnight or one in the morning, Clyde would drive out and relieve me. He then stayed outside baling until three or four in the morning. Work stopped when the dew started to settle, as dewy hay could mold if it was baled. And mold killed the hearty protein-packed flower ends that the cows thrived on.

No matter what time I finished baling—and there were nights when I was left out there until three in the morning—I still had to get up at five thirty for chores. School was difficult those two or so weeks of hay season. I fell asleep in most classes. But the teachers understood. Many kids lived on a farm. And there were a couple of other seventh graders who had to help their families during hay season, too. The difference between them and me, however, was that they usually stayed home from school those two weeks so they could sleep during the day. In truth, I wouldn't have stayed home even if I'd been allowed to. I'd rather have sat dizzy-eyed through a math class, my brain as soft as cotton, than sleep at home with Clyde and Cookie lurking around.

The bales were picked up a few days later in daylight. That's when Norm joined the party. While Clyde drove the fields in a flat-bed truck, Norm and I picked up each bale and bucked it onto the bed. The bigger the circle that had been cut, the bigger the bale. They ranged in weight from forty-five to sixty pounds. With my knees bent for propulsion, I was able to buck any size bale straight up onto the truck, side by side with my brother.

Sometimes during hay season, when I was finally going to bed, I feared I'd actually die from exhaustion. My heart might simply say *enough,* and that would be the end.

One night when I came in from baling hay, I ran into Cookie in the hallway outside the bathroom. I stumbled into the wall right in front of her.

"What's your problem?" she asked.

"I'm dying from exhaustion." I went into the bathroom to brush my teeth. My mother came in while I was still brushing and stood behind me. My body, which usually tensed up when Cookie was within arm's reach, was too tired to respond. Still, I took note of what was around me. She could smash my face into the sink. That would hurt. She could smash my face into the medicine cabinet mirror. That would hurt, too, and might cause more damage if the glass broke. She could grab my hair at the nape of my neck and throw me down to the linoleum floor. That would probably be the least painful option. But Cookie didn't do any of those things. Instead, she shook a pill bottle, like a little maraca, in my ear. I looked at her in the mirror. She smiled.

"For you." My mother had recently begun having ailments that were only evident to her and the doctor a few towns away who she convinced to write her regular prescriptions for what I later learned were Percocet, Quaaludes, and Valium that she combined into brain- and body-numbing cocktails. I didn't really mind, as it made her more mellow and relaxed than alcohol.

"What are they?" I took the bottle from her hand.

"Pills." Cookie smiled. It was a tight smile. A needling smile. It conveyed no joy. "In case you want to end it all."

I didn't know if I was being set up for something, or if she was serious. "You mean kill myself?" I opened the bottle and looked in. The pills were different sizes and colors. It was the sample platter.

"Yeah. Don't fucking sit around and complain about

how tired you are. Do something. Go for the eternal sleep!" Cookie laughed.

I took the pills and left the bathroom. There was an old dresser next to my bed. I put the pills there, right near my head, where I could see them when I lay down. That night, as I was plummeting into sleep, I considered what my mother had said. With my body worked into a rubbery exhaustion and my mind mushed from no rest, it didn't seem like such a bad idea to go into an eternal sleep. It would be a relief to get away from Cookie and her rages, from Clyde and his bow-legged body pressing against me in the milking parlor, from manure up to my knees, from cat hair on every part of my body and all my clothes.

But when I looked outside of all that, outside of life on the farm, I saw school, friends, my brother, the church. And I saw my sisters, whose voices were always in my head. How could I ever disappoint them by checking out before I'd even checked into the future they had hoped for me?

I knew if could do all the work and tolerate Cookie's beatings for one day, then I could do it for another day. And if I could do it another day, I could do it another week. And if I could do it another week, I could do it another year. And if I could do it another year, I could do it until I graduated from high school.

And then: freedom!

The pills were left next to my bed. I stared them down every night. And every night I made the same decision.

The morning after Cookie gave me the pills, she told me she was picking me up after school at 2:45.

"Why?" I asked.

"You have an appointment." My mother tapped out her ash onto the floor.

"Where?"

"For fucksakes, Rosanne, be standing outside at two forty-five. You'll know where we're going when we get there."

At two forty-five, I was standing outside waiting for my mother. It was hot out, so I pulled off my sweatshirt and tied it around my waist. Cookie pulled up around three, banging the station wagon into the curb. Her eyes were pulled shut from the bottom lids up, like a lizard's eyes. I wondered how she could see.

"Get in." She was as loaded as I'd ever seen her.

"Do you want me to drive?" I figured a station wagon couldn't be any harder than a truck or a tractor.

"Getinthefuckingcar." Cookie was so drunk she couldn't separate her lips enough to separate her words.

The station wagon lurched and stopped so many

times, my stomach was rolling when we pulled into the parking lot of the doctor's office.

"Why are we here?"

"You're just like your pathetic sisters." My mother got out of the car, leaving the door open behind her. I leaned across the seat, shut her door, removed the keys, and then got out of the car.

The nurse looked nervously at my mother, who was weaving across the reception room. She quickly ushered us into the exam room. I sat on the crunchy paper-covered exam bed, and Cookie dropped into the chair at my feet. I was still nauseous from the ride, or maybe it was the anxiety of being in public with Cookie when she wasn't pretending to be a good Mormon.

Dr. Phillips came in smiling. He put his hand out to shake Cookie's, but she didn't seem to notice, and he quickly pulled it away.

"How are you ladies?" he asked.

"I'm fine," Cookie said. "She's a slut."

The word was like a punch to my gut. I felt myself contracting inward with a howling embarrassment.

"Pardon?" He looked at my mother, and so did I. Cookie stood.

"She's been slutting around and we need to get her on the pill." My mother pointed to my crotch as if that would better illustrate her point. I wanted to shrink up so tightly I'd transform into a black hole and simply vanish.

The doctor turned to me; his wrinkled face had a cast of pink. He nervously twitched his lips before he spoke. "How old are you now?"

"Twelve," I said quietly.

"Are you having intercourse?"

"No. I haven't even kissed a boy." I barely had the breath to speak.

"She's a liar!" Cookie said. "Look at her! Look what she's wearing!"

"It's a tank top," I said. "Everyone's wearing them."

"Of course," Dr. Phillips said.

"She's a slut and she needs to go on the pill. I don't want any little babies getting dumped off on me to raise!"

"Are you planning on having intercourse?" Dr. Phillips asked.

"No. Well, when I'm married, I guess." I stared at my knees.

"She's lying! Look at her. Look down there! Can't you see by looking at her pussy that she's been slutting around?" Cookie pointed at my crotch again.

The doctor swallowed, and the walnut of his Adam's

apple shifted up and down. "It would be unorthodox and wrong for me to do what you are asking. I think we're just going to have to trust her."

I wanted to weep with gratitude. Instead, I continued to focus on my knees, my eyes darting up every now and then to Dr. Phillip's kind, wrinkled face.

"Trust her?" my mother said. "You can't trust her!" And then Cookie veered into single-sentence blather and said, "This girlsalyingslutlikehersisters! Whores! Every single fucking oneofthem! I'm not leavingthisfuckingoffice until you do somethingabouther! Anything! We've gotta stopherfromsluttingandwhoring!"

The doctor paused for a moment, as if he were translating in his head and then he said, "We'll just put her on the pill as a precaution then." He turned to me and said, "And it will prevent you from getting acne. So you can think of it as skin medicine, okay?"

"Okay." I smiled. I could tell Paige and Jasmine it was skin medicine, too.

My last night of baling that spring, I woke up at nine to a silent house. It was Friday and Norm had gone out to a party around the time I'd gone down for my nap. I went into the living room and saw Cookie snoring, passed out on the couch. There was only a single beer can on the coffee table, so she must have been knocked out on pills. Clyde was probably sleeping. He'd told me earlier that he'd relieve me at midnight.

I threw on my boots, grabbed a Mountain Dew and sunflower seeds, then got in the truck and drove out to the field where I climbed onto the baler. By the third round of Madonna's "Lucky Star," I was too tired to really belt it out. I stopped for a minute and looked up at the sky. It was less velvety and less twinkly than it had been all week. Maybe there was some cloud cover. Tonight, the sky looked like a thick black cape with tiny pinholes letting in light from the other side. Ahead of me the field was eerie and beautiful with the tractor headlights on it—a giant, golden wedge, flat and shimmering.

I flipped over the Madonna cassette to the B side, hit *play*, and then stepped on the gas to bale another circle of cut hay.

Rather than dreading an interaction with Clyde, I felt pure happiness when I saw the bouncing headlights of his truck heading toward me earlier than scheduled. In less than ten minutes I would be asleep in my bed.

I cut the engine, turned off my Walkman, climbed down out of the tractor, and crunched across the dry hay stubs toward the truck I'd driven out. Clyde pulled his truck up right in front of me, blinding me with his headlights. I put my arm up over my eyes and waited for him to cut the lights and engine, which he finally did.

"Keys are in the ignition," I said when he walked toward me. I turned to leave, but Clyde stepped in front of me and grabbed each of my shoulders.

"I told you the keys are in the ignition." I shook my shoulders to get his hands off me and dropped the Walkman.

"Lie down." Clyde grabbed my shoulders again.

"What?" My heart revved up.

"Take off your sweatpants and lie down." Clyde's fingers pressed into my shoulders like clamps; he was pushing me toward the ground, but I pushed back even harder.

"No!" My stomach revved up too.

"NOW." Clyde moved one hand to the back of my neck and grabbed my hair, the way my mother usually did. He pulled me down until I lay on the pointed hay bits.

I turned my head and looked at the fallen Walkman. I didn't remove my sweatpants.

Clyde kneeled his bow-legged body down at my feet and tugged my sweatpants to my ankles. My legs were pinned together, as straight as an ironing board.

"You're a beautiful girl. Nothing like your mom." Clyde worked my underwear down to my knees.

I shut my eyes and pretended that I wasn't in my body. Whatever was happening on the hard, crisp ground was separate from the me that was *me*.

Clyde put his mouth in a place that I never knew men put their mouths. After the drive across the country, Norm and I had seen my mother put her head down there on men many times. But I didn't know that men bowed over women like that, too. "Does that feel good?"

I didn't answer. I didn't think about if it felt good or not. *I* wasn't there. Instead, I was at the Happy House. I was with Cherie, Camille, Gi, and Norm. We were picnicking under the willow tree. We were eating fresh, cool watermelon. We were listening to Madonna sing about lucky stars. And we were laughing.

I didn't know what made this thing Clyde was doing "over" or "done," but at some point Clyde had finished, for he sat up and flashed his paint-white teeth at me. I pulled up my underwear and sweatpants, picked up the Walkman and hurried to the truck. Clyde was saying something behind me, but my head was so crowded with revulsion and confusion that I couldn't hear his words. It was only a jangled buzzing that was coming out of his mouth. I started the truck and drove off so fast the Walkman bounced off the seat and landed in my footwell. I remembered Clyde telling me once to make sure nothing was in the driver's side footwell because if it got caught under the brake and you couldn't press down the pedal, you'd easily crash. Just then, driving back to the house, I hoped the Walkman was sitting under the brake. I hoped I'd end up driving straight into the house, crashing through the mudroom and into the cat-hair-covered living room. Clyde would know what had gone down during my final minutes alive. My mother probably wouldn't even wonder.

My real return home had no drama. I parked the truck in front of the house, then reached down below me and picked up the Walkman.

Blue was waiting on the porch. He followed me into the house where I found my mother still passed out on the couch, her mouth hanging open as if she were playing the grape-catching game. I took Blue into my room and called him up onto my bed. With my face buried into his thick, soft fur I released a deep, stuttering cry.

"At least it's over," I said to Blue. There was an idea in my head that Clyde would never try that again, that what had just happened was the worst that could happen.

I was wrong. That moment on the hay field was only the opening night in a long-running performance.

When Clyde wasn't committing these acts, we both did an excellent job of pretending things were normal. At home I was on high alert at all times, my body tensed and ready to run even if I was just sitting on the couch doing homework.

Clyde tried to keep things smooth between us with a mind warp of compliments and flattery. He must have sensed that of everything I needed at that time in my life, at twelve years old, recognition was near the top of the list. And so I accepted his praise while fighting against the things he did that were so vile I had to mentally remove myself until I felt invisible. This created a world where I was both seen and unseen. Built up and destroyed. Myself, the hard-working girl who liked to be told she was pretty and strong. And not myself, the girl lying on the field in the dark of night or the glare of day—whenever and wherever Clyde could trap me alone. The only place where I felt whole and complete was with my friends at school.

To keep me quiet, Clyde told me that if I revealed this secret to anyone, things would be worse: He'd incite my mother to beat me for imaginary crimes; he'd give me even more chores to do each day; he'd double his efforts to get me alone.

I didn't consider running away. In a town of 360 people there was no place to run where I wouldn't be found. Two high school kids had shot themselves dead the past year. Even though I didn't know those kids, I thought about them from time to time. I figured we had something in common. They too knew that running away wasn't an option.

Like all the other injustices in my life, this one I bore as well as I could. And I prayed for my sisters to find me. To save me. To take me home to them.

17
Ditched

Two wonderful things happened in the fall of eighth grade. The first was that I joined the cheerleading team and had the great joys of practice and games to keep me away from the house. The second was that my sister Cherie bought a ticket to Idaho.

Like an Advent calendar in my head, I counted down the nights until Cherie's visit and prayed every morning that nothing would prevent her from showing up.

When the day finally came, I went with Cookie for the two-hour drive to the airport in Boise. Cookie bitched and complained the whole drive. The arrival of Cherie brought up old grievances I hadn't heard since Gi's visit: we kids had destroyed her body, sucked her dry, ruined her life, taken all the good she had in life and *turned it to shit*. I barely listened. My head was singing, bubbling, overflowing with the anticipatory joy of seeing one of my sisters.

Cookie parked the car and we waited together at the gate. I was worried I wouldn't recognize my sister, or that she wouldn't recognize me. But as soon as she stepped out, I knew it was Cherie. Her brown hair was long and shiny, her eyes were scrunched up into bright stars, and she was smiling at me like there was nothing in the world that could make her happier than just seeing me.

Cookie grabbed my sister first and gave her a firm hug. Cherie looked past Cookie's shoulder and winked at me. When my mother released her, Cherie came to me and hugged me so hard I felt like we were merging into a single person, a single heartbeat. Just like when I saw Gi for the first time in several years, seeing Cherie stunned me into silence. But even if I could have spoken, I wouldn't have been able to articulate what I was feeling: this connection and feeling of love was so true and pure, it sustained me.

The drive home was easier than the drive there. My mother was unusually sweet. A rare family showing of the Cookie who showed up at church on Sunday, or the Cookie who sat in the living room with Sister Elson and Sister Price each week.

In spite of her civility and cheer, it amazed me that my mother didn't ask a single question about any of her daughters. Cherie told us everyone's news, however. Camille, now married, was a doting mother who loved caring for her family. Cherie herself was no longer with her husband but had loads of wonderful friends, was working at a deli, and loved her coworkers. And Gi was doing great in college. I felt so proud of my sisters. When I grew up, I wanted to be like each one of them, and like my brother, Norm, too. I'd have Gi's brains and ambition, Camille's cheerfulness and good spirit, Cherie's determination and grit, and Norm's ability to let the bad things blow away like insignificant dust. From my mother, I'd take nothing. Not her drinking and pill-popping, not her violent streak, not her devotion to unworthy men, not her thieving and hoarding, not her selfishness and self-centeredness. The creation of her five children was her greatest act in life. And those children alone, the fact that we were alive, was all I'd take from her.

Cherie helped me with the morning and evening chores every day of her visit. Just as it had been with Gi, nothing felt difficult with my sister by my side. Cookie quickly slipped back into her angry self, and eventually she was more bold than she'd been when Gi was here. Still, Cherie wouldn't let her touch me. Each time Cookie lunged for me, or grabbed my hair, Cherie pulled Cookie's hands off me and stood in the way. As loud as Cookie shouted, Cherie went louder, stronger, more fierce. It was like having a lion by my side. And whatever words came out of Cookie's mouth, Cherie doubled them, upped them. My oldest sister had no problem saying *fuck you* to my mother. Her courage amazed me.

The day before Cherie was scheduled to leave, Cookie decided she needed to go to Oregon, where she liked to grocery-shop tax-free.

Cookie was standing in the kitchen gathering her purse, cigarettes, matches, and a bottle of something she pulled out from the back of the bottom cupboard when she said, "I'm going down below."

Cherie and I were eating breakfast before we went out for morning chores.

"Below what?" Cherie asked, and I laughed.

"It means going to Oregon," I said. "That's what people say out here."

"You're driving to Oregon today?!" Cherie said, and I hoped her surprise wouldn't make Cookie change her mind.

"This isn't New York," Cookie said. "You can drive

for hours, drunk off your ass while smoking cigarettes and steering with your knees to give your legs a break, and still you won't hit shit out here."

Cherie laughed. And then she said, "All right, Mom, be safe and don't kill anyone on the road."

This was the gentlest interaction they'd had in about three days.

After finishing the morning chores, Cherie suggested that we clean the house. It bothered my sister that we lived like squatters in a place so filthy you'd expect to find graffiti on the walls. We turned on Top 40 radio as loud as it would go and started cleaning. First, with a dust pan and a trowel from the garden, we scooped up the cat droppings that had been ignored for so long there were piles that had turned white and chalky with age. Next was the cat urine. I had grown used to the smell as it was a constant, but Cherie said there was not a room, including the bedrooms, that didn't have the sharp, ammonia edge of spraying and pissing cats. On our hands and knees we scrubbed the floors in the kitchen, dining area, and mudroom, and the carpet in the rest of the house with the exception of Cookie and Clyde's room. Neither of us would open the door to that room.

We used Comet and scouring pads on the walls

to get off the crusted food from when Cookie threw dinner, the grease from cooking, and cigarette smoke. I had forgotten that the walls had been white when we moved in. They'd changed to the color of a wet tea bag.

We cleaned the bathroom, and we organized the mudroom as well as Cookie's papers and sewing projects she left scattered around the house. As a final act, we went fly-hunting, chasing down as many as we could with a flyswatter in my hand and a spatula in Cherie's.

When we were done, my sister and I sat at the table and admired our hard work. The house smelled like lemons. It actually looked like a home where people might be happy. "If Mom could stop beating on you, it might not be that bad living here."

"Yeah, but there's still Clyde." I looked at the table. My face was burning.

"What's he doing?" Cherie put her hand on my wrist until I looked up at her.

"You know." I shrugged.

"Where? When?" Cherie's eyes were like fire. She had Cookie's rage in her, but it wasn't directed at me. And it wasn't for no reason.

"He touches me in the milking parlor when Boone isn't around. And when he can get me alone in a field . . ." I was mumbling.

"The fuck?!" Cherie pulled her hand away, looked

toward the door, and then looked back at me. She was blinking hard. Her eyes were watery. "The fuck!"

"Sorry," I said.

"What?! Don't say sorry! This isn't your fault, you did nothing wrong! It's *him*." My sister was shaking her head like she was saying *no, no, no* as she thought about something. "Do you have your period already?"

"Yeah. Why? Shouldn't I?"

"I don't want you to get pregnant and have to suffer."

"He doesn't do *that*," I whispered. "He told me it's not a bad thing he's doing because he doesn't do *that*."

Cherie just stared at me, her mouth half open as if she didn't get what I was saying. I leaned closer to my sister's face and whispered to her the terrible and strange thing Clyde did to me—it was always the same—the act he'd done that first night in the field.

"Does Cookie know?!"

"Clyde said he'd tell her I was lying if I told, and he'd make sure she beat me bad."

My sister's face was electric with rage. "These people make me sick!"

"Me, too," I said.

"I've gotta get you outta here." Cherie leaned over and hugged me. "And I will. I promise."

I blinked and tears released from my eyes. And then Clyde came into the house. He stood in the middle of the living area and turned a slow circle. I dropped my head so he couldn't see my tears.

"I'll be damned," he said. "Looks like a different house."

"It is a different house." Cherie's voice was sharp and cold, but Clyde didn't seem to notice.

"Not sure Cookie's gonna like this." Clyde laughed and went to the kitchen, where he poured himself a glass of milk. When he finished his milk, he walked out. My sister lifted both her middle fingers and slapped them back and forth in the air toward Clyde's back. I covered my mouth and laughed as I cried.

Cookie came home a few minutes later, a bag of groceries in each of her arms. "Help me get this shit outta the car," she barked.

Cherie and I fetched bags from the station wagon. When we came back in the house, Cookie was standing in the kitchen looking around.

"What the fuck happened here?" she asked.

"We cleaned up," Cherie said. "Look on the ground: no cat shit!" Cherie walked back out to the car and I followed her.

We came in with the next round of bags.

"Where are my papers that were here?" Cookie pointed to a spot on the counter.

"Here!" I showed my mother where I'd stacked her

papers on top of the side table against the wall near the dining table.

"Where's the dress I was sewing?" Cookie asked.

"Here." Again, at the side table, I showed my mother where I'd put her fabric, needles, threads—all her notions neatly organized next to the sewing machine, which was in its case. I followed Cherie out to the car again.

Cookie's face was hard as a stone when we came in with the last bags of groceries.

"Who the fuck did this?" Cookie pointed to a whip-thin grease and tobacco streak on the wall.

"We cleaned the walls," Cherie said. "That's a spot we missed."

"Well, no one would notice it if you hadn't cleaned the fucking wall!" Cookie charged toward me and Cherie stepped out, blocking me from her.

"Outta the way!" Cookie pushed at Cherie, but Cherie pushed back. "OUTTA THE FUCKING WAY!" my mother yelled.

Cherie wouldn't move. It seemed Cookie had met her match. Cherie cocked back her fist and was ready to go. They screamed at each other, and then the punching and kicking began. Each one got louder than the other as they fought. Cookie went to the usual places with her insults and names. She called Cherie a *whore, cunt,* and a *twat.* She said that every single one of her daughters was an *ungrateful whoring bitch* who just wanted to *steal her beauty and steal her men.*

Cherie shouted about Cookie being a terrible mother, abusive, mean, unloving. And then she said, "And you're fucking evil, Mom, to let Clyde do what he's doing to Rosie!"

"WHAT?!" Cookie stopped punching at Cherie and stood facing her, panting. "What is that lying little bitch saying he's doing to her? Because all I fucking see him doing is give her a roof over her head and food in her big, lying hole of a mouth." It was a dare. My mother was daring my sister to say it aloud.

Cherie's lips were trembling. She was crying but still upright and strong as she spoke. "You know exactly what Clyde's doing. You are a terrible, sick woman who oughta be in jail."

I could see both Cherie's and my mother's chests rising and falling as they gulped for air.

And then Cookie said, "I'm going to fucking kill you," and she lunged at my sister.

Cherie ran. And I ran, too. I grabbed my sister's hand so she would run where I led her. My mother was right behind us, screaming, "I'm going to fucking kill you two!" We dropped hands and ran faster.

I looked behind me to see Cookie galumphing back

to the station wagon. Cherie and I both stopped running and watched as our mother got in the car and started it up.

"She's not—" Cherie started, and then we turned and ran as the station wagon came barreling toward us. It seemed our mother had every intention of actually running us over.

With the car gunning behind, Cherie and I cut off the driveway and into the field. Cookie accelerated and drove after us, straight across the rutted earth. She was leaning out the open window hollering, "*I WILL FUCKING KILL YOU.*" I was screaming and so was Cherie. We raced side by side, our feet hitting the ground in tandem. If our mother was going to hit us, she was going to hit us as one.

We ran straight toward a barbed-wire fence that enclosed one of the pastures. It was an electric fence of three strands of wire running between posts that Norm and I had planted in the ground the previous summer. The electricity had been broken for months, but there was no need to fix it as the cows had already been trained from whatever little zaps they'd received when it did work. I lifted a loose wire between two posts and my sister slipped under. Then I crawled under, too. And we kept running.

I almost tripped when I looked back to see the station wagon crashing through the fence, dragging the loose posts for a few yards. The fencing around the car slowed the station wagon, and Cherie and I gained some distance as we approached a ditch that ran across the property. The ditch was about four feet wide. I knew I could leap it and hoped my sister could, too. Paige, Jasmine, and I often flew across the ditch, our feet pointed in an attempt at grace.

The station wagon suddenly zoomed in closer, the fence now left behind. I could feel the heat of the engine.

"Jump!" I yelled. Cherie leapt just behind me. We both fell to the ground as we landed, then hurried upright and started running again but stopped at the screeching sound of a crash. My mother's station wagon had nose-dived into the ditch.

"Shit," my sister said. We jogged back a few feet to make sure our mother was still alive. When the door of the nose-down station wagon opened, Cherie yelled, "Run!"

We took off again, finally stopping when we reached one of the barns. My sister and I both collapsed over our knees, gasping for air. Cherie sat down first, her back against the outside of the barn. I sat beside her. We were facing the house in the distance. Cherie wrapped her arm around me, and I could feel her whole body shaking. I turned in toward my sister, my head against her shoulder, and realized I was shaking, too. Cherie and I looked at each other and then we started sobbing.

As painful as it was to have had to outrun our mother, who wanted to kill us with her station wagon, there was a sweetness to this moment simply because I wasn't going through it alone.

Cherie and I sat outside the barn for hours. From our vantage point we saw Clyde help Cookie into the house. We saw Norm come home and go out again. And then we saw Clyde walking across the field carrying Cherie's suitcase. He dropped it in the dirt in front of us. My sister and I both stood.

"I think it's better if you two don't sleep in the house tonight," Clyde said.

"You touch my sister again and I'll make sure you end up in prison."

Clyde turned and walked away as if Cherie hadn't even spoken. I wanted to run after him, leap on his back, and start kicking and punching. I knew if I did that, Cherie would jump on, too. She'd have no problem taking on Clyde. But once she was gone, I'd have to face Cookie and Clyde alone. The attack would be turned on me, multiplied, amped up, and I would end up the loser.

"*YOU'RE A FUCKING PERVERT!*" Cherie yelled

after Clyde. I could tell by the stiff way he ambled back to the house that she made him nervous. I wanted to clap my hands and cheer.

My sister was a superhero.

Cherie and I took turns carrying the suitcase, which had no wheels or pull bar. I was used to carrying two fifteen-pound jugs of water, so I could easily manage her bag.

We walked to the only hotel in town. Once we were in our room, Cherie closed the drapes and I double-locked the door: bolt, bar. There was one bed in the room, and we got in it together and turned on the TV. Within minutes, after our bodies eased into the comfort and safety of the room, we were relaxed enough to have fun. Like it had been all week while mucking stalls, milking cows, and scrubbing grime, the joy in being together was irrepressible. It wasn't long before we laughed ourselves to sleep.

There was a knock on the door the next morning. I put my eye to the peep hole and saw Norm's face, warped as if I were looking at his reflection in the back of a spoon.

"Mom with you?" I asked.

"She's in the car. Open up!"

I opened the door, and Norm came in. Cherie was still in bed, the covers up to her neck.

"NORM!" My sister shouted, and she patted the bed so he'd come and sit beside her. Norm was a little bashful with my sister's affections, but he went to the bed anyway and slouched down beside her as she sat up.

"You missed a good show last night," Cherie said.

"I heard." Norm was grinning.

"Mom out there waiting for us?" I asked.

"She said she's done fighting and just wants to get Cherie to the airport." Norm got off the bed, opened the curtain, and looked out the window. "You better hurry."

I hated that my sister had to leave, but I knew there was no choice.

When we walked out of the hotel, Cherie and I were both surprised to see Cookie in the station wagon.

"I can't believe it's still running," Cherie said.

"Clyde and I towed it out," Norm said, and he got in the backseat.

Cherie scooted in beside Norm, and I sat on the other side of Cherie. Cookie tilted the rearview mirror and looked back at us. She opened her mouth as if to speak, then retilted the mirror into place, lit up a cigarette, and pulled away from the curb.

My mother smoked almost a pack of Virginia Slims on the two-hour drive. No one said a word, but Cherie held my hand and squeezed it from time to time as if she were giving me messages in code.

At the airport, when she hugged me good-bye, my sister whispered in my ear, "I'm gonna get you out of here. I promise."

18
Light Extinguished

After Cherie's report, Gi was even more worried about me than she'd been before. She started sending me letters at Paige's house where Cookie couldn't intercept them. Often, Gi put money in the letters with the instruction that I was to spend it only on myself, on something that made me happy.

Early that winter, Gi was finally able to locate a social worker in the county and convince him that he needed to look in on me. His name was Mr. Petant, Gi told me in a letter, and soon he would figure out everything and get me away from Cookie and Clyde. Following that letter, when I said my prayers at church, I always added a little prayer for Mr. Petant. I prayed that he would be strong in the face of my mother and Clyde, that he would be able to see the truth, and that he would do what was best for me. Waiting for him was like waiting for an archangel to descend. I believed in him. And I believed he'd save me.

Finally, one winter day I came into the house after school before I did my chores and found a man in khaki pants and a button-down shirt sitting on the couch talking to Cookie. They each had a cup of coffee, and there was a plate of lemon cookies on the coffee table. My mother was smiling and using her gentlest church voice. Her legs were crossed but she'd gained so much weight that her top leg didn't hang down, rather it stuck out at an angle as if she were in the middle of doing a kick.

"Rosanne, this is Mr. Petant." My mother waggled her red-tipped fingers toward me, as if asking me to sit down beside her.

"How are you?" Mr. Petant looked nothing like the archangel I had imagined him to be. He had eyes duller than old coins, and his face was pink and shiny. He reminded me of a fish. A dead fish.

"Fine." I sat where my mother directed me.

"Seems your crazy sister's drinking again and she's gone off her meds." Cookie looked at me, her eyes zinging the message that I needed to stick with her story.

"Oh," I said quietly.

"Rosie, are Clyde and your mother abusing you?"

Mr. Petant was looking at his notepad as he asked this. My mother rested her hand on my thigh. Her fingers were tense, alert, as if she was about to use her claws to scrape bloody stripes into my leg.

"No." Of course I wanted to say yes. But when I was that close to my mother, with her hand on my flesh, there was a terror, a threat, that was too powerful for me to fight against.

"No?" He looked up from the notebook. "No one's beating you or touching you in inappropriate ways?"

I felt the pressure from my mother's nails in my thigh. "No," I said.

Cookie put her arm around me, hugged me, and kissed the top of my head. "Of course not," she said.

"I'm sorry to bother you," Mr. Petant said. "We just have to look into it when we get a call like this."

"Oh, I understand," Cookie said. "And I'm sure you understand, too. Regina's so messed up on drugs and alcohol—and she's mentally ill! We couldn't have her livin' with us."

My body felt thick and heavy. The conversation between my mother and Mr. Petant sounded far away, as if they were on a shore and I was listening to them from underwater. Everything sounded bubbly, muted, buzzing. Inside I was screaming, punching, fighting against the weight of that water.

Mr. Petant stood, and Cookie walked him to the door. A little fire inside me flickered and I got up and ran to the door. If I could be alone with him for just one minute, I could pull up the courage to say aloud, to this complete stranger—a grown-up man!—what Clyde and my mother were doing to me.

"I'll walk you to your car," I said.

"Of course," Cookie said. "We'll both walk you to your car."

My mother held my hand, her nail carving into my palm as we walked with Mr. Petant to his burgundy four-door car. We stood together, watching until the car was out of sight. And then I ripped my hand from Cookie's and ran as fast as I could through the snow to Paige's house. I knew the beating would come anyway. I Just needed to put it off for a few hours. I needed to call my sister. Collect, of course.

Gi was incensed. Outraged. Furious.

"Why would he ask you *in front of her*?!" she shouted over and over again.

"He didn't even look at me," I said. "I mean, I would have winked or something."

Gi hurried off the phone as she wanted to call Mr. Petant and the social worker in New York who had taken me and Norm away from Cookie. Maybe if those two talked, Mr. Petant would understand the situation.

"*Je t'aime times a million!*" Gi said before hanging up.

"*Je t'aime times a zillion!*" I said.

The following day, my back and ribs throbbed from the beating I got when I had finally gone home. After school I walked to town to use the pay phone near Sheryl's Shop. It was cold in the booth and my breath frosted the glass walls. Again, I called my sister collect.

"*Mia bambina*, I miss you so much." Gi's voice sounded sad. She wasn't speed-talking as she often did when she was angry or excited.

"Did you talk to Mr. Petant?"

"Oh, *bambina*." Gi started crying.

My heart pounded. "Did he talk to the social worker in New York?"

My sister sobbed as she told me the story. The social worker in New York refused to call Mr. Petant since I lived out of state, and Mr. Petant refused to call to the social worker in New York because, he claimed, there was no need. He had already talked to my school, and the school reported to him what Cookie had said when Regina had called them our first year in town: Gi was a mentally unstable, chronic liar; an alcoholic who liked to stir up trouble. For Mr. Petant, it seemed, two false stories equaled one complete truth. He instructed Gi to never phone his office again. The case was closed, he told her. Don't even try.

"*Mia bambina*," Gi said. "I promise, I'll get you out of there one way or another."

The thrust from day to night, and night to day, mirrored my emotional blackness at home and ethereal lightness at school. My friends and teachers never could have guessed that after I got off the bus near the farm, the bubbly, spirited girl often went silent. Shut down. Cold. At times the briny fog of depression didn't lift until my first interaction on the school bus. It was like I was living inside a terrible nightmare and only woke up at the sound of Paige' or Jasmine's voice.

And even with Norm at home, there was no escaping the one-two punch from Cookie and Clyde. Norm knew about the beatings—he did his best to stop them, but often his interference made things worse. My brother had no idea what went on in the milking parlor or on the fields, however. I couldn't say the words to him that I had said to my sisters. There was a privacy, a modesty between my brother and me that wouldn't allow me to expose that to him. Besides, he was managing his own puzzle of torture from Cookie, who alternated between affection and tenderness for Norm and humiliating criticism and mockery of him. My brother's escapes were friends, video games, and art, at which he excelled.

Norm was also a good farmer, like me. Though he was much more stoic and strong when it came to what I thought of as the two hardest tasks: separating the calves from their moms and castrating the bull calves.

Between the calf corral and the cow corral was a walkway with a farm-style rustic entrance of two posts about three-quarters as high as telephone poles, across which ran a thick beam with Clyde's initials carved in it. In this walkway was an old metal chute, rusted and creaky. It looked like a big trough, but it enclosed the calves on all sides with a head restraint in the front. The chute was used to dehorn, castrate, brand, and inoculate the calves before they were old enough to go into the bull pen or cow pen. Norm and I had been exempt from this chore the first couple of years on the farm. The year I was thirteen, however, Clyde decided that my brother and I were as capable as any farmhands he could hire and were brought in to help turn the calves into steer.

"It's not a good day to have testicles," Clyde said, as the three of us walked to the chute. Boone was already there standing at a small metal table with a stack of the razors, used to castrate; the gouger, used to dehorn;

and the needle, used for shots. A shooting fire burned within in a circle of rocks just past the chute. The branding iron lay across the rocks, in the center of the fire.

"Do we give them painkillers?" Norm asked. His brow was furrowed into nervous folds.

"Nah, they're cattle, not kids," Clyde said.

"They're my little brothers and sisters," I whispered so Clyde couldn't hear. I'd fed every single one of these calves by bottle since they were weaned from their mothers. I knew them by sight, by the sound of their moos, by the white patches some of them had over their eyes, by the funny out-turn of one's hooves, and the giant long legs of another. I never named them because Clyde had told me not to, but I still knew them as individual souls. I knew their personalities.

"Can't we just give them some pain pills or something?" I asked.

"Now, where are we gonna get something like that?" Clyde asked.

Norm and I looked at each other, each pursing our lips so we wouldn't snicker. There were enough pain pills in Cookie's nightstand drawer to knock out all the cattle on Clyde's eighty acres.

I stopped below the overhanging beam and watched Boone lead one of the bull calves into the chute. The animal walked in easily, and then Boone lifted the rusty metal sides and locked him in so he couldn't move. I went to the front of the chute so I could see his face. This was the calf with a heart-shaped white spot on his forehead, above and between his eyes. He was a sweet one, who when he head-butted me, did it so gently that his new horns never jabbed. I thought of him as a mama's boy, but not in a bad way, in a gentle way. He just wanted to be loved.

"Does he have to be clamped like that?" I asked.

"Anyone would have to be clamped like this for what we're about to do." Clyde was at the tools now, inspecting each one.

I looked the calf in the eye and he mooed very quietly, like a question. My stomach was as clenched as if I were stuck in the chute. I couldn't see the difference between Clyde trapping me in his rubber apron or forcing me on the ground in the field, and this moment for the bull calf. Both created a total loss of control. A total loss of agency. The humiliation of having your body clamped, prodded, probed, and manipulated, without regard to the mind and soul attached to that body.

"I don't want to do this," I said to Clyde. I was stroking the bull calf's forehead. Norm was examining the tools; I could tell my brother was stealing himself against what was about to happen, creating a different focus so he could go through with it.

"I'll do it for Rosie," Norm said. "She can go do something else."

"You're both gonna do it." Clyde turned to me and said, "Do you want an apron? Or do you want to take off your shirt?" Clyde winked, and I quickly turned my back to him.

"Of course I'm not going to take off my shirt." My shirt already was marked up by farm work. Norm took off his shirt. Boone and Clyde were in rubber aprons. This was the bloodiest chore on the farm.

The calf nudged his head to my hand, to remind me I was petting him. "I don't want to hurt him," I said.

"Just give her a break," Norm said.

"There are no breaks on a farm," Clyde said.

"Rosie," Boone said, "you are the best farmer I know. The strongest girl I've ever met. You can do this." Boone was one of my biggest supporters. As with my teachers, I could not bring myself to disappoint him.

"Okay." Maybe if I was the one to do it, it would hurt the bull calf less.

"We start at the rear and work our way up to the head." Boone pointed to the calf's rump, where Clyde was waiting, his white teeth flashing that milky smile.

Clyde said, "Get over here. This is one thing you need to get exactly right."

Norm and I both squatted at the calf's hind quarters so we could see Clyde's hands at work. With a razor, Clyde sliced off the tip of the calf's scrotum. The calf let out a holler that sounded shameful. I cringed and my stomach clamped up. Clyde reached his bare fingers into the scrotum, pulled out the testes, and snipped them off so they fell in his hand. Again, the calf wailed. Clyde stood and tossed the testicles onto the fire pit to cook.

"Now the horns," Clyde said, and he handed me gougers that looked like a gardening tool with a circle-bladed snipper at the end. I stared at the gougers, my stomach swirling as the calf continued to cry.

"I'll do it," Norm said.

"Let Rosie do it," Clyde said. "You go second." Clyde put his hand on my back, which propelled me to the front of the calf where Boone was waiting.

With his hands over mine, Boone opened the gouger for me and then placed it so that the circular blade was on either side of the horn. "You don't want to get too close to the scalp or they can bleed a lot," he said. "Think of it as a tree stump you want to leave behind."

I closed the gouger and cut off the wedge of new horn. It was as long as a pack of cigarettes, triangular almost, with a dull point. Boone shook some white powder into the wound to help stop the bleeding.

"Now the other one," Boone said.

I placed the gouger around the other horn and clipped. This time a stream of blood squirted up at me and the cow gave a wailing moo. Boone poured on the white powder and Clyde laughed. I blinked in my tears and swallowed the stone in my throat.

"You were a little too close that time," Boone said. "But don't worry about it, you'll get the hang of it soon."

Clyde handed the branding iron to Norm and he stamped Clyde's initials into the calf's rump. The calf moo-cried again and I tried to soothe him with strokes and gentle words.

"I'll do the shot, too," Norm said, and he lay the branding iron back on the fire and took the syringe from Clyde's hands. I could tell my brother was trying to give me a little break.

"Right there, right on the hip," Clyde said. Norm stuck in the needle and the calf barely flinched. That was a relief.

This routine went on for hours. I felt like I was partaking in a ritual of abuse while being abused myself. I wanted to wail right along with the calves.

Norm, who was always better than I was at blocking out the brutalities in our life, got into the spirit of things and ate the grilled testicles with Boone and Clyde. I was harangued into trying one, too. It tasted no different than any other chewy, crunchy piece of rough beef I'd had.

By the end of the day, Norm's torso was covered with blood, as were the aprons Clyde and Boone wore, and my T-shirt as well. Norm and I were left alone to clean the tools and wipe down the chute.

I was nearly silent as we worked, stunned.

"It'll be okay," Norm said.

"When?" My rag was so drenched I seemed to be painting the chute with blood rather than cleaning it.

"Well, we could always end things for ourselves," Norm said.

I looked up at him to see if he was serious. "You ever think about that?"

"Yeah." Norm laughed, as if he were saying *no duh*!

"How would you do it?" Talking about this made it less heavy, easier than just thinking about it.

Norm nodded toward the beam that created the archway between the corrals. "I'd hang myself right there. I've already thought it through."

"You have?"

"Yeah. There's a roll of rope in the bull barn. I'd take that rope and hang myself." Norm smiled, but it was an anxious smile that let me know he wasn't kidding.

"Is there enough rope for me?" Together we could make this a joke.

"Hell yeah," Norm said. "I'll even tie the knot for you." And now I laughed.

"We could take some of Mom's pills to ease the pain," I said.

"We could drink all her hidden liquor, take all her pills, and then do it totally wasted." Norm smiled for real this time.

"Yeah, but first we'd open every pen and barn and let all the animals run free."

"Even the chickens," Norm said. "Who are so dumb they'd probably rather live with Clyde and Mom then run free." We both smiled.

"Oh, and we'd have to roll all the vehicles into the manure pit," I said. Now we were cracking up.

"We'd take Mom's Frankie Valli records," Norm said. "And we'd throw them in the manure pit as well."

"This is gonna be so great," I said.

My brother and I continued to laugh as we listed what we'd dump into the manure pit before we killed ourselves: Cookie's knickknacks, all the stored junk for Prismatic Fantasies, Clyde's John Deere baseball caps,

Clyde's work boots, the sewing machine, and every piece of farming equipment there was.

When we were walking back to the house, Norm said, "You know I'm serious about hanging myself there."

"Yeah," I said. "Me, too."

19

Out of Idaho

At the end of the drive to our house, near the road where the school bus pulled up, was an idling, white four-door car I'd never seen before. It was March of eighth grade, I had on a thick sweatshirt and my backpack, stuffed with homework.

I slowed at the car, a little hesitant, as my experience with idling cars was limited to Mr. Nettles and the Mafia.

Carefully I peered in the window. It was my sister Cherie, who was frantically waving her arm at me to get in. The school bus was driving straight toward us, about to pull over for me. I opened the passenger door, threw my backpack into the backseat, got in the car, and shrieked with joy.

"You're back!"

Cherie tore onto the road and drove away before the bus caught up to us. She reached one hand over and pulled me in so I could hug her while she was driving.

"I told you I'd come back for you!" my sister said.

"Where are we going?!" I was overjoyed to see my sister, but a little nervous, too. I'd never played hooky before.

"New York." Cherie looked at me and then picked up my hand and squeezed it.

"What do you mean *New York*?"

"We're taking you back."

I was shocked. All I'd wanted was to get away from Cookie and Clyde and now that it was really happening, I was terrified rather than relieved.

"But how? What do I do about school? What about Norm? I mean, how I do I just leave?"

"It's okay, Rosie. We're gonna take care of you." Cherie glanced back and forth between me and the road. She looked worried. "I bought some donuts and coffee. Eat something. It will help calm you." Cherie pointed with her thumb to the backseat. I leaned over toward the back and pulled up a bag of donuts and a coffee from a box on the floor.

"Do we have plane tickets?" I reached into the bag, pulled out a chocolate-covered donut, and took a giant bite.

"Yes. Hand me a coffee."

I gave Cherie the coffee and she gulped down some sips.

"Cookie's going to kill me."

"Rosie, you don't understand. She's not going to kill you because she won't be able to reach you. I'm taking you to New York. To live. For good."

Even though I understood each individual word that came out of my sister's mouth, the way she strung the words together didn't make sense to me. It was like Cherie was telling me she was moving me to the moon.

"Where will I live?"

"With me, in my apartment. And you'll go to school there and everything."

"What are we going to tell Mom?" No one I knew had the steely nerve of Cherie. Nothing scared her.

"We're not telling her anything," Cherie said. "Now don't freak out, but there's a wig in that bag on the floor—" My sister pointed to the floor at my feet. "Put it on so no one recognizes you."

I stared at the bag but couldn't bring myself to reach for it. Cherie pulled the car off on a dirt road. She pulled up the emergency brake and cut the engine. "It's going to be okay. We're going to take care of you."

"All right." I nodded. "What about Norm?"

"Things aren't hard for him the way they are for

you. He doesn't have Clyde molesting him. And Mom really doesn't beat him as much."

I nodded again, then reached down and picked up the bag. There was a long-haired, curly red wig; a pair of Ray Ban–looking sunglasses; and a T-shirt that said NEW YORK. If I could have laughed, I would have. Instead, I just changed into the shirt. Then Cherie helped pin up my hair and adjust the wig.

"It's all over now," Cherie said, as she tucked in stray strands of hair. "The abuse, the beatings . . . everything. You're done."

It didn't feel done. It didn't feel over. I didn't feel anything that I recognized as a normal feeling. It wasn't quite anxiety, but I was worried. And it wasn't quite fear, but I was apprehensive. More than anything, I felt numb. Cherie hugged me. Then she started the car and we took off for the Boise airport.

I had a hundred *what-ifs* and *what will happen whens* running through my head. How would the cheerleading team operate without me? Would Paige and Jasmine be mad at me for leaving without a word? And what about the calves? Who would feed them, and would that person stroke their heads and talk to them and make sure they felt loved? Would my teachers think I was a dropout? A slacker? Pregnant and running away?

"You think Mom called the police?" I put on the sunglasses, flipped down the visor, and looked at myself.

"Mom won't realize you're missing until you don't come home from school. But wear the wig in case we drive past someone you know or run into someone at the airport."

Cherie did most of the talking on the way to the airport. Like my mother, she smoked cigarettes, but she tapped her ash out the window and stubbed the butts into the ashtray. I tried to focus on what my sister was saying, on what the plan was, but I couldn't get past the idea of my disappearance from everything I knew and everything that was familiar. I'd seen a movie once about a guy in the Witness Protection Program and decided that *that* was what was happening now. Like someone relocated without a trace—someone who was avoiding being killed—I was being erased from Idaho. I was avoiding a death, too, I decided, either by Cookie's hands or my own.

At the Boise airport we returned the rental car and then went to the terminal and got in the security line.

Cherie handed me my boarding pass and whispered in my ear to relax, act normal. But it was hard to act normal with a giant, curly, red-haired wig on my head.

The security agent looked at my boarding pass, then looked at me. "How old are you?" he asked.

"She's thirteen," Cherie said.

"What grade are you in?" he asked.

"Eighth," I said.

"You're tall," he said.

"Tallest one in our family," Cherie said.

He handed the boarding pass back, and my sister and I walked past him to the conveyor belt where I put down my backpack. It wasn't until I had walked through the metal detector and put on my backpack again that I realized my legs were shaking, my knees almost buckling.

Cherie grabbed my hand and we walked away quickly, as though we had just escaped being arrested.

"I *have to* itch my head," I said. There was the sensation of ants crawling all over my scalp under the wig. A tingly, prickly, maddening itch.

We hustled into the ladies' room and then went together into the largest stall at the end. I reached up under the wig and scratched my head with both hands. It felt so good, I did it again and again and again. Once I was done, the wig was hanging from a single bobby pin half off my head and my hair was frizzed out.

"Okay," Cherie said. "You look like you just rode

on the highway on the back of a motorcycle with no helmet. While drunk."

I smiled, and I wanted to laugh, but I was still in the fog of shock and unable to emerge from it.

Cherie gave me the window seat on the plane and she sat in the middle. My sister fell asleep instantly. She had flown in from New York the night before, and had barely slept as she waited for morning.

It was my first time on a plane, but I couldn't focus on that fact. Instead, I wondered what was happening in Oakview. What Paige and Jasmine might have thought had happened. If the school had called my mother to see why I was missing. What Cookie might say or do— would she drive around town looking for me? And what Clyde and Boone would do without me there to help with the afternoon chores? It was somewhat like imagining my family after my death—something I had done many times before.

My sister woke up just before we landed. "Look." Cherie pointed out the window to the Statue of Liberty standing on an island below us.

"That's so cool," I said, and it really was, but still, I couldn't feel anything except a general numb terror.

"You okay?" Cherie asked.

"What if Cookie's standing at the gate when we get off the airplane?" I asked.

"Impossible," Cherie said.

"Or Clyde."

"Impossible," Cherie said again. "They couldn't get to the airport any quicker than us. They probably are just now finding out that you didn't go to school."

"Do you think they're going to come out here and drag me back?" I imagined that my mother had the strength and willpower to yank me from New York to Idaho by the hair on the nape of my neck. It was her own special leash—that base of hair—and she used it whenever she felt the need.

"They won't know where you are." Cherie stopped talking as the plane bumped once and then smoothed out and glided across the runway.

Camille and Gi ran to me when we walked off the plane. They each took one of my hands and we rushed to the parking lot, no one talking as if that might lead to our discovery. When we got in the car, my sisters hugged me and kissed me and said everything they hadn't said in the airport: they missed me, everything would be okay now, they'd all take care of me. I was still veiled in a fear-drenched cloud and could barely speak out loud.

"Oh *mia bambina amore*," Gi said, and she kissed me again until my face was wet with her tears. "Are you scared?"

I nodded. Gi held my hand tight during the ride. I was silent, and my sisters chattered quickly about the flight, the drive, the dinner that was waiting at Camille's house, and Camille's son, Frankie, whom I'd soon meet.

Camille's house smelled so good and warm. Her husband, Frank, had made spaghetti and meatballs. He carried the baby while we loaded up our plates and sat at the table. I'd never seen a man act like this; I was fascinated by his kindness.

We ate spaghetti; everyone talked and no one yelled. There was no food thrown across the table, no one grabbed my hair, and I didn't have to rush outside after dinner to do more chores. When I started to do the dishes, Gi stopped me and told me to sit down. I needed a night off, she said. She was right. I hadn't had a day or night off work since we moved in with Clyde. I almost didn't know how to sit and do nothing. But when I did it—when I sat on Camille's couch and did nothing—I felt my body go limp and still. It seemed like something was seeping out of me. And maybe something was. The murky fear, anxiety, and dread I'd been feeling were slowly escaping, like air from a pinhole leak in an inner tube.

I went to bed still silent and stunned. But when I woke up the next morning, I felt more like myself than

I'd ever felt with Cookie and Clyde. I was with my sisters. *My sisters!* I tried to keep my joy contained, however, as I didn't trust that it wouldn't end at any minute.

My sisters decided I needed brand-new school clothes and not their castoffs or anything from the throwaway bin at the Salvation Army. So on my first full day in New York, it was decided we'd go to the mall. Camille's husband Frank and little Frankie came, too. In the car, I sat on Gi's lap, even though I was bigger than she was. My sister played with my hair and rested her cheek on my back and I felt loved and secure.

Everything looked familiar when we reached the road the mall was on. "I've been here before, right?" It was like visiting a recurring dream. I both knew where I was and felt completely lost.

"We once lived across the street here; it's the Smith Haven Mall." Gi pointed out the window. "Over there. That was where you were riding the mare when the stallion tried to mount it."

I could see it all clearly now. And I remembered the smell of the Hostess cakes the Mexican workers gave us on cold mornings.

Little Frankie was asleep in his car seat, so Camille, Frank, and Gi stayed in the car to wait while Cherie took me shopping. Gi, the organizer, wanted to work out the schedule and plans for . . . well, for the rest of my life in New York.

The mall seemed bigger than any field I'd ever been on. Everyone looked dressed up and confident. The New York accents stood out in a way that my mother's didn't. My friends in Idaho pointed out Cookie's funny way of speaking, but I had stopped hearing it long ago. *Did I ever talk like this?* I wondered, and then I remembered Flavia Feliciano saying I spoke funny. But that New York accent, however strong or light it may have been, was long gone. As my sisters pointed out, I sounded like I was from Idaho.

Cherie and I picked out jeans, a heavy winter coat, a pink top, and a red sweater. I worried about how much money Cherie was spending, but she insisted that she, Gi, and Camille wanted to spend money on me.

"You're our sister," Cherie said. "We'd spend any amount of money to make you safe and comfortable."

"I'll pay you back," I said as the cashier was ringing it all up.

"No you won't," Cherie said. "I know you'd do the same for any of us."

I tried to imagine Cookie showing love and caring for me or my sisters. And I couldn't. My mother showed love for her cats—petting them and talking to them like cuddly babies. She showed love, of some sort, I suppose, for Clyde—touching him all the time on his crotch, in particular, and rubbing up against him. Although maybe that wasn't really love. And she could be nice to Norm at times, too. But it always felt precarious, as if at any minute she might criticize him for not being the farmer Clyde was. Maybe Cookie just didn't know how to love people. Maybe she never learned it.

After three days, Gi and I moved out of Camille's house and into Cherie's apartment, where I would be living. Gi was taking a few days off from school to get me settled. Soon I'd be enrolled in the eighth grade at the school near Cherie's apartment, and Gi would go back to college.

When Cherie, Gi, and I were having dinner that night, I realized how different I felt. It was as if a hundred-pound shell had been removed from my back and I could suddenly feel the wind and the sunshine around me. I no longer jumped every time the phone rang, or ran to the bathroom and hid each time there was a knock at the door. Living away from Cookie and Clyde now seemed possible, and I felt hopeful that soon I'd be in school and making new friends.

Cherie and I were laughing at a story Gi was telling us about a friend at her school when the phone rang. I looked over at it but didn't even think about who might be on the other end.

Cherie answered and Gi kept talking. Then I heard Cherie gasp. Gi got up from the table, went to the phone, and put her ear against the receiver. I ran to her side and tried to listen in, too, but there was only room for my sisters.

"Fuck!" Cherie hung up the phone. Gi's almond eyes widened into circles.

"What?"

"Uncle Nick's been calling Camille," Gi said. "Mom called him and said that she's called the authorities and there's a search out for me and you."

"But you haven't run away from anything," I said.

"She's saying I kidnapped you," Gi said.

Cherie said, "If Mom's house burned down in Idaho and Gi was in Hawaii at the time, Mom would still blame Gi."

"I don't even remember Uncle Nick," I said. "Why does he even care?"

"He doesn't," Gi said. "He just a terrible, perverted man who hates women and girls. He's been mean to every single one of us since the day we were born, just because we're not men."

"He's an asshole," Cherie said. "A motherfucking asshole."

"Don't worry, *bambina*," Gi said. "We're gonna keep you safe."

But I did worry. And so did my sisters. None of us slept well that night.

The next day, while Cherie was at the deli, Camille called and said that Uncle Nick had showed up at her house. Frank told him that as far as he knew, Cherie lived out of state, Gi was at college, and he had no idea where Rosie was, but Nick didn't believe him. Frank was worried that Nick would call around and eventually find out that Cherie was nearby.

I could barely eat that day. After hearing more of Gi's stories about Uncle Nick—how dismissive he was of women; how mean he was to his wife; how when Gi was a little girl he didn't allow her to speak, and if she did speak, he called her a snob and a bitch—I was even more scared of him.

Gi tried to keep me occupied. We read books and watched TV; she studied for midterm exams and showed me what she was working on at school. But I was only ever half there—just waiting for the mysterious Nick to blow down a wall and come stomping in like a rabid, half-crazed ogre.

The following day the phone calls to Cherie's apartment started. Now the ogre had a voice I could hear over the answering machine. It was an angry, impatient voice with an accent like my mother's: dropped Rs and Gs, a nasally twang. Nick started out demanding that Cherie call him. The third time he left a message, I knew we were dealing with someone as dangerous as my mother when he said, "Pick up the FUCKING phone, you bitch! Pick up the FUCKING phone!"

Gi quickly walked around the apartment straightening things up. My sister was panicked.

"Let's go," she said finally, and we ran out the back alley. Gi stopped at a pay phone and called Camille. She left a message on her machine telling her we'd be hiding at the mall.

At the mall, my head darted like a bird's at every dark-haired man I saw. I was looking for Cookie in the male, ogre form. *Pretty in Pink* was showing at the mall. Gi bought us tickets and we went inside the dark theater and sat in the back row so we'd know if anyone came in. Every time the door opened, my eyes shot over to the wedge of light and I tried to discern the shape, the face, the expression of whoever had just entered.

In the middle of the second showing of *Pretty in Pink,* we decided to leave the theater. I kept my head down and my hand tightly in my sister's as we navigated our way through the mall crowds. And then my sister said, "Oh shit. Shit, shit, shit."

A man with a long pointy face and two policemen by his side were coming toward us.

"Run!" Gi said, and we took off back into the movie theater and then out the emergency exit of the lobby where there was an industrial-size Dumpster.

"Get underneath it," Gi said, and she lay on the ground and scooted below it. I lay down, too, and shimmied in beside her. There was a rotten, sharp smell. It wasn't anything like the manure, fertilizer, and muck from the pens at the farm. This smell was edgier, harder. I squeezed my sister's hand and shut my eyes.

Soon it was dark out. And though I knew it was probably chilly, too, I couldn't feel that. All I could feel was my heart thumping, the heat of my sister's hand, the hard, gritty ground at my stomach.

"Why can't we hide behind the trash?" I whispered.

"Too obvious," Gi said.

There were sounds of footsteps, people leaving the mall, cars starting and driving away. We saw what was likely a boy in boots come out the squeaky back door of the movie theater, a bag of trash hanging low near his ankle. He heaved the trash into the bin. It barely made a sound as it landed; still, I clenched Gi's hand as if it were going to break through and hit us.

And then we heard Cherie's voice.

"Regina? Rosie? Come out! Come out now!"

"Shhh," Gi said to me. "She's with Nick. He's forcing her to call us."

"How do you know?" I whispered.

"Because I understand the Calcaterras. Nick is every bit as cunning as Mom."

Cherie kept calling for us and then her voice faded as it got farther and farther away.

More cars left the mall. And soon it felt as if we were alone in the parking lot, a pile of mall trash above us. I knew Gi was so determined she'd have stayed there for a week if it meant I didn't have to go back to Cookie and Clyde.

When all was quiet and the parking lot was nearly empty, Gi whispered, "Let's go."

I scooted out and my sister slithered out behind me. We ran to a pay phone outside the mall where Gi called Camille.

Camille was hysterical. Uncle Nick told her the police had figured out everything and if she didn't return me to Idaho, they were going to press kidnapping charges against all of my sisters, and Frank, too. Camille could lose custody of her son, Frankie. A meeting was called at Camille's house so my sisters could work out a plan.

Eventually, after much crying, it was decided that my sisters couldn't risk being charged with kidnapping. Fighting a case like that could take months, or years—time where I'd be placed with Cookie and Clyde anyway. And not one of them had enough money to hire a lawyer. There was no choice but to return me to Idaho.

While I cuddled with them and listened, my big sisters talked into the night. Gi was determined to find a legal way to get me away from Cookie and Clyde. Cherie was determined to go back to Idaho so she could break all the bones in Clyde's hands and smash up a few of his other parts as well. And Camille was determined to find a peaceful way to make me safe. She suggested we find someone in Oakview to take me in. I knew, but didn't have the heart to tell Camille, that in a town of 360 people, no one would humiliate Cookie and Clyde by taking me in against their will.

I drifted away into my head, into Idaho, where after this interlude, I would likely be even worse off. I knew I couldn't bring home the beautiful clothes my sisters had bought me. Cookie would probably burn them in front of me, or wrap my new jeans around my neck and try to strangle me with them.

Unless Cookie had removed them, the bottle of pills

was still on the dresser next to my bed. I could always take those, I realized, and beat my mother to the final punch.

The following evening, Cherie and Gi took me to Uncle Nick's house as agreed. He had promised that if I showed up there that night, he would make sure no charges were pressed against my sisters.

Uncle Nick opened the door with two barking, teeth-baring Dobermans by his side. With his black hair and long ruddy nose, my uncle looked exactly like the dogs.

"Say good-bye to your sisters," Nick barked, just as ferociously as the dogs.

"We're not leaving her," Cherie said.

"Fuck you, you little bitch." Uncle Nick reached his arm toward me and both my sisters lunged in front of me.

"We're staying here with her," Cherie said.

"I'm not letting you little whores in my house," he said, and now I knew that it was a family trait—the degrading, demeaning name-calling.

"We're not leaving her," Gi said.

Uncle Nick stared down my sisters. He turned and kicked at the dogs so they'd move out of the way. The three of us entered the house. It smelled like mold and dog pee. The canine version of the smells in Cookie's house. Nick's wife, Jennifer, came out and was nervously smiling. She had a broken, soft voice. Nothing she said sounded true, but it did sound like she wanted it to be true.

"Your mother misses you so much, Rosanne," Aunt Jennifer said.

"Where are we sleeping?" Cherie asked. We'd already had dinner and had showed up as late as possible.

Aunt Jennifer had a nervous, twittering walk as she led us to the guest room. She opened the door, and the three of us went in. Aunt Jennifer shut the door behind us.

There was a couch folded out into a bed with two pillows; a sheet; and a grayish, likely once white, pilly blanket folded at the foot of the bed. Spread across the bed were photos of naked women. Hundreds of photos, each around the size of a piece of school notebook paper. Uncle Nick worked in printing and was an amateur photographer. These were, we assumed, photos he'd taken.

"Don't look." Cherie turned my head so it was facing away from the bed, but I'd already seen enough. They weren't art photos; they weren't in black and white or gracefully composed. Uncle Nick's pictures were of body parts, hairy as beasts, dehumanized, open and exposed.

"We're not sleeping on that bed," Gi said, and she pulled the sheet out from under the photos and spread it out on the floor, which was covered in a green shag carpet.

"You think the pillows are okay?" Cherie asked.

"No," Gi said. "We'll use our coats rolled up."

We lay on the floor in our clothes, pushed together like three spoons. Throughout the night my sisters and I cried off and on, laughing at times when our crying harmonized.

In the morning, when we came out of the room, Uncle Nick held the dogs back and gave us each the once-over, as if he were examining something he wanted to purchase.

"You three diking it out in there?" he asked.

"You're disgusting," Gi said. Cherie lifted her middle finger at him.

My sisters wouldn't let me get in a car with Nick, so he followed us to the airport to make sure they really put me on the plane.

We sobbed at the airport, me the hardest. Our words were muted by our choking cries. I felt just as I did at eight years old when we lived in the Toad House and the social worker ripped me from my sisters to deposit me at the Callahans'.

When I got on the flight, I sucked in and held back the crying. I needed to shore up, insulate, put a shell around my heart. I couldn't think of anything good that might be on the other end of the flight.

20

Into Idaho Redux

Among the punishments handed down after the *sisternapping*, as everyone in Oakview was calling it, was that I was now responsible for mucking every pen on the farm until, according to my mother, the day I died. I wondered if she really thought I'd live out my life with her. After New York had been snatched from me, it seemed that there were only two ways out: death or college. In the weeks following my return I would have said it was a toss-up as to which exit I'd take.

Still, I survived that summer by spending as much time as possible with Paige and Jasmine.

Many nights, after Cookie and Clyde went to bed, I rode my bike to Paige's house. If there was a rock on her mailbox, that meant her father had gone to bed and she could get out undetected. No rock, and I'd turn around and ride home.

One summer night, after sleeping a couple of hours, I tiptoed out of the house and headed down to Paige's. The rock was there. I flicked my lighter several times and Paige soon leapt from the second floor into the bushes that lined the side of the house. She climbed out, pulled the twigs and leaves off herself, and then hopped on her bike. We took off.

There were no streetlights on the road so I held a flashlight in front of me and steered with one hand. Paige liked to ride in the middle of the road where it was smoother, but I always preferred the side so we could dump our bikes and leap into the grass if a car came. If anyone saw us, they'd surely report it to our parents.

"Car!" Paige shouted as headlights peeped from behind us.

We turned into the side of the road, crashing the bikes into the ground and then rolling down flat. I killed the flashlight, and we waited until the car had passed.

The bruises and scrapes we got from this routine weren't even noticeable on two bodies that dealt with animals, wheelbarrows, tractors, and pitchforks. And then, for me at least, there were the marks left by Cookie and Clyde. Once I pulled a chair into the bathroom and stood on it so I could examine my naked body in the mirror. It was a map of scrapes, bruises, scabs, and scars. A landscape with a visible memory. Only in a farming community would these marks go unnoticed. Every kid who lived on a farm was as banged up as I was, even when their parents never touched them.

That night in town, we met an older boy named Lucas. Paige gave him some money and he went to Sheryl's Shop and bought us our first six-pack of beer: Miller Lite, as that's what Jasmine told us she drank the first time she tried alcohol. Paige and I spirited the beer away to the phone booth on the most central corner of downtown, the place where I called my sisters collect. There was a patch of grass around the phone booth. We sat on the grass, alternately running into the phone booth every couple of minutes to chug from our hidden stash.

I loved the way the beer eased me into a floppy bone-lessness. Fully drunk, I had a vague awareness of my body not drunk, the stiffness I usually carried. Threats were such a continuous part of my daily life that I was always clenched in anticipation. Until that night, with the alcohol running through me. Paige seemed to love it, too. She was chattering like a monkey, jumping from one subject to the next.

We were on our backs, staring at the stars, when Paige asked, "What do you think the tourists would think of what happens in the hot springs?" Travelers often stopped in Oakview on their way to Perilous Peak. And when they did, they were directed to the hot springs.

"Tourists prob'ly skinny-dip, too." My words were slurred.

"I'm not talking about skinny-dipping. I'm talking about the bloodless pig dipping!" Paige kicked her feet up into the air and let them drop again.

"Yeah, that would be bad if they knew." I thought that the next time I talked to my sisters on the phone I would tell them about the bloodless pig dipping. How the local farmers paid certain hot spring owners money to soak their recently blood-drained pigs in the springs long enough for the skin to separate from the bones. It's easier to butcher pigs when the skin is loosened. My sisters would howl with laughter at this—they always found the details of small-town Idaho fascinating.

That night we stayed out until just before sunrise, when we rode our bikes to my house and started on my chores. It wasn't too hard to do the work on no sleep and with a mild hangover. As we were mucking out the bull pen that day, Paige and I decided that we liked drinking. Neither of us could think of any good reasons not to do it again.

When high school started that fall, I joined everything I could that might keep me out of the house and away from Cookie's beatings and Clyde's perversions. I was on the cheerleading squad, the yearbook staff, and the volleyball and track teams. Additionally, I was in the Girls Athletic Association, the Pep Club, and the band, where I played the clarinet. I was vice president of the freshman class and an active member of the LDS youth group. On top of all that, I competed in spelling bees and talent shows.

When Clyde bought me my first horse, Meeco, I added 4-H Club to the list of activities that kept me out of the house. I knew the horse—traded for a beef cow, a bull, and a couple hundred bucks—was a guilt gift from Clyde, as if what he was doing to me would be okay if I had a horse. I wanted to reject Meeco on those grounds alone, but I didn't. I'd been yearning for a horse since the sixth grade, when I had learned to ride on friends' horses. And a rejection of the gift, I knew, would only have brought more beatings my way. Cookie loved to point out how ungrateful she thought I was.

Meeco was a brown Appaloosa with a spotted white

rear. She looked like she was wearing a cute polka dotted skirt. She came with a well-worn saddle, though if I didn't feel like saddling her up, I rode bareback, holding onto her mane. On the weekends, and after school if I had time before chores, I trained her for 4-H shows. Like Shadow and Pup, Paige's inseparable goat and dog, Meeco and I, too, were inseparable on the farm. If I was outdoors, she was with me, following my steps from the barns to the milking parlor to the calf pen. She had a sweet disposition and a calming influence. Just sitting on her back, leaning forward, and stroking her shimmering coat made me feel safe.

Although Norm and I were in high school together, he a senior and I a freshman, I barely saw him. Norm had actively disengaged from our mother that year, as if he were prepping her for his departure to art school the following fall. He was the only person other than Clyde who could manage Cookie. And his easygoing way with her gave Cookie the illusion that they were friends. The more Norm detached from Cookie, the kinder she was to me. It was a strange time, as if my mother was testing me out as her new companion. Cookie was clearly lonely without my brother, and I was the nearest person who might be able to fill that loneliness.

It was during an evening of relative companionability with Cookie that I decided to bring up Clyde. We were in the kitchen, and Cookie was making stuffed peppers. She was a sophisticated, inventive cook—I loved everything she made. Like sewing, it was a skill I didn't know she had until we were settled with Clyde.

"Mom," I said, "can I ask your advice for a friend?"

"Sure. Lay it on me." Cookie put the baking sheet with stuffed peppers into the oven. She shut the oven door and then pulled the cigarette pack from her cleavage, tapped one out, and lit it.

"Her stepdad is molesting her," I said. "And, you know, it's disgusting. She doesn't like it."

"She doesn't like it, huh?" Cookie laughed. "Who does?"

"Exactly. No one."

Cookie nodded her head slowly as if she were thinking.

"Can't she just stay away from him?"

"She has chores with him. And she runs away from him, but he catches her and he tells her he's gonna beat her worse than her mother already does."

"I hope she's on birth control," Cookie said.

"He doesn't do that," I said. "He does other stuff."

"Pervert." Cookie snorted.

"Yeah," I said.

"Why doesn't she tell her mother what he's doing?"

"Her older sister told her mom once. But her mom didn't believe her."

Cookie blew smoke straight toward me. "Really?" Her voice had the upturn of suspicion.

"Yeah. Really. What do you think she should do?" Though I was talking entirely and truthfully about myself, a friend from school had recently confessed to me that her father was abusing her. I was shocked by her story. Somehow I had thought that I was the only one to whom these kinds of things happened. I wanted to tell my friend that Clyde was doing things to me, too, but the words wouldn't come out of my mouth. As she spoke, I experienced her pain so keenly that I reverted to the silent kid in the rocking chair again— stuck inside myself. I comforted her the best I could, but still worried I hadn't comforted her enough.

"Rosie. Is Clyde touching you?" Cookie wasn't angry as she said this. And she wasn't drunk. She was calmly smoking a cigarette. The last low rays of sun streaked in through the window. The smell of cooking peppers pleasantly overwhelmed the smell of cat pee. A cat rubbed himself against Cookie, walking back and forth, his torso arched around the post of her leg.

"Yeah. Clyde does horrible things to me." My lungs

stuttered as I took a deep breath. I watched my mother carefully. I wanted her to hold me. To tell me she loved me. And, amazingly, she gave me a hug. And stayed there, holding me like that.

"Oh honey." Tears ran down Cookie's cheeks. It was only the second time I'd seen her cry while sober. "I'm so sorry to hear this. And I'm so mad at that bastard!"

She was mad, but it was a different mad. A sane mad. My mother was in control of herself. I shut my eyes for one second and hoped that Cookie was all better. She'd get rid of Clyde. She'd be proud of me. She'd love me. Everything would be okay.

"It's really awful, Mom." I cried, too, half of me feeling the sadness and half of me feeling a certain joy in having an honest moment with my mother. It was the first time she'd taken what I said as truth. It was the first time we'd cried together.

"When did it start?" Cookie pulled out of the hug. She grabbed a piece of paper towel from the roll and blew her nose several times.

"When I was twelve."

"Fucking son of a bitch." Cookie blew her nose again.

"I tried so hard to stop it," I cried.

My mother rested her hands on the counter as if

she had to hold herself up. She was still crying, lightly though. "I'm calling Randy." Randy Cooper was the local sheriff.

I nodded my head, *yes, yes, yes.* I was so shocked that my mother was helping me out. I wondered then, if she cut out all the pills and alcohol, was there a reasonable person hidden inside her?

"He's a piece of shit. A pervert!" Cookie blew her nose once more and then picked up the phone and dialed the sheriff's number, which we had listed on the wall with other emergency numbers. Just as he answered, I heard Clyde come into the house. I hurried to the mudroom to distract him. I didn't want anything to prematurely end my mother's conversation with the sheriff.

"Clyde, the clutch on the tractor was grinding earlier today. Can you show me how to fix it?" I asked.

"Can it wait until after dinner?" He kicked off his boots.

"Not really since I need to use it in the morning and it'll be too dark out to look at the engine after dinner. It would be better if we checked it now."

"Well, why are you telling me now? I just took my boots off. Dinner's almost ready."

"I forgot to tell you earlier."

"Why don't you see if Boone is still around, he could

help out that cute little hiney of yours," Clyde reached around and tried to pinch my bottom. I darted out of his reach. "Make sure you don't kill the engine with all that grinding." Clyde winked at me.

I stepped into my boots while trying to block Clyde's way. When I heard my mother end the call, I stepped aside, then turned and watched as Clyde wobbled on his bowed legs into the living room.

I grabbed my sweatshirt and went out to the barn to see Meeco. It was chilly out, and I was wearing a tank top, but I was so nervous that I was hot. I tied the sweatshirt around my waist and hopped up on Meeco's bare back. She shimmied her hair as I settled on her, my head buried in her silky mane. Then, as if she sensed my anxiety, Meeco stepped back and forth a couple of times, rocking me into calmness.

When I came back into the house, Sherriff Cooper was in the living room with Cookie and Clyde. He was on the chair, his back to me. My mother and Clyde were side by side on the couch. Holding hands. There was what looked like a glass of water on the table in front of Cookie. But I knew it wasn't water. My mother didn't drink water. It had to have been vodka.

Cookie and Clyde looked up at me. Their faces were as hard as hammers. Clyde shook his head, his lips pursed so that his lower lip popped out. My mother put her cigarette in the ashtray, then reached into her mouth and plucked a wayward piece of tobacco off her tongue while keeping her beady bat's eyes trained on me.

The sheriff turned in his seat, glanced in my direction, and then stood.

"Rosanne, can I talk to you alone for a few minutes?" Sheriff Cooper approached me, his jutting belly leading the way. He waddled, as if his thighs were uncomfortably rubbing together.

"Yeah." I looked back and forth between the sheriff and Cookie's and Clyde's hard faces.

"Let's go for a little stroll." The sheriff held out an arm in an *after you* gesture. I walked out the door and he followed.

"Where are we going?" I asked.

"Keep walking," he said, his boots making a shuffling sound on the ground. The wind was blowing, but I was still nervously hot.

When we reached the bull pen, Sheriff Cooper stopped walking. The bull was standing in the middle of the pen watching us as if there was something to see. I always felt sorry for him. He seemed so lonely being kept away from the steers.

"Your mother told me what you said," the sheriff said.

"Yeah," I said. "He's been doing that kind of stuff since I was twelve."

"Since you were twelve, huh? Let me ask you this. How long have you known Clyde Hapner?"

"Um, I guess since right after I turned eleven. I'm fourteen now, so three years?"

"Hmm. Okay, so you've known him for just about three years. I've known him over a decade. Which one of us do you think knows him better?" He took a step closer to me so his jutting belly almost hit me. I leaned back into the rails of the bull pen.

"I think I do, since I live with him." My voice quavered. It was unusual for me to be so bold with an authority figure, but this was urgent. He needed to know the truth.

"Well, you know what I think?"

"What?" My lips trembled.

"I think you're trying to stir up trouble so you can get out of chores, that's what I think."

"I'm not!"

"Don't interrupt your elders."

"Sorry." I looked behind me to see where the bull was. He charged every now and then for no good reason.

"Clyde Hapner is a good man, an honest man, and a man of integrity. Maybe he's fresh with his comments sometimes. We all are. But if you don't want him lookin' at you, then I suggest you cover yourself up. I'm not sure what you expect when you're walking around town in those little itty-bitty shirts like the one you have on now."

My arms moved instinctively across my chest, but I couldn't feel myself. I was numb.

"Okay," I said. I wanted him to get far away from me. I wanted him to turn his head so he couldn't see how hard I was shaking.

"Now, I don't want to hear any more out of you about this, or you're the one who's gonna be in trouble. You hear?"

"Yes," I said. My teeth were chattering, and I knew it wasn't because of the chill in the air.

"Yes, sir," he said.

"Yes, sir," I repeated.

I stayed out by the bull pen while the sheriff walked back to his car. He lived on the farm just north of us. I should have known he wouldn't believe me over Clyde. Once he'd driven away, I slowly walked back to the house. Maybe if I pretended that nothing had happened, Cookie and Clyde would pretend nothing had happened. Maybe this was too embarrassing for Cookie to beat me over it in front of Clyde. And maybe

Clyde, since he was guilty, would give me a little break in the punishment.

"The clutch's okay," I shouted out from the mudroom. I took off my boots, and then entered the living room. No one was there. The cooked stuffed peppers sat on a plate on the counter. Four cats surrounded them and were licking at them.

"Mom?" I said.

"Here." My mother's voice was coming from down the hall. "Come here!"

I found Cookie and Clyde in the bathroom with the door open. Clyde was sitting on the tub and directed me to sit across from him on the closed toilet seat right next to where Cookie was standing.

"Sit your ass down." Cookie waggled her red fingertips at me. "You've got some explaining to do."

"Why the heck would you say that about me, Rosie?" Clyde's voice was gentle; he sounded hurt and surprised.

"Because it's true." The shaking in my lips started up again.

"Why would I touch a girl like you when I have your beautiful mother available to me night and day?"

Cookie smiled at that remark. She made it seem as if we were in competition for Clyde and she had just won.

"Tell the truth," I said to Clyde. "Tell her what you do to me!"

"Don't you talk to him like that!" My mother grabbed my hair and yanked me down so that my head hit the linoleum floor. Clyde stood and stared at me for a minute as if he was trying to decide what to do. And then they both started kicking. It was a barrage so intense, it felt like twenty people were attacking me. There wasn't a part of my body, no matter how I turned and curled, that wasn't being hit. I prayed for silence, blackness, quiet, death! Dying was the only imaginable way out of the intense pain hailing down on me. Within only a couple of minutes, it was as if my prayers were answered, and I was no longer with my body. No longer able to feel anything.

It was the middle of the night when I regained consciousness. I groaned, tried to sit up, and felt a storm of pain up my back. A sound came out of me, but it wasn't quite a scream. My mouth was filled with fluid and I turned my head toward my pillow and spit up something. I wiped my mouth with my hand and could feel that my lips were swollen, split open, and covered with what I assumed was blood.

"Blue," I said. But there was no movement from the

floor. When I turned to peer over the bed, imaginary razors cut into my skin. Blue was missing.

It felt like every bone in my body was broken as I moved to the door. It was locked. From the outside. I hobbled back to bed.

The next time I woke up, it was light out. I turned my head slowly toward my pillow and saw that it was covered in blood. There was blood on my hands and arms, too. I tried to sit up but couldn't. Everything hurt, from my skin to my muscles to my organs.

My bedroom door swung open and Cookie filled the doorway. "Get your sorry ass outta bed!"

I opened my mouth to speak, coughed, and then spit up chunks of cakey blood. "Can't."

"Can't? Can't?" Cookie laughed. "Oh yes you can!" My mother rushed into the room and yanked me up by my arm. The pain was so intense I had to focus on not vomiting.

"Just give me a minute." I scanned the floor for my socks but could barely see out of my swollen eyes.

"Your little trick backfired, didn't it?" Cookie picked up my tennis shoes and threw them at me. "And you know what's happening now? This week?"

I dropped to the ground and pulled on my socks. "What?" Even my lungs hurt when I spoke.

"We're getting married. Yup. Married! That man is so distraught over the lies you told that he wants to marry me just to prove how wrong you are!"

I shut my eyes. "Congratulations."

"Why don't you say it like you mean it?!" The dog ran into the room and jumped on me. Darts of pain flew through my body. It was so excruciating that I was silenced for a moment and had to catch my breath before I spoke.

"Congratulations." My face throbbed from the pressure of the word passing my lips.

"From now on, you call him Dad, you hear?"

"Uh-huh." The idea of it gave me pangs of pain that radiated down my back.

"And don't you dare say a bad word about your father in this town, get it?"

"Uh-huh." I was still on the floor and leaned my back against the bed.

"You have no say in this town because you are nothing. Got it?" Cookie leaned her top-heavy body over me now.

I nodded.

"Say it! Say you're nothing!"

"I'm nothing," I mumbled.

"That's right. Except our slave." Cookie laughed.

"My and your new daddy's nobody, piece-of-shit little slave!"

"Okay," I whispered.

"Now go out there and do your chores. Your daddy called Boone and told him not to come in today, so you gotta pick up his share of the work, too."

"Okay."

Clyde's head jerked back slightly at the sight of me when I walked into the milking parlor. Then he flashed his teeth and started talking as if nothing out of the ordinary had happened. My horse, however, didn't pretend that things were right. That morning, I leaned on her—too weak to climb onto her back—as I stumbled from the calf pen to the chicken coop to the bull pen.

When I was done with my chores, I limped back into the house and then straight to the bathroom where I held onto the wall to stay upright. It took a minute for my eyes to focus enough to see my face in the mirror. There was blood crusted in my nose. Blood crusted in the cracks of my lips. My eyes were bloodshot and puffed into slits. I washed my face, cringing with pain each time I lifted my arms, each time I touched my cheeks, chin, lips, brow. This beating would be impossible to hide under clothes. I'd have to blame the charging bull. Or I could say I tumbled off the tractor into a rock pile. Or maybe I'd say I was running and fell on the cattle guard—the grid of bars with trenches between them, embedded at the entrances and exits to Clyde's land. Every farm had cattle guards to keep the animals from wandering off. When you tripped on them, it was a hard landing if you hit those metal bars. A sure way to break up a human face.

For weeks the pain in my bones, in my spine in particular, persisted. I ignored it the best I could, trying to move my body, and my mind, even, as if nothing unusual had happened. The more I moved, the more I was able to forget about it.

There was something else I was trying to forget, too: the marriage of Cookie and Clyde at the courthouse thirty minutes away in a neighboring town. As commanded, I had served as the witness.

21
Harvesting Rosie

Cookie loved being Mrs. Clyde Hapner. She flashed that name around wherever she went: the hardware store, the little junk shops around town where she bought things on credit, the market where she grocery-shopped if she wasn't going down below.

At church every week, we appeared like any other LDS family: cleaned up for the day, friendly, faithful. Sometimes I looked at the people sitting near me and wondered if any family was hiding secrets as dark and violent as ours.

Amazingly, Clyde stopped touching me after he and my mother were married. I still couldn't relax around him as I was always waiting for the moment he'd lunge. In the fall, when Norm took off for art school in Florida, my anxiety around my stepfather ramped up even higher.

That year, in tenth grade, I kept up all the extra-curricular activities that kept me out of the house. Additionally, I worked on Meeco. Each evening, after chores, I rode Meeco across the fields as fast as I could. For those few short minutes, I felt an exhilarating liberation. Sometimes I imagined that Meeco and I could run all the way to New York. All the way to my sisters.

Just before Christmas, I took on one more activity: hanging out with Gavin.

Only Paige and Jasmine knew about my relationship with Gavin. He was in his twenties, owned a small ranch and was beautiful to look at with straight, thick brown hair that hung over one eye. He was one of the kindest people I'd ever met. And unlike the boys my age there was nothing goofy or odd about Gavin. It was like he was fully formed, completely developed, a person who wasn't trying to figure out who he was. He *just was.*

Late at night, if I wasn't meeting Paige and Jasmine to hang out at Sheryl's Shop or sit on the grass near the phone booth, I rode my bike to Gavin's house. We drank beer from time to time. And we had sex. What happened between us was so intimate and real it didn't resemble, even in shadow form, the things that Clyde had done to me in the field and in the milking parlor.

Though Gavin was older than me, I was the one in charge. This isn't to say I bossed him around the way Cookie bossed me. It was that nothing happened unless I wanted it to happen. He never touched me unless I wanted him to touch me. We only drank if I wanted to drink. If I wanted to just sit with him on his couch watching TV with my head tucked into the warm spot on his chest, then that's what we did. Out around town, when I ran into Gavin, we stopped and chatted and there was always a charming twinkle in his eye. But he never let on that we were seeing each other. I'd told him that my mother would take our relationship as further proof of the slutting, whoring tendencies she'd been accusing me of since I was eight.

I felt almost as close to Gavin as I did to Paige and Jasmine. And as it had been with my friends, I kept the beatings and the years of molestation a deeply hidden secret. Something only my sisters and the two perpetrators themselves knew. Once, Gavin remarked that I had more farm injuries decorating my body than any farm girl he'd ever met. Still, he didn't suspect that anything more than Cookie ranting and raving at me was going on at home. He just thought I worked harder and was tougher than everyone else.

Each day that followed a night with Gavin, my life was a little easier to manage as I felt the glow of him on my skin and carried that glow with me wherever I went. It was like he had infused me with something, a fuel that kept me going through the terrors at home.

One night, when I planned to sneak out later to meet Gavin, Clyde called me into the living room. I was wearing a nightgown, as if to convince my mother and Clyde that I was in for the night. The TV was on and Cookie appeared rapt. Clyde had one arm across my mother's shoulder; he looked over the back of the couch at me.

"You forgot to close the bull pen," he said.

"I did?" I didn't doubt him. I had been drinking more and more, and smoking pot, too. It was all a glorious escape, helping me leave my body so I could float in my head through chores, dinner with Cookie and Clyde, beatings from my mother, and the echoes of beatings that I carried with me at all times. That day, I'd smoked pot before the evening chores. I was surprised that closing the bull pen was the only thing I forgot.

"Yes. You did. And do you know how hard it was to corral him back in?" Clyde took his arm off Cookie.

"I'm really sorry." I was. I did know how hard it was to corral him back in.

Cookie finally looked away from the TV. She elbowed Clyde and said, "And you're gonna stand for that? You're her father now."

"I'm thinking," Clyde said. He looked at Cookie, then picked up his glass of milk from the coffee table and gulped it down.

"Well, I don't have time for this shit." Cookie stood and rushed toward me. She slapped my face with both hands, back and forth, and then pulled me to the ground by my hair. Clyde sat on the couch watching. My mother kicked me once, hard, in the gut and then looked back at Clyde on the couch. "You're her fucking father now, you gotta do this, too!"

Cookie grabbed my hair again, this time pulling me up off the floor. She led me by the hair until I was bent over Clyde's knees. He lifted his hand and started paddling my bottom as if he were driving a spike into hard dirt. Cookie continued to kick me, but she couldn't raise her leg high enough to get much force. I turned my head into Clyde so she wouldn't kick my face. He then lifted my nightgown and continued to violently spank me while my mother screamed and tried to land her pill-wobbly kicks.

The humiliation was far greater than the pain. It was like a fuzzy mold that instantly coated me from the inside out. That my mother would take part in this ritual shouldn't have shocked me, but it did. I thought of the pills on the dresser next to my bed. In my head, I could see myself swallowing all of them and then going to sleep. A solid, peaceful, permanent sleep.

When they were done, Clyde and Cookie were both panting and sweating. I yanked down my nightgown, went into my room, and got dressed. That night at Gavin's house, I did three shots of vodka. Then I lay in his bed and let him fold himself around my back like a human shell.

"Don't move," I whispered. "Let's just lie here."

"Whatever you want," Gavin said. It was what he always said.

I considered telling him about what had happened, but when I started to say the words, they soured in my mouth. It was too grotesque to say aloud. And the longer I lay with Gavin, the more I forgot about Cookie and Clyde. Being in his arms could erase just about anything. I was happily, perfectly, contentedly in the present.

Unfortunately, Cookie and Clyde quickly worked the spanking into the beating repertoire. I threw my nightgown away and wore sweatpants to bed from then on.

The summer before eleventh grade, Boone offered me his old Chevy truck for only a hundred dollars. He knew I wanted my own truck, and though this one was worth more than that, he was willing to let me have it for what it had cost him to get it running again. My guess is that the only reason Cookie and Clyde agreed to the purchase, and provided the money for it, was that Boone made the offer standing in our living room, with all of us present. How could Clyde say no and still pretend he was a doting stepfather?

I loved having my own wheels, and I even loved how beautifully beat-up this truck was: originally it had been black or blue, but there were so many rust and paint-over-rust spots that it was as multicolored as a calico cat.

Just a couple of weeks later, Clyde once again had the chance to prove himself in the community as an upstanding stepfather. A neighboring farmer had an old, unbroken white Arabian named Ghost that he didn't have time to train. The neighbor knew I showed Meeco at 4-H and thought I might enjoy a second horse. Clyde agreed to trade two steer and some hay for Ghost, as long as he came with the rusty two-horse trailer Clyde had seen abandoned on the farmer's property.

I was thrilled with Ghost. He was massive, surly, and stubborn. But unlike my massive, surly, stubborn mother, Ghost adapted to my needs. He learned to listen to me. He learned to trust me. And he learned to love me. I loved him back, just as I loved Meeco.

After hours and hours of training Ghost, I finally hitched the two-horse trailer to my truck and took him out to shows along with Meeco. When I left home with both horses like that, I felt like I was on a road trip with my two best friends.

Everyone got a participation ribbon at these events, so that never felt like much of a reward. But the couple of times Meeco and I placed second and third in reining and showmanship gave me a boost of confidence and a little bit of pride. I would have done it all even if I never won a thing. Just being away from the farm, with two enormous, elegant creatures I loved almost as much as my sisters, was a prize in itself.

In spite of the fact that they had paid for and allowed me to keep the horses, Cookie and Clyde showed no interest in my ribbons and never even asked how I did in competitions or in any other extracurricular activities I participated in. But Boone was generously curious about my riding, showmanship performances, and many other things I did away from the farm. He wanted to see my ribbons and hear the details about the competitions. And, in spite of Boone's firm belief that "a football field is a terrible waste of a good cow pasture," he and his wife showed up at their son's football games. And always, when they were in the stands, they hollered out for me too as I leapt in the air with the cheerleading squad.

This mattered to me far more than they ever could have known. At the time, I often felt that my accomplishments were worthless unless someone I cared about acknowledged my efforts. My teachers and coaches at school provided the feedback I needed with their abundant praise and encouragement. Academically, I was pointed out as one of the kids who should be heading to college. And Paige, Jasmine, and Gavin made me feel as if everything I did was spectacular. Whereas I was invisible at home, I was entirely visible outside of it.

22
Mothering Cookie

B ecause of my early-morning farm chores, I was
rarely allowed to sleep out of the house. I was allowed to have friends stay over, though, and in eleventh grade Jasmine stayed with us frequently. I was
amazed that anyone, even someone from a farm town,
could tolerate the cats—there were more than forty by
then. There was no escaping the smell of cat piss and
cat droppings that littered the floors and carpets. And
the cat hair could not be contained. Boone once told
me that he watched Clyde pour milk into his cereal one
day, and a cloud of cat hair floated up above the bowl.

Cookie, high as ever on pills, was frequently happy
that year. To my mother's delight, Norm had returned
home from college. Cookie and Clyde had "borrowed"
his student loan and scholarship money. And since they

had yet to pay it back, Norm had no way to cover his tuition. My mother's happiness over Norm, along with the presence of Jasmine, brought out Cookie's best self. She was funny, charming, entertaining. She cooked big meals and told stories of go-go dancing and singing backup. She even taught Jasmine and me a doo-wop dance that we performed in a talent show at school.

I had told Jasmine enough Cookie stories for her to know that what she saw was only a brief performance. But I hadn't told enough stories for her to know how mentally ill my mother and Clyde were. How they regularly held me down so they could whip and beat me. To Jasmine, Cookie was all fun with an occasional drunken mean streak.

It was in Jasmine's presence, while Cookie was doing what I thought of as *The Cookie Show*, that my mother offered to sew the Owl costume for the school mascot. Moments later, after Jasmine gushed over Cookie's generosity, my mother offered to sew my junior prom dress as well. Now I gushed. I was so taken aback that I offered to pay for the fabric. Cookie insisted that *she* buy the fabric, but I knew that soon enough, with Jasmine out of the house, she'd want some money from me.

Now that I had a truck and a little more freedom, I needed money for gas and alcohol. Jasmine needed money to buy a prom dress. Unlike Paige, she wasn't able to sew something as complicated as a formal gown. So we started a housecleaning service and drew up a couple of fliers. We dropped them off downtown and within a day we had a single weekly customer, Craig Harrison, who paid us ten dollars an hour each to clean his house. I'd met Craig a couple of times before because he was a friend of Clyde's.

At Craig's place, Jasmine and I put on Top 40 radio as loud as it could go and sang and danced while we worked. Since his bathroom repulsed us both, we did it together as fast as we could, and only when a song we both loved was on. In spite of the bathroom, cleaning Craig's house was relatively easy work compared to mucking out stalls, stables, pens, and corrals. Physically, it was much easier than hauling farm equipment and buckets of water. Emotionally, it was a vacation compared to castrating bull calves.

One morning when Jasmine was helping Clyde and me in the milking parlor I brought up that we'd been cleaning Craig's house.

Clyde stopped what he was doing; he pulled his head back and smiled.

"You're cleaning Craig's place? Why didn't you tell me?"

I hadn't told him because I spent as little time as

possible with Cookie and Clyde and barely spoke when I was with them.

"He's disgusting!" Jasmine said. "His place is a mess!" I wondered what Jasmine thought of the acres of cat droppings and dead, desiccated mice decorating the floors of my house.

"Ah, he's a good guy."

"I guess," I said. "We don't really talk to him. He leaves us cash on the kitchen counter."

"Listen." Clyde put an arm on each of our shoulders. "I'm sure he'll pay you a lot more than ten bucks an hour if you pretty girls give him a little something special on the side."

Jasmine screamed and then started laughing. The Craig we'd met would never do anything of the sort.

"That's disgusting." I shrugged away from Clyde's arms and then attached the suctions to the next cow on the ramp. Jasmine kept laughing and snorting. She couldn't figure out if Clyde was entirely serious or not. And I wasn't about to set her straight. Clyde's dirty little comments always reminded me that his dirty little acts weren't that far behind us. In fact, the memories of those acts felt like scars deep inside my body—internal welts that I would permanently carry with me.

A few days later, Cookie drove down below and bought yards and yards of fabric to make my prom gown. It was going to be one-shouldered and ruffled, like what a Spanish castanet player might wear. But instead of being red and black, this would be black and white.

At the first fitting, I stood in my underwear next to the dining table where the sewing machine was as Cookie zipped me into the dress. The satin was so creamy and shiny that it looked wet. My mother hadn't finished the hem and had yet to apply the ruffles to the skirt and the one shoulder. But a bodice had been assembled, the zipper was attached, and the neckline was finished.

The zipper stopped between my shoulder blades. Cookie tugged it up. She tugged again.

"Fuck!" she said.

"What?"

"Your fucking shoulders! You've got fucking football player shoulders!" My mother kept tugging.

There wasn't an ounce of fat on me. You couldn't find an inch on my body to pinch. But after farming from age eleven, I had shoulders as strong and wide as some boys'. During my short escape to New York, my sisters were impressed with my powerful shoulders and sculpted arms. They made me feel proud of my strong physique. To my mother, however, I was flawed.

"Take it off! Take it fucking off!" Cookie pulled the two sides where the zipper wouldn't close and ripped the dress open.

"Mom!" I turned, trying to keep the dress intact.

"TAKE THE FUCKING THING OFF!" Cookie beat at me as she pulled the dress apart, tearing it off my body. I fell to the ground as she yanked at the fabric; I was trying to get out of the dress in order to get her angry fists and claws off me.

When I was finally out of the dress, Cookie picked it up and whipped me with it. It didn't hurt at all, but I worried about the destruction of what I hoped would be a beautiful gown. I begged her to save the work she'd done already.

"Save it? Are you fucking kidding me?" My mother threw the balled-up dress into the kitchen sink. She opened the cupboards and removed piles of bowls and dishes, dropping them on the counter or the floor. Some broke, others survived.

"What are you looking for?" I wanted to retrieve the dress but knew that if I got any closer, I'd make the situation worse.

"None of your fucking business." Cookie pulled out a bottle of rum and overturned it on the dress. I gasped.

She took a match from the counter and lit the dress on fire. I worried she'd grasp the fireball of the dress and throw it at me. She didn't. She stood there and watched it burn. I stood behind her, watching as well.

The next day, Cookie went down below again and bought more fabric. When that dress was too loose in the hips, it, too, was destroyed. This time cut into pieces.

It wasn't until the third fitting that my mother's work wasn't destroyed by her angry hands. She cursed me through every stitch on that gown—that I was ever born, that I was a girl who wanted a dress, that I was ungrateful, that I had my father's height and shoulders, that I didn't deserve even an inch of satin.

In the end, it was a magnificent creation. Cookie possessed a talent equal to Paige's. But I would have been happier cleaning more houses and buying a simple red gown like the one Jasmine bought in Boise.

23
Out of Perilous Peak

My senior year, I was voted student body secretary, named editor of the yearbook, joined the Natural Helpers Club (where, ironically, we were trained to help abused and at-risk teens), and was nominated as a Homecoming Princess. It seemed I had finally maxed out on the number of activities I could do while still working on the farm, riding Meeco and Ghost, and secretly meeting Gavin late at night. The only way to do more would be to stop sleeping. Already, I slept less and less.

And I drank more and more. I'd always been a part of the Oakview High party scene. But now it was like I was in a party competition, pushing to make the championship play-offs. Keggers, beer bongs, speed shots, pot in chocolate chip brownies, speed, and mushrooms—I turned none of it away. The alcohol and drugs were like a giant wet sponge that wiped everything down and rubbed away the hardest edges of my life. Already, I did so much hard work with compromised strength—cheerleading after having been beaten so badly my body felt like it was on fire every time I moved; 4-H and other shows when it hurt to place my battered body on my horses' backs; farm chores when I couldn't lift my arms above my head because, I feared, Cookie had dislocated my shoulder—that to do anything while drunk or high only made it easier.

I don't know who came up with idea, but soon enough my group at school was using farm syringes to inject oranges with vodka. We ate the oranges throughout the day. I liked to peel mine in first period math, and then eat one or two sections in each class. I'd have a nice buzz going until I got home from school and could sneak some of Cookie's hidden liquor. Even though my mother, who was obviously addicted to pills at this point, claimed she no longer drank, there was always enough booze in the house to satisfy a weekend binge.

The evening after Halloween, when I was still hungover from the night before, Cookie came into the milking parlor while Boone and I worked. The cows mooed and shifted as my mother's cigarette smoke wafted in their faces.

"Boone, I need to have a word alone with my daughter." Cookie dropped her cigarette butt on the cement floor and smashed it out with her shiny red boot that looked entirely out of place on the farm. My stomach clenched. Cookie appeared ready for a fight.

"Whatever you have to say to Rosanne, you can say right in front of me." Boone didn't look toward my mother; he just hooked up the suctions to the next cow and acted as if she hadn't asked anything of him. I moved in closer to him so that his body was blocking me from Cookie.

"Get the fuck outta here!" Cookie said.

Boone paused for a second, staring my mother down. Then he turned away from her and carried on. "Camille, I have a job to do here and I'm not going to stop just because you have something to say to Rosanne." Boone had no idea what had been going on all these years. But he certainly knew my mother had a temper. And he'd probably guessed that she slapped me, as many kids in the area got a slap every now and then.

"Then you're fired." Cookie reached into her cleavage, pulled out her cigarettes, and lit a new one.

"I work for Clyde," Boone said. "He can come out here and fire me if he'd like."

"You're a fucking pain in my ass, you know

that?" Cookie blew out smoke. Then she barked, "ROSANNE!"

"I'm right here." I leaned my head out from behind Boone's shoulders.

"I just heard from a little birdie that you've been partying night and day like a dumb little drunk."

My whole life, everything my mother had accused me of was entirely untrue of me while being entirely true of her. She first called me a slut at age eight, when she was picking up different men in bars every night and I hadn't even developed my first crush. She'd been calling me a pig and a slob since we'd moved in with Clyde, and she was the one who had forty cats that acted as if they were outdoors when they were sitting in the middle of the living room. She called me lazy while she slept in most days, had no evening chores, and never got up in the middle of the night for hay-baling. She called me stupid, and though I don't actually think she was stupid, whenever she said it to me, I wondered if that's what she believed about herself.

But now she was saying I was *a dumb little drunk*. As much as I wanted this to be true of her instead of me, for the first time, I couldn't honestly deny the charges. And so I lied and said, "I'm not drinking."

Cookie stepped around Boone so she was on the other side of me and said, "You're not? Then why did your school just call me and tell me that they're stripping you of all your stupid clubs and activities?"

"What?" The jolt in my stomach was so strong, it felt like Cookie had kicked me.

"You think you're a high-and-mighty princess at that school. Well, think again." Cookie took a deep drag off her cigarette. "No more cheerleading, no more yearbook, no more pep club or whatever the fuck it is you do over there." Cookie tapped out her ash onto the floor. I watched it fall and felt like my whole soul, my entire being, was falling with it. Without the escape of my activities, my home life was about to turn from brutal and dehumanizing to profoundly brutal and dehumanizing.

"And Clyde and I are taking your truck away," Cookie said. "You've given us no choice. Now what do you have to say for yourself?"

I shook my head. I had nothing to say for myself or for anyone else. I felt myself go silent, locked in my head, shelled up to hide from what was going on around me. I was back in the rocking chair at the foster home. The little girl without her siblings.

"Well, let me tell you this." Cookie clenched the cigarette in her teeth and took another step toward me. She reached her hand out, grabbed my hair at the nape of my neck and started to slam me toward the cement floor when Boone turned and latched on to both of Cookie's wrists until he had wrested her away from me.

"Enough!" Boone snapped.

Cookie spit her cigarette out onto the floor and yelled: "Get the fuck off me!"

"You get on back into the house," Boone pointed to the door. "I'll talk to Rosanne about the drinking."

"Fuck you, you're fired!" Cookie gave Boone the finger and then left the milking parlor.

I was so grateful that Boone had stood up for me that I was trembling with emotion. I wanted to hug him, but he wasn't a hugging guy.

Neither of us said anything for a moment. And then Boone said, "You been drinking?"

"Yes." I felt ashamed.

"You get it under control now, you hear?"

"Okay," I said. "I promise."

"I'm proud of you, Rosanne. You're like a daughter to me. But I'm real disappointed that you've been drinking'."

"I'm sorry." I blinked away tears.

That night I lay in bed and stared at the suicide pills. I couldn't imagine any other way out: I had no money; no means to make money since my truck had been taken away and I had to work on the farm; and no one to legally turn to since the sheriff was Clyde's pal and the county social worker believed everything Cookie had ever said. Even my sisters, who loved me more than anything, couldn't help without risking their own children being taken away. I'd disappointed Boone, and I'd probably disappointed all my teachers. On top of that, college, which had been the Great Escape I'd been working toward, was feeling impossible. If Norm, who Cookie appeared to love, wasn't able to stay in school because Cookie and Clyde had taken his loan money, how would I ever hold on to loan money?

I picked up the pill bottle and shook it. Then I opened it and poured the contents out into my palm. Tomorrow morning, I decided, I would ride each of my horses as a way of saying good-bye to them. And then I would end my life.

Before I fell asleep I thought about everyone I loved: my sisters and Norm first and foremost; Boone; Gavin; and my teachers and all my friends at school. Especially Paige and Jasmine. Since I'd been in Oakview, Paige and Jasmine re-created with me the sister relationship that provided the love and support I craved. They kept me afloat and paddled me to shore whenever I felt I was drowning. But now, it was too late for them to swim after me. I was like a bloodless pig dropped in the hot spring.

When I rolled over in my bed, I caught sight of the

pile of clothes on my floor. Some belonged to Paige and Jasmine. I needed to attend one more day at school, I thought, so that I could return their things. Neither one should have their clothes disintegrate beneath the endless cat urine, droppings, and hair.

In my first period class, Jasmine handed me a vodka orange. I handed her the blue-and-white-striped sweater I had borrowed. Paige sat on the other side of me. To her, I returned a denim skirt she had sewn and three tops that had been passed back and forth between us so many times, I wasn't really sure who the original owner was.

Near the end of that class, Mindy Paletto, the special ed teacher, stuck her head in the room and called me out of class.

I shoved the rest of the vodka orange in my mouth and chewed it quickly as I stoically packed up my backpack. They could strip me of whatever school positions they wanted. By dinnertime, *I* would no longer *be.*

Ms. Paletto and I walked quietly down the hall to her office. She was a tall woman with the same permed hair and short bangs of just about every girl in the school. When we entered the room, Ms. Linden, the girls' basketball and volleyball coach and my psychology teacher, was waiting for us. Ms. Linden's hair was short and sporty. She usually had a huge smile. Now she wasn't smiling.

I sat in the chair closest to the door. I figured if I had to, I'd run out and end the meeting.

"Do you know why we called you in, Rosanne?" Ms. Linden said.

"Yeah." I leaned back in the chair. The vodka from the orange was filling my head with a nice padded mushiness.

Ms. Paletto said, "You can't be a student leader with cheerleading, yearbook—"

"Student government," Ms. Linden said.

"Student government," Ms. Paletto repeated.

I slumped in my seat and said in a bored monotone: "Pep squad, track, basketball, band." I liked both of these teachers so much, but I just wanted this moment to be over with. They were about to take away my life and I, in turn, had to end whatever was left of me.

"Yes," Ms. Paletto said. "You can't be in a role-model position while making so many poor choices with alcohol. The younger students look up to you. The choices you make influence them."

"Sorry," I mumbled. I looked at the clock hanging on the wall and remembered how funny it was that I didn't learn how to tell time until I was eleven.

"Do you have to be somewhere?" Ms. Linden asked.

"No." We were only two minutes in and I was done. *Pull the plug,* I wanted to yell. *Turn on the electric chair, let the guillotine fall, shoot the rifle!*

"We had a faculty meeting yesterday, and it was decided that you were to be stripped of all your positions." Ms. Linden tilted her head and tried to make eye contact with me. I continued to stare at the clock.

"We don't want to do this," Ms. Paletto said.

I shrugged.

"Rosanne, please," Ms. Linden said. "We want to help you."

I shrugged again.

Ms. Linden continued: "We care about you. Just tell us what's going on in your life, why you're partying like this, why you're blowing everything up."

"This is going to hurt your chances of getting into college," Ms. Paletto said. Her voice was going up; she seemed upset, and I felt bad that I was causing her pain.

"There's no money to go to college anyway," I mumbled.

"There are lots of ways to get money for college," Ms. Linden said. "If you'll only tell us why you're being so self-destructive, why you're acting out this way, maybe we can help you. And maybe we can figure out a way for you to hold on to some of your positions."

I shut my eyes.

"Is there something going on at home?" Ms. Paletto asked.

I didn't move.

"Rosanne," Ms. Linden said. "Open your eyes. Look at me."

I looked at her.

"Tell us what's going on at home."

Both women stared at me. I was about to kill myself and no one knew my entire story. My sisters knew the most, but certainly not everything. Norm knew only what he'd witnessed. Cookie didn't believe anything that didn't involve her. And Clyde, who knew all the horrors of the milking parlor and the fields, had no idea what had come before him. Everything was inside me and it would all die with me. But I wanted it to be known. I needed to believe that when I was gone, at least the story of me—the true story of me—would remain.

"There's a lot going on at home," I said. And both women took a deep breath and scooted back in their chairs as if to give me the room to speak. And so I spoke. And I told them everything. And I cried. And I knew that teachers weren't supposed to cry at school because it made them seem unprofessional, but when I saw tears in their eyes, I understood that they were on my side. Telling my story gave me a helium lightness. It felt like I'd released an unfathomable weight from my body. Just as I'd always needed someone to see my achievements so that I could see them myself, I realized that I needed someone to see the abuse I'd suffered, too. Not so I could see it myself, but so I could see myself separate from the abuse. A whole person in spite of it.

"Where are the pills that you were planning to take?" Ms. Linden asked.

"Next to my bed." Where my mother frequently saw them and never moved them.

"What if we just move you out of there and into my spare room?" Ms. Linden said. It was the plan my sister Camille had hoped for. The plan I had thought would be impossible.

Ms. Paletto nodded her head in agreement.

"My mother will never allow it." Of course I'd love it. I'd get to see my friends and do my activities but never see Cookie and Clyde.

"Considering the alternative, the legal steps and the public humiliation that she and Clyde could face if we take this on, she just might," Ms. Paletto said.

"Can I bring my horses?" They were all I'd miss from the farm.

"No, I'm sorry," Ms. Linden said. "And you'll have to stop partying, too."

"I can do that," I said. Giving up my horses was the only painful part of getting away from Cookie and Clyde. But I had to do it; my life depended on it.

While Ms. Linden and Ms. Paletto left to go speak with my mother and Clyde, I stayed at school and worked alone in the yearbook room. I didn't want to go to cheerleading practice where Cookie could storm the gym and humiliate me in front of the cheer squad. Still, it was hard to focus. I kept my eyes on the door, waiting for Cookie to burst in and drag me out by my hair.

After an hour, Ms. Linden finally showed up. She had two thumbs up and her giant smile was back. I ran to her and we hugged.

"What happened?" I asked.

Ms. Linden sat at the table. I took the seat opposite her. I could tell she didn't want to tell me how things had gone down.

"It was strange." She shook her head.

"Did she scream at you?"

"No." Ms. Linden went on to tell me that she and Ms. Paletto had gone to the farm and found only Clyde at home. They were appalled at the filth in the house. Neither would discuss me with Clyde since he wasn't my legal guardian. They left with a promise to return later in the evening.

Ms. Linden dropped Ms. Paletto off at home and then went to get gas. Cookie was at the gas station. Ms. Linden got out of her truck, and my mother rushed to her and told her that she needed help with me. I was a juvenile delinquent, Cookie said, who stayed out all night partying, and she didn't know how to handle me.

Instead of confronting my mother, as she had originally intended, Ms. Linden told Cookie she could offer her spare room to me—free room and board. She'd take me off Cookie's hands and set me straight. Cookie agreed immediately, and Ms. Linden followed her back to the house.

"I was surprised by how quickly she packed your clothes," Ms. Linden said gently, as if knowing this might sting. "I mean, in less than five minutes all your stuff was in garbage bags and the bags were in the back of my truck."

I didn't feel hurt the way Ms. Linden expected I might. Of all the things my mother had done, this was the least of it. But I was confused. Was Cookie really giving in so easily? Could it be that my mother was truly done with me? Maybe she and Clyde weren't fighting this because I wasn't as essential as I had been on the farm. Now that my brother wasn't in school, he was able to work there full-time. Much of what he did in the day was stuff I'd been doing after school for years.

And maybe Clyde, now that he no longer trapped me in the milking parlor or on the fields, was done with me. It seemed too easy to be true.

Ms. Linden drove slowly and calmly. Her house was quaint with flowers in front and shutters framing the windows. It was a mobile home but was so cheery and solid looking, it took me a minute to realize that. Also, it was on a cul de sac and not in a mobile home park.

"You ready to do this?" Ms. Linden asked.

"Totally," I said.

"You think you can live here?" She looked up toward the house.

"Yeah!"

"You're going to have to call me Alaina now," she said.

"You're going to have to call me Rosie," I said, and we both laughed.

"And I'm very serious about the drinking and drugs. And no boys, either. I'm sorry."

"So am I." Gavin might as well have been a drug, a beautiful, multicolored, smoke-filled fantasy. I loved him, but I was ready to let him go.

We grabbed the garbage bags from the back of Alaina's truck and hauled them inside.

The house was clean, and the sheets on my bed were

fresh and crisp. I couldn't stop thinking about how strange it was that when I'd woken up that morning, it was the last day of my life. And now I was still breathing, I'd moved out of Cookie and Clyde's, and I had all my activities, none of my chores, and no one around who might beat me.

After I unpacked, we went grocery shopping and Alaina let me pick out anything I wanted. I couldn't decide what kind of cereal I'd most like, so we came home with three different boxes. None of them were puffed rice.

I slept until seven. It was glorious. And when I walked into the kitchen, there was a pot of coffee brewing. Alaina sat at the kitchen table; it looked like she was doing paperwork for school. She shut the notebook she was writing in and smiled at me. "Cereal?"

"Yeah."

"It's on the counter."

The three boxes were lined up. I picked up the Special K and then opened a few cupboards until I found a bowl. When I poured in the milk, no cat hair floated up. It was just milk and cereal.

I sat at the table across from Alaina. She slid a spiral-bound notebook over to me. On the cover was a picture of Ziggy the Pinhead, a cartoon character who was popular that year.

"That for me?"

"Yup." Alaina said. "It's for you to write it all down."

"Write what down?" I asked.

"Everything you think, feel, hear, see, and remember. Write it all down. I'll never open it and read it. That book is your sacred place where you can say whatever you want."

"It's gonna be one sad book."

"No, it's for the good stuff, too! All the great memories you have of your friends and your life at school."

I lifted the notebook, opened it to the first page, and stared at the blue lines. I had so much to say. I knew I would fill that book.

24

Exorcism

Every day that I woke up at Alaina's house seemed like a miracle. And with all the time freed up from not doing farm work, not partying, not seeing Gavin, and, sadly, not riding my horses, I put more effort than ever into my schoolwork and activities. And I got a job, too. I was waiting tables at Beanie's Diner, where everything was so slow—the customers, the cooks, the cashiers—that I sometimes felt like I was the only living thing around.

I should have felt relieved and happy, but I was tense, on guard. I couldn't believe this freedom wouldn't end soon. In each class, I snapped my head toward the door every few minutes, expecting my mother to fill the doorframe with her big hair, her big voice, and her big nails reaching toward me. I continued to watch for her even after Norm, in one of his regular phone calls to me, assured me that Cookie was now so strung out on pills that most days she never even left the couch.

It wasn't surprising when Cookie started phoning Alaina at school and asking that I be returned to her. But it was surprising that she wasn't calling Alaina a bitch, a twat, a whore—any of the things she'd called me and my sisters over the years. Instead, Alaina told me, Cookie was almost sweet on the phone. She said she missed me and loved me and asked if Alaina would please return me to her. Even when she claimed to have hired a lawyer so that she could get permanent custody of me, she wasn't screaming. The last statement was proof of her pill-stoned confusion. My mother had never lost custody of me. She'd simply agreed, while filling her station wagon with unleaded gas, that I could live with Alaina.

Alaina never seemed worried about the return, or the rise, of Cookie. But I couldn't shake my mother from my psyche. And then I got a long letter from Gi, the most thorough person in our family. She made a point-by-point analysis of my situation that reassured me in ways that nothing else could. Gi offered logic: *If the woman cannot pay her phone bill, then she definitely cannot afford to pay lawyer's fees.* Gi offered insight: *She is determined to control your life because she is not able to control hers . . . to see you having long-lasting friendships with your peers eats at her.* Gi offered encouragement: *You are an extremely strong and independent young lady. . . . Go to college, otherwise the choices for your future will be limited. . . . Don't give in or give up.* And Gi offered love: *I love you and am always thinking of you. . . .* Je t'aime, mia bambina.

Armed with this letter, I started to believe that, like my sisters, I might soon be in control of my own life.

That confidence faltered when Cookie called Alaina and calmly told her that Clyde had a gun and she had asked him to use it to get me back. We had no idea whether Clyde knew of this plan or this was just an idle threat by my mother.

"Does he really own a gun?" Alaina asked. We were in her truck driving home from school. She was nervously biting her bottom lip. And she frequently checked the rearview mirror as if someone were following us. This was the first time Alaina appeared shaken up.

"Every farmer owns a gun," I said.

"Shit," Alaina said, and then she smiled quickly at me.

"Yeah, shit," I said, and we both smiled. The student-teacher relationship had all but dissolved and within a few short days Alaina seemed more like a mother to me. An interested and caring mother.

"Does he have that kind of personality? Would he show up waving a gun around?"

"I dunno," I said. "He's definitely had to kill a few lame animals. But I don't know if he'd shoot a person." And then I thought about everything Clyde had done to me, the way he treated my body, my mind, and my soul. And I said, "You know what. I think he would shoot a person. I think he doesn't see people as people. Or, at least, not women and girls."

"Yeah," Alaina said. "I've got a feeling you're right."

When we got home that night, Alaina and I circled the house, locking all the windows and doors. We pulled the curtains shut, too, making sure there weren't any cracks where someone could peer in on us. While I made pasta for dinner, Alaina called around and came up with a list of homes I should run to if Cookie, or armed Clyde, showed up at her house. It was an undercover operation, Alaina said. I was to tell no one at school where I was staying on any particular night, so that no one would be able to report my whereabouts to my mother or Clyde.

"The doors to these homes are open to you, twenty-four hours a day." We had just sat down to eat. Alaina slid a piece of paper across the table to me. Ms. Paletto was on there, as were several of the other teachers at my school. If there was a gun coming, I had an army at my back.

The day the Oakview High Natural Helpers Club left for a mountain retreat, I relaxed in a way that was so rare for me it felt unfamiliar. Cookie and Clyde wouldn't know where I was and so couldn't come and get me. I'd be entirely safe from everything that had threatened and harmed me since the day in New York when the social worker hauled me and Norm off to the Callahans'.

Alaina was the faculty leader for Natural Helpers, but instead of driving up with her in her truck, I rode on the bus with my friends. Jasmine, who was in the club, too, brought a boom box and we sat in the back of the bus and played music. As Jasmine and I sang along with her cassettes, dancing in our seats and hooting at passing cars out the bus windows, I felt unshackled, liberated. It was the way that alcohol used to make me feel, yet I was sober. When AC/DC's "Whole Lotta Rosie" came on, Jasmine and I screamed and sang together as loudly as we could, rocking so hard it felt like the bus was jolting with our movements. This was true freedom. And I wanted it to last forever.

At the retreat, there were scheduled activities in the

morning, free time before and after lunch, panels in the later afternoon, bonding and trust-building games every evening, and a campfire each night where the group talked about everything they had figured out or learned during the day. In most discussions that week, I had experienced some form of what was being discussed: alcoholism, drugs, mental illness, abandonment, foster parents, being taken away from siblings, physical abuse, emotional abuse, sexual abuse, humiliation, and being shamed and not believed when reporting a crime. The only things I hadn't experienced first-hand were the eating disorders. I wondered then if having been starved and forced to search for food at such a young age had prevented me from ever developing an eating disorder.

Near the end of the retreat, Jasmine and I took out a canoe. We started off quietly paddling around, but soon we were fooling around, one of us standing up and rocking the canoe while the other one screamed. It was when we stood up together that the canoe flipped and we were plunged into the cold water. Of course we thought this was hilarious, and we laughed continuously as we swam the canoe to the embankment and then climbed out. Our tennis shoes squeaked with water, our clothes clung to our skin. We disrobed down to our underwear and then ran, wet balls of clothes in our hands, through the camp to our cabin where we could change.

That night, I woke up in my bunk bed with a fire burning in my spine. Jasmine was on the bunk above me, and eighteen other girls filled the rest of the beds in the long room. They were all sleeping. Someone was snoring softly. And the wind was blowing a branch against the screen window, making a noise that sounded like *shhhh*.

"Jasmine," I whispered. I tried to lift my foot to kick the bottom of her bed, but the fire roared through me and I gasped. "Jasmine!" I said louder.

Jasmine flipped over the edge of the bed, her head hanging upside down, and stared at me. "What?"

"Help!" I tried to get up and the fire flared as if gasoline had been thrown on it. "I can't move and I'm in so much pain I want to scream."

Jasmine flipped out of the bed and ran off to get Alaina. A few other girls stirred awake, and soon everyone had gathered around the bed and was trying to figure out what was wrong or how they could help.

When Alaina stepped into the cabin, I started crying. I told her about having fallen into the lake earlier in the day. I suggested that maybe the cold water had done something to me.

Jasmine was sent to get more help and several counselors quickly arrived. Together they carried me, as gently as possible, to Alaina's truck, where I lay curled up on my side, my head on the armrest. It was decided that I would be taken to the emergency room of the hospital an hour away.

Alaina drove slowly off the rutted dirt road of the retreat. Once we reached the main road, she hit the gas, the car humming in a different key as she accelerated.

"You okay?" Alaina looked over at me. I could barely turn my head her way.

"Maybe we should go back and I'll sleep it off." It was hard to speak through the pain, but the night was so quiet and dark, Alaina could have heard me breathing.

"I don't think you can sleep this off," Alaina said.

"My mom doesn't like me to go to a doctor."

"Your mom's no longer in charge," Alaina said.

Alaina was quiet for a few moments. "Why doesn't your mom want you to go to the doctor?" I could tell by her overly calm voice that she was coming up with theories.

"I dunno," I said. "She's probably afraid of what they would find if they actually checked me out."

"I see." Alaina's mouth was pulled tight. She looked worried and that made me worry, even though it was hard to have a thought beyond the pain.

"We don't have to tell her," I said.

"Yeah," Alaina said. "When we get to the hospital, let's just say I'm your mother."

"Okay." I loved the sound of that. It even eased the pain a bit.

In the hospital a nurse helped me change into an open blue gown and I was examined and then wheeled into a room where my body was x-rayed.

After the X-ray, a doctor with deep black eyes and a nurse whose loopy curled hair was like a cap on her head came into the room and stood by the bed. I had been given some medication that began to numb my pain and my senses. I wondered where Alaina was and why they hadn't brought her back to the room.

"Rosanne," the nurse said. "Doctor Abrams has examined your X-rays and sees skeletal injuries that indicate severe physical abuse." She spoke very slowly and clearly, as if I might have trouble understanding her.

"Several of your vertebrae are cracked and you have two cracked ribs," the doctor said. I felt oddly detached from this information. Maybe it was because the physical abuse was no surprise to me—I'd been enduring it for years. Now that I was living at Alaina's, I was actually free of it.

"Who did this to you, Rosanne?" The nurse asked.

I put into practice everything we at Natural Helpers

had learned to reject when I said, "I was bucked off my horse. That's all." The cover-up lie was pure instinct. Other than the day I confessed everything to Alaina and Ms. Paletto, my entire life had been a cover-up lie.

"You were bucked off a horse?" the nurse said.

"Yes." As soon as I said it, I wondered why I was keeping up the lie. It could be because I was on pain-killers, surrounded by strangers, and I hadn't yet figured out how to speak openly about my mother.

"There are what appear to be whip mark scars on your backside," the nurse said, her voice getting a little sharper. I could tell she was a mother who had little patience for untruths.

I stuck with my story, instinct over logic again, and said, "I landed on my crop. That's what the whip marks are from."

"This is a safe space," the nurse said. "You can tell us how you got these injuries." I had just heard the term *safe space* for the first time at the retreat. And now she was using these words with me.

"You don't get a whip mark from landing on a crop," the doctor said.

"If you tell us who did this, we can put an end to it. We can take care of this." The nurse looked at me, her eyes blinking hard. I wished we could start from the beginning and I'd just tell them it was Cookie and

Clyde. It was hard to remember that I was free. And it was hard to get used to the idea that being free meant speaking the truth.

"My mother and stepfather have been regularly beating me," I said. "But it's already been dealt with—"

The nurse picked up the phone in my room, dialed a number, and said, "Someone grab that mother from the waiting room before she runs!"

"Wait!' I said. "*She's* not my mother!"

She held the phone against her chest and looked at me. And as if on cue, Alaina opened the door and stepped into the room. "Well?" she said. "What'd you find?"

"Are you her mother?" the doctor asked.

"Yes, I'm her mother," Alaina said.

The doctor's face darkened, as if he were suddenly standing in a shadow. He stepped closer to the bed and I had a feeling that he was deliberately creating a barrier between Alaina and me.

"She's not my mom!" I said.

"Ma'am," the doctor said. "Let's talk in the hall."

"I swear that's not my mom," I said, and I shut my eyes as the drugs were making me drowsy. It was almost like talking in my sleep when I said, "My mom's name is Cookie . . . Camille. . . . Calcaterra . . . Brooks . . . Hapner."

It was almost an hour later when the nurse woke me and helped me get dressed. I was being released.

Driving away from the hospital, Alaina and I laughed about the mix-up.

"That nurse almost cried with relief once she understood that you'd already been removed from the house," Alaina said. "It took me half an hour to convince her that the situation had been dealt with. I mean, if they had called the police, you would have been thrown into the foster system in Boise—away from school, your friends. . ." Her voice trailed off.

"Where were people like that when I needed them?" I asked, and then I blinked and was asleep again.

The pain problem was resolved by simple anti-inflammatories. I never had such extreme pain again and I always wondered if the reason it flared up like that then was because it could. There had never been the luxury of feeling pain with Cookie and Clyde. There were always more chores to do, more beatings to take. Any pain I had needed to be ignored or masked with alcohol and drugs. It was only in my sobriety, and in the absence of Cookie's and Clyde's threats, that I could really feel it.

Or maybe that night was the one great, final release of pain. All of it. From every beating, every year, everyone. My exorcism.

25

Unbridled

By January, Cookie's calls to Alaina were infrequent. And when she did call, Alaina said, she sounded so doped up, she could barely form a simple sentence. Finally, I exhaled the giant breath I'd been holding since I'd left the house last fall. The small pleasures of living at Alaina's now gave off an even bigger spark. I felt a giddiness each time one of my sisters called, and I could talk freely without having to stretch out the phone cord and hide, or speak in code, or pretend it was someone else on the line. And whenever Norm stopped by to visit, I didn't feel the anxious tension I'd always had when he had showed up at my friends' houses as Cookie's messenger, telling me to come home and feed the chickens, or to come home and find the wayward bull, or to come home because I'd left my shoes in the hall and my mother had stubbed her toe when she walked into them and was holding a belt and ready to whip me. When my friends came over, I thrilled at the ease I felt now that I no longer had to worry about being embarrassed by my pill-stoned mother talking to the cats in her half-baby, half-screeching voice. And everything in my body relaxed knowing that no one would say something sexually suggestive to my friends the way Clyde did when he worked his pervy thoughts into thinly veiled statements about our youth or prettiness.

Even working on my application to Idaho State University at Pocatello had a feathery weightlessness as I did it in the serenity of Alaina's house. I felt safe from the mockery my mother doled out whenever I had dared to dream of a life beyond the milking parlor. Gi and I talked on the phone frequently then. While she fretted over the application deadline, I fretted over the sentences in my essay. Alaina didn't fret about any of it. She had unwavering faith in me and my abilities.

That spring I ran to the mailbox every day after school. There were often letters from Gi, and bills for Alaina. The letters made me happy, but I didn't want to answer them until I'd heard from Pocatello.

And then the day came when there was a thick packet in the mailbox. I held it in my hand, staring at my name. My heart thumped quickly, like a rabbit

trapped in my chest, urging me to rip open the enve-
lope. I pulled out the cover letter and read the word
Congratulations!

"I'M IN!" I screamed as I ran into the house. I
wanted to call my sisters and Norm and tell them right
away. And, surprisingly, I also wanted to call Cookie. I
realized then that no matter what she'd done to me, no
matter how she'd beaten and abused me, part of me still
wanted my mother's love and approval.

I picked up the phone and called Alaina, who was
still at school. She screamed and hollered down the hall
to Ms. Paletto, "Rosie's going to Pocatello!" Then she
said, "Call your sisters direct right now! Don't worry
about the long-distance charges!"

I dialed Gi's number first. She screamed, "*MIA
BAMBINA!* I'm so proud of you!"

I called Camille and she screamed, "FRANK!
FRANK! ROSIE'S GOING TO COLLEGE!"

I called Cherie and she screamed, "HOLY SHIT! I
KNEW YOU'D DO IT! I JUST KNEW IT!"

I called Norm and he said, "Ah, Rosie, that's great,
but I'm gonna miss you."

"Will you tell Mom and Clyde?" I asked Norm.

"Do you want me to tell them?"

"I guess. I dunno why, but I want them to know."

"They'll steal your loan money if I tell them," Norm said, and we both laughed.

"Do they know that we hang out sometimes? Do they ever ask if you've seen me?"

"Nah," Norm said. "It's like Gi, Camille, and Cherie. They just pretend you never even existed."

"Wow." I was starting to feel myself shutting down and closing up.

"Yeah, but who gives a shit about them," Norm said. "You're goin' off to college!" And just like that, the joy in my brother's voice brought me back to my wonderful day.

That night I lay in bed and let myself cry with happiness. College had always seemed an impossibility— something for rich kids, people with parents who helped them study for the SAT and got them math tutors. When Mrs. Connors, the librarian in Caldwell, had said she imagined I'd go to college, it seemed so far away, I could barely imagine still being alive by then. But there was I was: alive, safe, and happy.

In June, my sisters sent me money for graduation. I combined that money with what I saved from waitressing to buy myself an old, used Mustang. Once I had the car, I felt a whole new level of exhilarating independence. No one could stop me from going anywhere

I wanted or doing anything I wanted. I truly had been freed.

Once a joiner, always a joiner. And so, at Pocatello, I joined a sorority (Sigma Sigma Sigma) and the Homecoming committee, and I tried out for and was chosen to be Benny the Bengal, the school mascot, for my sophomore year.

My sisters sent me letters at school and called regularly to check in. I felt so grown up when I talked to them. I was still Gi's *bambina,* but I was no longer the baby. Norm snuck the occasional call from Cookie and Clyde's phone. And once he called in a panic because Paige Paisley had told a few people she was trying to decide between joining the army and marrying Norm. She was joking, only about the Norm part, but the rumor spread so quickly that my brother couldn't go into town without running into people who wanted to congratulate him on his engagement. The congratulations didn't stop until Paige finally did join the army and was shipped off to training.

The most surprising thing that happened that first year at Pocatello was that Cookie started sending me cards and letters. In her impeccable, slanted Catholic school handwriting, she told me the things I'd ached to hear when I lived with her: she loved me and she was proud of me. She also said she hoped we could make things right between us.

Alaina called regularly and even managed to visit me a few times. She claimed to be astonished by how hard I worked between going to classes, manning the information desk in the student union, and waitressing on the weekends. It was all fun. I loved talking to people, and barely considered any of it to be work. Work, in my mind, was what I'd done on the farm before and after school. Work was baling hay at one in the morning before a seventh grade American history exam.

That winter, Cookie and Clyde sold the farm and moved two hours south to Prairie Valley, Idaho, where Norm joined them to live on a smaller farm. Alaina speculated that they moved because they were shamed out of town. Everyone knew I had been living with her my senior year. And eventually they all knew why as well.

As for the forty cats, Cookie told me in a letter, Clyde got rid of all but three. There wasn't room enough for them in the new place.

I imagined Clyde killing the cats and tossing the dead cats into the manure pit. He was heartless with the animals and always flashed his white teeth when he dumped whatever animal had died that year into the pit. I worried about my horses. More than once, I called Norm to make sure Meeco and Ghost were really alive and that

Cookie and Clyde weren't just pocketing the money I sent each month to feed my horses. I asked my brother to stroke the horses' necks and noses, and to let them know that I still loved them. He groaned and moaned at the request but always promised he'd follow through.

The summer following freshman year, after nine months of my mother claiming she wanted to reconcile, I agreed to spend the summer with Cookie at her and Clyde's farm. Alaina and Gi both adamantly advised against it, but they hadn't been getting the *I love you* and the *I'm so proud of you* letters from Cookie. They didn't know how sincere she sounded. Also, Cookie had promised to pay for my work on the farm. With free room and board for the summer, I'd be able to save some money to take back to Pocatello the following year. And just as important was the fact that I'd get to spend time with my brother and with my horses, whom I hadn't ridden since I'd left the house to live at Alaina's.

The first couple of days at home were pleasant. I no longer was fearful of my mother, and I could tell that she sensed it, that she knew that if she even tried to slap me, I'd get in my car and leave. Clyde wasn't a threat either. The idea that he and my mother "owned" me had completely vanished. I didn't like him any better than I ever had, but my stomach no longer clenched when he walked into the room. I knew I was in control of my body. Not him.

Norm seemed to be doing well with Cookie and Clyde. He was living and working on the farm, but they treated him like an equal. Also, he'd already made new friends in Prairie Valley.

I loved being reunited with my horses. As if no time had passed, Meeco followed me around the farm, as faithful as a dog. Ghost, with his massive white body as firm as a statue, watched us from the corral.

One morning when my brother and I were milking the cows together, I reminded him of how we had planned to hang ourselves on the beam between the calf and cow pens.

"Do you still think about that?" I asked.

"You mean that we wanted to do that?'

"No. Do you ever still think about killing yourself?"

My brother paused with the suctions in his hand. A rush of air went through me as I worried for him. And then he said, "Nah, I'm okay now. Do you still think about killing yourself?"

"No," I said. "We're so lucky that we never went through with it."

"Yeah, we are." Norm attached the suctions, and we never discussed this again.

I tried to tell Cookie about school, about my classes, my friends, the papers I'd written, and my future as Benny the Bengal, but she wasn't interested. Half-conscious on the load of pills she took each day, Cookie would rather watch TV than talk. When I asked about her daily life and the goings-on in Prairie Valley, she waved her floppy hand, lit a cigarette, and said, "Same ol' shit, different town."

After a week of working, I brought up getting paid. We were eating dinner; Norm wasn't home. Cookie had made lasagna; I was loving the home-cooked meal.

"Paid?" Clyde asked.

"For my work," I said. "We had agreed that I'd be paid for my work this summer."

"Well, let's see," Clyde said. "After we deduct room and board and the cost of those two damn horses that should have been shot years ago, I think we come out to you still owing us a couple hundred every month."

"I thought I was going to live here for free." I looked at Cookie.

"Oh, honey." Cookie's stoned eyes were almost shut. There was a string of lasagna cheese on her chin. "I know we planned on that, but times are really tough and we jus' can't afford it." Cookie smiled. She put down her fork, pulled her cigarettes from her cleavage, and lit one.

"So you want me to work like I've been doing every day *and pay you?*"

"Naaaaah." Cookie tapped out her ash on the uneaten salad on her plate. "We'll let what you owe us slide. Right, Clyde?"

"I suppose." Clyde stabbed his fork into the lasagna and took a bite that filled both his cheeks.

"Bu' honey," Cookie said, "we're in such bad trouble here, we were hopin' you could get another student loan and then loan it to us so we can get outta debt."

"Yeah, sure, I'll do that." Not only had Norm's academic career been killed, but his credit had been ruined when Cookie and Clyde got hold of his student loans. After seeing what had happened to my brother, there was nothing that could compel me to hand over my loan money to my mother and Clyde. But if I wanted my stay there to be relatively peaceful, I had to pretend that my money was headed their way.

I rose from the table and cleared the dishes. Clyde left to do chores, and Cookie went to the couch. She smoked and half-consciously watched *America's Most Wanted* while I cleaned the kitchen. When I was done with the dishes, I sat on the couch beside my mother. I couldn't see anything on the TV. I couldn't hear anything. There was an incredible buzzing in my head; it felt like my brain might pop out of my skull.

"Mom," I said finally. "You were going to pay me to work. Remember?"

"You're getting' free room and board, *remember?*" Cookie's dull eyes remained on the TV show.

"I'm your daughter. Is it room and board when it's your own kid?"

Cookie turned toward me and slowly said, "Honey, we'll let the room and board slide. Just get us the student loan money, okay?"

The buzzing in my head exploded, and then all went silent and I could perfectly and clearly see my life behind me, my life currently, and my life in front of me. It was like a movie shot in the sharpest focus and playing in the darkest theater. I couldn't misunderstand what I was seeing. And what I was seeing was that my mother only wanted to reconcile so she could get the student loan money.

I remembered the letter Gi sent to me shortly after I had moved into Alaina's. I'd read it so many times then that I'd almost memorized it. *Just keep on standing up to her . . . don't give in or give up.*

My sisters had always been right. My mother would

never change. I'd never get what I wanted or needed from her. It was time to truly let go.

The next evening at dinner, Cookie and Clyde asked me if I'd gotten the loan. I had already told Norm that they were angling for the money, and he knew I wasn't really going to give it to them. Still, I couldn't make eye contact with my brother as I lied and said the bank was working on it. Of course I hadn't gone to any bank. Instead, I had gone to a pay phone and called Alaina to ask if she could take on the task of finding a retirement home for Meeco and Ghost. Thankfully, Alaina agreed. She knew it was impossible for me to make private phone calls with Cookie stumbling around the house all day. If my mother knew I was going to send the horses away, she'd sell them to a dog food or glue factory. Or maybe she'd just take out Clyde's gun, walk the horses to the manure pit, and shoot them to spite me.

Over the next couple of weeks I did farm work, cleaned the house, helped make dinner, and rode my horses. I didn't say much to my mother and Clyde, but neither one seemed to notice. If anything, my mother was relieved that I'd given up trying to be her friend and set things right with us. She seemed much more comfortable now that she was calling me a dumb slut when I overcooked the peas, or a lazy pig when I slept in past the milking hour. We had essentially reverted to our old roles, though no one could lay a hand on me.

Whenever Cookie left the house, which was rare, or when she completely passed out on pills, which was less rare, I searched the closets and the barn, where she hoarded junk, for any relic of my old life. I found photos, riding ribbons, pressed corsages, cards from my sisters, and yearbooks. All of it was collected in a garbage bag and stored in the trunk of my Mustang. I laughed when I thought of Cookie saving up all the things she had stolen from Jackie in a garbage bag under Jackie's couch. But this was different. I wasn't stealing anything. I was erasing my trail. My hope was that once I'd left with my stuff, the only thing my mother would have of me would be the thoughts in her head.

Every night at dinner Cookie and Clyde asked how the student loan was coming along. Every night at dinner, I told them that it would probably only be a couple more days. I came up with the story that the bank was questioning why I was taking out a student loan in the summer when I wasn't paying tuition.

"They just want to make sure that I'll use it for tuition," I said.

"Oh yeah," Cookie said. "We'll pay you back before the tuition's due."

I kept this prattle up long enough for Alaina to find a good equine retirement home—which she did in California. I had to keep it up even longer as I waited for the horse trailer from California to make its way to Cookie and Clyde's farm in Prairie Valley. During the wait, I spent as much time as I could with Meeco and Ghost. I groomed them every day, and every day I told them what I'd learned through my sisters: that not even the distance between New York and Idaho—or the Earth and the moon—can take away the power of real love.

The horses were to be collected one morning around breakfast time. By then, I had said good-bye to Norm and had everything packed and ready in my car. A blanket had been thrown over my things in the backseat so that Cookie and Clyde wouldn't notice.

My stomach was clenched and roiling when I woke up that day. And by five that evening, when the trailer still hadn't arrived, I was sick with anxiety. Norm had gone fishing with friends. Clyde was in the milking parlor. Cookie, high on pills, was in the kitchen slowly beating a piece of meat with a mallet.

I was peeling potatoes while staring out the kitchen window when the truck towing the trailer backed up the drive. I threw the peeler into the sink, dropped the potato on the counter, and started toward the door.

"Who the fuck is that?" Cookie asked.

"I'm sending the horses away," I said, and then I rushed out of the house and met the driver, a man who looked every bit the cowboy with a hat and boots.

Although the big good-byes had happened over and over throughout the day, I still cried with heartbreak as I kissed each of my horse's velvety cheeks and stroked their strong necks. Meeco seemed to feel my sadness as she pushed her neck into me, half around me as if to give me a hug. Ghost was stoic as ever.

When I handed over the reins, I noticed Cookie watching out the kitchen window. I caught her eye, and she turned her back to me. I knew that in Cookie's slanted world, the idea that I was shipping the horses away before she could sell them or kill them was a win for me and a loss for her. My guess was that she was going to pretend it had never happened and in that way she could think of herself as still being the one on top.

My keys were looped on my finger as I stood in the driveway and watched the trailer pull away. I had planned to drive off, back to Pocatello, without a word.

But instead of getting in the car, I shoved the keys in my jeans pocket, and walked out to the milking parlor.

Clyde looked old and slightly shrunken. What little hair he'd had had thinned so much over the years that he was now fully bald. His blue eyes had faded to a murky gray. His teeth, though, were still as white as whole milk.

"Clyde," I said.

"You comin' to help?" He was attaching the suctions to the last cow in the line up.

"No. I want to tell you something."

"Oh yeah?" Clyde turned toward me, one hand resting on the cow's belly. His bowed legs reminded me of giant parentheses.

"I want to tell you that you ruined my childhood—"

"What?" Clyde took a couple of steps toward me, and I held up my palm.

"You call yourself a man of faith"—I raised my voice—"but there is no church on Earth that would have anything to do with you if they knew what you did to me, and what you did to that widow's daughter before me. And, who knows, maybe there were loads of other girls."

"Oh, Rosie, what the heck are you sayin'?" Clyde put his arms out like he wanted to hug me.

I backed away. "Don't come near me, Clyde. You're not allowed to touch me."

"Why are you sayin' these things?" Clyde stared at me with wet eyes. "I took you in as a daughter. I supported you."

"Don't pretend that you don't know what I'm talking about!" I took another step back and stared straight into his foggy eyes.

"I was a father to you," Clyde said quietly. He was aging before me: contracting, drying up into a cracked leather nugget.

"You molested me from the time I was eleven. And then you beat me when you stopped molesting me." There was nothing that could diminish the strength I felt from stating exactly what had happened.

"I taught you everything you know—" Clyde pointed at the cow in front of him.

"You taught me things I should never have known, things no child should ever, ever know! You're a pedophile. You should be in prison."

"Don't say that. Don't say things you don't mean." Clyde took another step, and I backed away.

"I take it back. Prison would be a vacation compared to living out your life with Cookie. You deserve every miserable minute of her." I left the milking parlor, surging with courage, and walked straight into the house. Cookie was setting the table.

"Don't set a place for me," I said. "I'm leaving."

"What about dinner?" Cookie opened the oven and peered in. She had a cigarette clamped in the corner of her mouth.

"I'm leaving forever."

"You're moving out?"

"No, Mom. I'm leaving. I'm leaving you."

"What the fuck are you talking about, Rosanne?" Cookie took the cigarette from her mouth and tapped the ash out on to the floor. "What's your fucking problem?"

"My problem is that my whole life, I've been waiting for you to love me. And you never have."

"I fucking gave birth to you!" My mother put one hand on her wobbly hip.

"It took me so long to realize what my sisters already knew. But I know it for sure now. You will never love me."

"Jesus Christ, the slut is giving a speech!" Cookie had a smirk on her face. She pulled her head back and smoked her cigarette as if she were watching a performance she couldn't stand.

"You know, Mom, you had five amazing kids and you never saw the good or the joy in any one of them."

"Yeah." Cookie snorted. "Show me the joy in raising a snotty little slut like you!"

"Think of all the love you could have had from us," I said. "But you weren't about love, were you? You were, and you still are, all about misery."

Cookie made a sound that was half laugh, half snort. "What? Now that you're in college you think you're Rosie fucking Sigmund Freud?" Cookie took a deep drag on her cigarette, and a stoned but wicked smile crossed her face.

"It's sad to think that you're going to die in this terrible little house, with that terrible white-toothed man, and you'll never know what you missed with us."

"You done now?" Cookie asked, smoke puffing out of her mouth.

"Yes." I threw up my hands. "I'm done. Totally and completely done. Done with you."

I walked out of the house and got into my car. My mother didn't come after me. And I knew she wasn't watching from a window. But I was watching myself. There I was: grown up, strong, capable. And in charge of my own life.

The dust kicked up clouds around my tires as I drove away. I could barely see the farm in the rearview mirror.

When I turned onto the paved road, I rolled down my window and inhaled the sweetest air I'd ever breathed. I thought of pumping my fist out and chanting, *I was here, but not to stay, I didn't like it anyway.* And then I thought, *Nah, done with that, too.*

Afterword

UNBRIDLED · 97

My three kids come in and out of the kitchen as I write this. Lexi, at fifteen, is tall with brown hair that swishes across her back. She's currently texting on her cell phone and simultaneously telling me that her dad, my husband, and I need to come to her basketball game tomorrow night. This is her biggest worry: that Bobby and I make it to her game in time. Lexi doesn't know what it's like to get up at five thirty and do physical labor before school. She doesn't know what it's like to be terrified in her own home.

My ten-year-old son, Brody, is growing and eats so much I can barely keep enough food in the house. But I try. I stop at the grocery store most days after work. When I forget something, which I often do, Bobby runs to the grocery store after work, too. Brody can eat half a box of cereal over two hours of playing a video game.

He drinks milk straight from the carton and leaves bowls of soggy cereal in the sink. When I came home this evening, I passed a bag of Doritos on the couch, abandoned last night by Brody. For my youngest son, a crisis of hunger is when we've run out of Cocoa Pebbles and he has to resort to puffed rice. Brody thinks he's hungry, but he doesn't really know hunger and that's how I want it to be.

My oldest son, Daniel, calls Bobby *Bobs*. Bobby isn't his biological father, but Daniel doesn't really think about that. At seventeen, when he's not in school, he's busy producing music on his computer or working with Bobby building computers. Although lately, he's been spending a lot of time with his girlfriend. Daniel is in the kitchen now, pulling everything out of the electronics basket, looking for a charging block. I look up and watch for a minute. And then I laugh. The kitchen is disorganized, a little messy, but there is no cat hair decorating the dishes; there are no dried cat droppings or desiccated mice to kick under the kitchen table; there is no cigarette smoke fogging the air, and no ashtrays overflowing with lipstick-blotted butts; there is no anger, or fury, or rage. Daniel might be upset that he can't find a charging block, but his search in this kitchen is as messy and chaotic as his life currently gets.

Bobby has just come home from work. I hear him in the living room talking to Lexi and Brody. Soon he will come into the kitchen. He'll lean over Daniel and teasingly try to kiss him while saying something like, "Come on! Give me kiss!" Daniel will bob and weave and duck away from this giant man who never uses his bulk for anything but love. Once Daniel has escaped, Bobby will bend over me, hunched at the computer, and he'll kiss my forehead. He'll wait for me to look up and then he'll kiss my lips. Affection comes so easily for Bobby. And those two things—love and affection—are doled out by him every single day. Of course we fight sometimes. But there's never been violence. There's barely been yelling. And laughter is something that happens every day.

Getting here wasn't easy.

My sophomore year at Pocatello, my focus turned inward, on *not* being like my mother. This wasn't a thought that I had now and then throughout the day. It was in my mind continuously. Cookie haunted me like a ghost shadowing me wherever I went. I didn't want to drink like my mother, rage like my mother, do drugs like her, or date men like the ones she dated.

And even though Cookie and Clyde were a six-hour drive away, my body couldn't let go of the terror I had been raised on. When I heard a loud noise, I jumped, expecting a leather strap to fly into my backside. If I got a bad grade on a paper or showed up three minutes late to work, I trembled with a near-paralyzing fear. Against all logic, against what I knew to be true, my skin, heart, and muscles expected that my teachers, my supervisors, and my boss would beat me for my errors. The only thing that alleviated this terror was motion, action, activities that sucked up and used every molecule of attention I had. And so, I started doing more. I volunteered at several different organizations; I taught aerobics; and I attended every school game even if I wasn't acting as the mascot. I ran from one thing to the next so quickly there wasn't time to think. Or to feel. I honestly believed that if I moved fast enough, I could outrun the looming ghost of Cookie.

When moving fast didn't help, the stark sobriety—which had started at Alaina's house—came to an abrupt end.

I started drinking. I tried some of the drugs offered me. I sifted through brief relationships with morally questionable men. Until I stopped sifting and landed on a man I'll call Jeff.

Jeff believed in his right to enjoy the company of any woman who might come his way. This is how frantic and confused I was: I let this man move into the trailer where I lived.

One afternoon I came home and found Jeff and another woman naked together on the couch. The Cookie inside me erupted and spewed out in a stream of fire. I was a human blowtorch, roaring profanities like my mother. As if possessed, I started throwing things. First went the breakfast dishes on the kitchen table: a milky cereal bowl, a plate with toast crumbs, two coffee cups each with a little splattering of cold, beige coffee. Jeff and his lover ducked their heads as they tried to dress under the hail of breaking glass and ceramic. Next came the dishes from the sink. They were dirty, wet, and dappled with the sticky crust of past meals. Jeff and his lover, with their arms covering their heads, ran through the dish-hail toward the door. And that was when I picked up the bulging bag of trash and heaved it toward them. The garbage exploded into a smoldering trail that spilled out the open door behind them.

They were gone, but I wasn't done. I opened the kitchen cupboards and, still screaming, threw to the floor and broke every single dish I owned.

Then there was silence.

I stood in the kitchen, surrounded by broken dishes and garbage, my chest heaving up and down as I gasped for air. My knees buckled and I went down to the gritty, glass-strewn floor. I curled onto my side, my knees pulled into my chest, and sobbed almost as loudly as I'd been yelling. Something was wrong with me, but it felt separate than me. Like a virus that had entered my body. I wanted it out.

When I finally stood, I walked straight to the counseling center at school. That day, I started therapy with a kind, young therapist.

And I told him almost nothing.

I complained about my boyfriend, about the boyfriends before him, about the pressures at school. I said, "I don't know *why* I make such bad choices with men!" I didn't mention Cookie and Clyde. I didn't talk about my brother and sisters and what we had been through together. The counselor did the best he could with the wisp of information I gave him.

I can't explain why I didn't tell the therapist about my childhood and my family—my guess is that I didn't yet understand the connection between my past and my present. I did tell my best friend at school, Kenda, about my history—even the things my sisters and brother didn't know. We were the same year, both from small farming towns in Idaho, each with a complicated past. Kenda's confidence and friendship saved me— much the way my sisters did when I lived with them. The fact that I could be authentic and honest with just one person kept me afloat.

Near the end of my sophomore year, I started seeing

a man I'll call Tony. He was ten years older and seemed grown up and in control of his life.

Being with Tony was a challenge—being with anyone at that time would have been a challenge. I was blind to the chaos and damage I was carrying around with me. And Tony wasn't someone who was able to see me through, or see me out of, my history of abuse. I started losing the confidence I'd built up through my activities and successes. Every day when I went to school, I felt like all the people I passed deserved to be there, while I was an imposter. It wouldn't have surprised me if someone from the Pocatello administration marched into one of my classes and dragged me out by the hair. To make up for my imagined deficiencies, I started seeing tutors. Nothing but an A could prove my worth. And, like many women, I hurtled my fears and insecurities inward, onto my own body. Whereas I once felt powerful—strong enough to buck fifty-pound bales of hay onto a flat-bed truck—I began to feel inadequate, unshapely, oversized. After dinner each night, I excused myself to the bathroom, where I fingered my throat until I had vomited up whatever I'd eaten. If there was a crack in my confidence (and my confidence was about as firm as the San Andreas Fault), any disagreement or argument I had with Tony wedged inside of me until I splintered in two. The insecurities, the fears, and the chaos I was living with were familiar to me. It was what I had always known. And I understood my place in it; I was comfortable with it. With Kenda as my only confidante, my sisters and brother didn't know enough to steer me away from a malfunctioning relationship. And so, at nineteen years old, I married Tony.

During my junior year, I took psychology and sociology classes. While my friends were bored by the readings, making jokes about Pavlov's slavering dog, I was fascinated. I reread the assignments. I highlighted everything. I wanted to understand human nature, people, desires, urges. And I wanted to understand myself, my Pavlovian triggers, why I acted the way I did. Still, I worked doggedly at being everything Tony expected me to be. I also worked hard at school, pretending with my new friends that I was someone without a complicated past—a former cheerleader who grew up with a couple of horses.

Several months into our marriage, Tony came home late one night and a fight ensued. Like the all-out battle that landed me on the kitchen floor with my broken dishes, this fight, too, woke up the Cookie in me. It was terrifying to see my mother reincarnated, in a sense, through me. I was afraid of myself, of my own impulses. Especially the impulse that propelled me to marry someone who brought out everything I was working against inside myself.

I skipped my morning classes the following day and went straight to the counseling center. There, I collapsed into a delirious state of grief. I sobbed and tried to explain, the best I could in my fractured state, what was going on. The outpouring of emotion wouldn't stop. I couldn't pull myself together enough to stand up and go to my classes. By the end of that day, I had been checked into a psychiatric hospital where I stayed for a week.

I didn't call my sisters or Norm. They had all been so proud of me as I progressed in school; I worried I'd disappoint them. And I was embarrassed. It seemed pitiful that after all the ways they had supported me, and everything they had done for me, I would go out and undo everything.

I wasn't allowed visitors in the hospital; even my husband was kept away. When I checked out, it was not Tony I ran to, but Kenda—the person who could bolster me when I was feeling weak. It was clear to me then that I had to end the marriage.

My life was now different in so many ways. I started taking prescribed drugs (a mix that was adjusted over the next few years until we landed on just the right cocktail that I still take today), and I carried with me a diagnosis that I could barely whisper to myself. I was, *I am*, bipolar. No one I had ever known admitted to having any mental illness. I was twenty years old, and though I was living in Pocatello, I still had the sensibility I'd developed in Oakview, where there were 360 people who all claimed to be sane. Even my mother, as obviously mentally ill as she was, had never been referred to as anything other than an alcoholic. The word *bipolar* terrified me. It shamed me. I felt like I had to hide my true self more than ever. And so I told no one about my diagnosis.

The psychiatrist from the hospital referred me to a therapist named Linda Barnier. Linda tried her best to help me accept the diagnosis and the drug treatment without shame. She explained that having bipolar disorder was no different than having anemia or low thyroid. There were deficiencies in my chemical makeup. The pills helped balance out for what was lacking. People all over the world suffered similarly. Or maybe they didn't suffer because they regularly took their prescribed medication. I accepted Linda at her word and tried to see the diagnosis not as a failure on my part, but simply as something that just is. Still today, it's hard for me to admit that I have bipolar disorder. But maybe in saying it here and now, I can once and for all kick away the shame of my diagnosis.

The shame held by anyone and everyone with similar diagnoses.

With Linda's guidance, I was able to flay myself open, and lay out and examine the truth of my life. Together, we mapped my childhood, looking at it as clearly as possible so I could understand it better. It was fascinating to see my actions from a distance. It allowed me to be compassionate with myself, to stop taking the blame for the wrongdoings of others. I was just a kid who did the best she could under the circumstances she was in.

Linda encouraged me to go to Alcoholics Anonymous. I did, and was soon attending Adult Children of Alcoholics, as well. And since there were still a couple of unattended hours in my week, I also went to Co-Dependents Anonymous. Basically, if there were twelve steps in the program, I had my foot out ready to take the first step. These programs opened me up to the idea that the world is full of people with painful stories you might not be able to see on their faces or read on their bodies. It helped me to never judge anyone as luckier or more together than I. You never really know what's happened to any individual prior to the moment when their life converges with yours. And still, you don't know what's going on in their home, their personal relationships, and their private life.

In spite of the twelve-step programs, the drugs, and the therapy, Cookie continued to vibrate inside me; she was a nerve-racking phantom. When I told Linda that I still felt my mother in my gut, and I was still fighting against her, Linda said, "Rosie, stop focusing on who you *don't* want to be and start focusing on who you *do* want to be." It was simple advice, I know, but it changed everything. Instead of the ghost of Cookie dictating how I did and did not act, I just looked at myself and what I wanted from my life. And since I can't do anything halfway, I started making vision boards with words and phrases cut out of magazines. I hung the boards on my walls and stared at them, reading them over and over and saying to myself, *That's me, that's who I am.* While sitting below my vision boards, I wrote in my journal. Or journals. Everything I knew, thought, and felt. Everything that had happened to me for as long as I could remember. I also started making gratitude lists that helped me turn off the sound when my mind played the record of my failures and insecurities on repeat. Every night, I listed at least ten things I was grateful for. When a surge of fear or insecurity hit me during a class, I'd quickly write what I was grateful for in the margins of my books or in the corners of my notebooks. I've kept all my journals and just flipped through one looking for a gratitude list. Here's one from September 18, 1994: *I'm grateful for being a survivor. I'm grateful for being loved. I'm grateful for being able to go to school. I'm grateful for having a bed. I'm grateful for my friendship with Kenda. I'm grateful for having a suit. I'm grateful for having a roof over my head. I'm grateful for having Murphy, my cat. I'm grateful for having a vehicle. I'm grateful for having food.*

The cat is long gone, but I remain grateful for all those things. (Kenda and I still talk and see each other regularly, and I'm super grateful that I currently own more than one suit that I can wear to work!) Even now, when I'm slapped with a moment of frustration or anger, I sometimes write a gratitude list. The lists bring me into a peaceful present just as much today as they did when I was twenty.

After college, I continued my volunteerism and worked at paying jobs, too, including a summer as an Outward Bound Counselor. Eventually, I moved to Salt Lake City, Utah, where I worked in development for a national nonprofit. I quickly had friends, a social life, and a Christian church where I felt comfortable.

At that church, I met and fell in love with a man I'll call Chip. Within five months I was pregnant with my son Daniel. And before he was born I was married. No child wants to read about his parents' relationship, so I will skip over those details and go straight to the pregnancy. I was terrified. Though my sisters had taken wonderful care of me when they could, I still didn't understand what it meant to be a mother. I knew how to love; I loved my sisters and my brother. But I didn't understand how to love someone you were in charge of, someone whose life was in your hands.

For most of that pregnancy, I was off my medication and on bed rest. But I used the time well, putting all my force and focus on staying healthy so I could be a good mother. Kenda and Chip made regular runs to the library for me, bringing home the parenting books I had requested. I'd lie in bed and read these books over and over again, tracing the words with my pointer finger, whispering them like prayers. I envisioned myself doing the things I was reading about. I imagined the baby, sweet and soft in my arms. Happy, warm, and safe.

As soon as Daniel was born, a flood of love poured out of me. It was unlike anything I had ever experienced. It made Cookie's actions, her treatment of her five kids, all the more horrifying. How could anyone bypass this gush of love and turn instead to terror and misery?

Within a couple of months of Daniel's birth, it was very clear to me that the right thing to do for my health was to split up with Chip. He moved out, and I got a job at an Italian restaurant to support myself. My friend at the restaurant, Wendy Linford, introduced me to her family: her mother, Carolyn; her father, Alan; her brother, A.J.; and her sisters, Tiffany, Jennifer, and Jessica. Tiffany became my babysitter, but I grew close to everyone in the Linford household and they soon grew into my makeshift family. With Wendy, Tiffany, Jennifer, and Jessica, it was like I had re-created my sisters (plus one!). They are incredible, strong women who helped take care of me as I figured out how to be a new mother.

My best friend at work was the man who would soon become my husband, Bobby Maloney. Bobby was kind, thoughtful, and four years younger than me. In everything he did, everything he said, Bobby didn't resemble any of the men I had ever known. He was easygoing and made no demands. He didn't criticize me. He didn't look at me, or any woman he saw, as something to be conquered and controlled. I felt safe with Bobby in the same way that I felt safe with the Linfords.

Daniel quickly grew, and so did my friendship with Bobby. We'd been hanging out together for a full year before we kissed for the first time. It was a magical kiss, and I realized then that Bobby had always been in love with me; he was just waiting for me to notice. I also realized that he loved Daniel just as much as he loved me.

After two years of dating, I got pregnant. The second I knew I was having a girl, my fears revved up again. I immediately went to the library and checked out all the same books I'd read before, and added the few new titles that had come out since I had been pregnant with Daniel. I wondered if that surge of love I'd felt for Daniel wouldn't flow out of me when I was faced with a daughter. Maybe that's what had happened to Cookie, maybe that's why she could be kinder to Norm than the rest of us. Bobby was patient and loving as I frantically read and memorized the books. He told me over and over again that I was a wonderful mother and he didn't doubt me for a second.

During this pregnancy, before I was really showing and before I had to, once again, confine myself to bed rest, Cookie was diagnosed with terminal cancer.

I drove to the town in Idaho where Cookie and Clyde were then living. My mother was on a hospital bed in the middle of the living room. There were cats tiptoe-ing nearby, cat hair everywhere, cat droppings drying in the corners of the rooms—the usual. Cookie was gaunt and her skin clung to her bones like a wet sheet over rocks. She was only fifty-seven but she looked like she was eighty. I barely spoke to Clyde that day while I sat by my mother. She put out her hand and I held it. It was cold, but delicate, like holding a little silk bag of dice.

Cookie cried off and on all day.

"I really screwed up my life," she said.

"Yeah," I agreed.

"I really screwed you over, didn't I?" my mother cried.

"It's okay," I said. "I forgive you."

"But I just was . . . I screwed up!" she said.

"You didn't know how to be a mom." I rubbed my free hand on my pregnant belly. The cycle of Cookie's life was going to end right here. The baby inside me, like Daniel, was a new starting point.

"I'm so sorry." Cookie wept and continued to apologize. I forgave her as many times as she said she was sorry. I didn't tell her I loved her because I knew that I didn't. I loved my son, Daniel. I loved Bobby. And I loved the secret baby inside me.

That afternoon, two Native American men stopped in to visit. It appeared my mother—the alleged New York go-go dancer, the alleged backup singer to 1960s bands, the alleged Mormon, the owner of Prismatic Fantasies—was now Native American. Once my mother learned that there's no Hell in Native American culture, she wanted in. Cookie knew as well as I that if there was a judgment day and she were to face God, she wouldn't even be pausing in Limbo.

I stayed in a hotel that night, as I couldn't bear to sleep under the same roof as Clyde. The next morning, I sat with my mother again for a couple of hours. She sobbed when we said good-bye. Not even a tear came out of me.

Three days later, I woke up at three a.m. I sat up and took a deep breath that I could feel all the way to my toes. There was a beautiful lightness inside me and I knew my mother was dead. Just then, the phone rang. It didn't even startle me. I picked up the receiver. It was Clyde.

"Your mother just died," Clyde said.

"I'm sorry," I said, though I wanted to say, *I know.*

Clyde said, "She was a good woman."

"Hmm." I wasn't going to agree with that.

"Can you help me pay for the casket?" Clyde asked.

"No," I said.

"She's your mother," Clyde said.

"I don't care if you bury her in a cardboard box," I said.

"She said you forgave her!"

"I did," I said. "Let me know when the funeral is."

I hung up the phone. Bobby was awake, his eyes were wide open. And he was smiling at me.

Daniel and Bobby came to the funeral with me. Norm was there, heartbroken in ways I didn't quite understand. There were three Native American men present—one of whom banged a drum throughout the service. He was dressed in a traditional costume and had a long braid with a feather in it. There were also two women from the Mormon temple and a few youngish people who Norm said were from a "crystal chanting group." I guess my mother was covering all the bases. None of my sisters were there and I didn't blame them. If it had cost me a plane ticket, I wouldn't have come either.

The service took place in a dingy, small room of the Mormon church. One of the crystal men, wearing a white shirt with a Nehru collar, stood at the front of the room beside the plywood-looking closed casket. He spoke for a few minutes about my mother and how he had gotten to know her during her illness. Then he introduced me and Norm and asked us to speak. I stood and looked out at the group of fifteen or so. Jackie's son, Sam, surprisingly, had shown up. The others were strangers, people who had likely only met Cookie during the last few weeks she was alive.

"I'm grateful that my mother gave birth to me." I stared out at the faces as I tried to find something, anything, else to say. Not a single word came out. I looked down at Bobby; he reached his hand toward me and I took it. And then I sat.

Norm spoke. He said loving and kind things about our mother. She got much more than she deserved from my generous brother.

When Lexi was born, the burst of love happened all over again. I was relieved, overjoyed, almost high from the expansion of good feelings. I called my sisters and Norm to tell them of Lexi's arrival. Everyone was thrilled, but when I hung up the phone, I realized we had drifted apart. Maybe each of us was trying to prove that they could survive without the others. Or maybe we were all so tender from what we'd gone through we couldn't bear the reminders that were brought forth in just being in contact.

Ten has always been my favorite number, so on October 10 of that year, Bobby tried to surprise me with a trip to Nevada to get married. Baby Lexi and three-year-old Daniel stayed with the Linford family.

Turns out there aren't twenty-four-hour chapels littering the state. After driving all the way to Reno and back, Bobby and I still weren't married. But we did it the following week in the living room of a retired judge we found through a friend. Daniel was with his father that day, but baby Lexi was with us. It was a beautiful, loving, and authentic ceremony. There wasn't any pageantry, but there was so much love.

After the marriage, as I honed in on my family, I dropped all contact with my brother and sisters. Much happened in their absence. Most notably the birth of my third child, Brody. There were no doubts about my mothering abilities the third time. I felt healthy and strong, like I had become the person I'd always wanted to be, the person who would have emerged sooner had she not been hiding behind the fear, trauma, and overscheduled life. With three small kids, I was so devotedly consumed with motherhood it was almost like my past didn't exist.

Almost.

In 2009, I started yearning for my sisters and brother again.

I signed up for Facebook and went on to search for my family. Immediately, I found Gi and sent her a message, saved to this day.

I don't even know where to start. . . . Can you forgive me for becoming so withdrawn and so disconnected from everyone for years? I am so sorry to have missed everything. . . . I really have missed everyone.

Gi wrote back: *There is no need to ask forgiveness for anything. I missed you and have had a hole in my heart because of it.* As we continued to write, my sister told me she had been tracking me through blogs and postings at my kids' schools. Just as she had since the day Cookie brought me home from the hospital as a newborn, my sister had been watching over me. She hadn't reached out to me because she sensed what was true at the time—in order for me to fully heal and grow, I had to disconnect from the family. Still, Gi never backed away from her self-assigned role as my guardian and guide.

A few weeks later, I flew out to New York and for the first time since the late 1970s, Cherie, Camille, Gi, Norm, and I were gathered in the same house. This time, there was no threat of Cookie storming in, ready to beat us. No threat of Clyde or any of Cookie's other boyfriends. No one was hungry (far from it, in fact!) and there was no fighting. All that remained from our childhood was the joy we were able to feel when together. Like when Gi used to organize talent shows, or when Cherie would do my hair, or when Camille would make us dance the hustle together—we created a happiness that was impossible to quell.

I'm still in the kitchen, but I have to get up soon and serve the roast I stuck in the crock pot this morning. Daniel found the charging block and is probably now in his bedroom on the phone with his girlfriend. I can hear Brody talking to the TV in the living room. He's turned on the football game. My favorite team, the New York Giants, are playing. Bobby just walked in. He's taking plates down from the cupboard and putting them on the counter. That means one thing: Tonight, we'll each serve ourselves and then eat dinner in the living room while watching the game.

Bobby leans toward the doorway and shouts, "Kids! Dinner!" Then he looks over at me and says, "Dinner, babe. Giants!"

Before I can sign off the computer, my phone rings. It's Gi. She's at a store in Manhattan and wants to buy a pair of pants for Lexi. *What size is she?* Gi asks. Lexi walks into the kitchen to make herself a plate, and I hand her the phone so she can chat with her aunt.

Since we reconnected, my sisters, brother, and I have never strayed. At first no one talked about the past, about what we'd each been through. Then Gi published her memoir, *Etched in Sand,* and the conversation began. None of us got out of our childhoods easily or even in one piece. But we've all been putting ourselves back together since.

Together, our greatest pride lies in the wonderful and amazing children we are shepherding through life. These kids will never be abused, by any means or in any way, by my siblings and me. We five—with multiple last names but a common heart—are committed to protecting and nurturing all people in our care, including each other.

My sisters and my brother have always looked out for me. Now, I look out for them, too. We are each other's champions and cheerleaders. Through my siblings, I learned how to survive and how to love. Once I shed the unbearable weight of my mother, a beautiful space opened up and the love I already had expanded until my body was filled with it. Now, there is so much love inside me I can barely contain it all.

I love you, Cherie. I love you, Camille. I love you, Gi. I love you, Norm. The road may have been long, and at times it was lonely, but in the end, we are walking this road together.

Acknowledgments

Thank you to my children, Daniel, Alexis, and Brody, for giving me a lifetime of joy. I couldn't have been the mother I have been without the support of my husband and best friend, Bobby Maloney. Thank you for loving me through better and worse.

While spending endless days and nights working on this book, the bond with my amazing sister Regina has grown even stronger. I'm so grateful for everything you've done for me; there is no one else with whom I could have taken the difficult journey of bringing this story to print.

I want to thank my brother and sisters: Camille for guiding me upward, toward heaven and toward God; Cheri for endless and unconditional love; Norman for offering me love and laughter at times when both felt impossible.

With appreciation to our brilliant, hardworking publishing team at HarperCollins, Lisa Sharkey, Amy Bendell, and Alieza Schvimer, for their guidance, insight, and support; and for giving us the opportunity to tell this story.

Thank you to Jessica Blau for capturing the essence of my life in the beautiful voice you have. I love you!

I am forever grateful to Jenny Swenson and Carol Hill for saving me on what has become one of the most important days in my life. Thank you, Carol, for taking me into your home and helping me to become who I am today.

Love and thanks to Angela Young, Jessica, Jason, and J.T. for showing me how a family can work. And just as much love and thanks to Carolyn, Alan, Jessica, Tiffany, Jennifer, and A.J. Linford for taking me into your family, where I learned how to be a mother and a friend.

My best friend, Kenda Baron, has been an invaluable support throughout the years and for that I will always be thankful.

Eighmie Reeder and Debra Dibble were shining lights in an often dark childhood. I love you both and will forever cherish our time together.

Thank you to Flavia Feliciano and her family, the Toothmans, the Leonis, Kim Kretten, Koli Reed, Tina

Sheffield, Janel Green, Shamona Spreadbuy, Sarah Lo-araine Phelps, and Brad Bauer. Your goodwill is forever imprinted on my soul.

To Jim and Adrian Hust: thank you for your love and kindness. I know you are smiling at me from above. I will always love you both.

Thank you to Linda Barnier, whose therapeutic ideas changed my life when I most needed it.

Thank you to Idaho State University at Pocatello for providing the desperately needed health services I utilized as a student. Dave Meyer, Susan Duncan, and Julie Hillebrandt provided love and laughter during my time at ISU, too, and I am equally grateful to them.

Enormous thanks to my FirstDigital Telecom family, especially Alex Jackson and Wesley McDougal, who gave me the freedom to write this book without censure. You have created a warm, happy, safe work environment that is rare in the corporate world.

The teachers, librarians, school administrators, and food service workers of every school and library I ever visited sustained me in body, mind, and soul. These people are true heroes and should be thanked beyond the pages of this book. I'd like to call out particular thanks to Mr. VanOrder, Mrs. Anderson, Mrs. Nally, Mr. Munden, Mr. Wertz, and Mrs. Lunsford.

Many symptoms of mental illness can start at a

young age due to adverse childhood experiences. These experiences can affect the body and brain functions. To adults and children suffering from mental illness, I urge to you seek help from the National Alliance of Mental Illness, twelve-step programs, counselors, therapists, social workers, and clergy. These people *can* help you gain power and control over your own life. Mental health is a national problem that affects society as a whole. Please support the mental health services in your community. No one chooses mental illness. Together we should all choose to help improve the well-being of those in need.

—Rosie Maloney

Rosie, although I generally knew what you endured, to learn about it in the detail necessary to properly share your story was heart-wrenching and much more difficult than I anticipated. Hearing about your journey and how you managed to continue moving forward has made me admire you even more. I wish I could erase all those years apart and fill them with happy memories, but sadly I cannot. So instead you entrusted in me the ability to share your extraordinarily inspiring and powerful story. Enjoy this journey, and please know that this time you will not be walking alone, for I will be with you every step of the way.

With tremendous appreciation to my siblings, Cherie, Camille, and Norman, for supporting yet another published book about our family. Your confidence in my ability to properly share Rosie's story was relied upon page after page as I struggled through sharing what she endured.

To my companion, Todd, for your love, commitment, and patience and to your family for their unrelenting enthusiasm.

To Brezan, for enthusiastically embracing my writing this story during the same time that we came to be. Being your mom has been one of my life's greatest blessings.

For the unconditional close friendship of Melanie McEvoy, Ed Moltzen, and Reyne Macadaeg, and all my other dear friends, with whom we wade together through all life's adventures.

The path to *Etched in Sand* and *Girl Unbroken* was literally paved by my publisher and dear friend Lisa Sharkey. Your boundless encouragement of me has been life-changing. To our entire publishing team at HarperCollins, especially my übertalented editor, Amy Bendell, and assistant editor, Alieza Schvimer, together we continue to impact the lives of so many.

Jessica Anya Blau, you not only gave Rosie her powerful voice, but you did it with such ease, grace, sensitivity, and humor. For all that you did, I am eternally grateful.

I am emotionally indebted to all those who supported Rosie and provided her safe havens throughout her life. May the blessings you placed upon her perpetually be passed back to you and your families.

With tremendous graditude to my exceptional fourth grade teacher, Louise Muse, for safeguarding a poem I wrote forty years ago and personally returning it to me just at the right time.

To the *Smithtown News*, whose archives unlocked answers to questions that lingered for decades.

Finally, I wish to acknowledge the readers of *Etched in Sand*. You not only embraced my story but also proactively responded to it. Since the publishing of *Etched in Sand* in August 2013, readers have: become certified adoptive foster parents and adopted older foster youth before they aged out of foster care; changed the rules at food banks so unaccompanied children now have easier access to free food; volunteered as Court Appointed Special Advocates to give a voice to children in foster care; and spearheaded an event called #TeensGottaBelieve where a high school junior started a conversation with his peers and entire community about the plight of aging-out foster youth and how every foster child deserves a forever family. This list is not exhaustive, just a small yet powerful sampling of how readers have responded.

Readers also wholeheartedly embraced my book's theme that "no child is a lost cause" and the concept that they can positively influence children in need for that moment in time when they are before them. For young readers that are facing similar circumstances as those I experienced, it has given them hope. The latter has been *Etched in Sand*'s greatest gift and I anticipate it will also be that of *Girl Unbroken* as well.

Because we all have to believe.

—Regina Calcaterra